PETER KLEIN

BEYOND GOD

WHY RELIGIONS ARE FALSE, OUTDATED AND DANGEROUS

Web Address: www.beyondgodthebook.com

ISBN : Paperback – 978-0-6482581-1-7
        E-Book – 978-0-6482581-0-0

CONTENTS

PREFACE

When we turn on our televisions, we are unfortunately no longer surprised to hear about a mass-stabbing incident, a van being driven into crowds or bombs being used to kill innocent people. We are all tired of the "terrorist" attacks that are still occurring all too frequently around the world. You hear the same rhetoric from political and community leaders, yet nothing changes: the world is no safer, nor does it appear that an end to the violence is in sight, based on the current ways of dealing with the situation.

Many people are afraid of openly stating their views on such issues for fear of being negatively labelled. Yet the only way out of this mess is to have frank and open discussions about the validity of certain widespread religious teachings. Only a small minority of people instigate terrorist attacks, and these atrocities continue partly because not enough people speak out strongly against the sources of these people's beliefs. The unfortunate reality is that religious violence will continue as long as people are fearful of causing offence.

Even if you have not been affected directly by religious-inspired terrorism, it has almost certainly impacted on your life. The procedures for travelling, especially on aeroplanes, have become more onerous; attending large public events involves bag checks and screening; and many schools and businesses require extra security that was not needed only 20 years ago. The early 21st century has seen a gradual recession of our daily freedoms because of fear of various religiously inspired groups.

This is, however, not new. Although Islamic fundamentalism is the current main offender, before that Christianity espoused intolerance of others, and widespread bigotry and hatred was preached openly from pulpits. These preachings led to inquisitions, pogroms, the Crusades, entrenched anti-Semitism, forced conversions, and the killing and torturing of heretics, witches and homosexuals and other minorities. Before that, if we are to believe the stories in the Bible, genocide in the name of a god was also a part of the history of Judaism. Almost all religions have perpetrated violence in the name of their beliefs or gods.

The aim of this book is to share evidence and information about the history of humankind and life on Earth and the origins of some of the most important religious beliefs. At their core, most religions, particularly the three main monotheistic religions (Christianity, Islam and Judaism) have common ideas about the age of the universe, the first appearance of life on Earth and, even more importantly, how humans came to be ("made in god's image") and our relationship with other creatures. Until we accept the truth about this most important foundational information, we will never escape the many problems that are caused by religious teachings.

We will continue to be affected by these issues as long as we allow religious leaders to hold a level of educative power way beyond what they should have. We need to be teaching our children not only what to think, but more importantly *how* to think. We need to teach them how to accept or reject information and assess evidence for phenomena or beliefs. The scientific method is the only way of "knowing" these things; other views and "understandings" are purely *beliefs*. Until we do this, we will always be slaves to others and their teachings.

We must remember that only a few hundred years ago most people thought we lived on a flat planet, with the Sun circling us. It was only after this long-held view was questioned and the scientific method was developed that we realized that this belief was in fact false. Questioning produced evidence that enabled us to see the truth. This book is all about questioning existing beliefs, in particular those associated with religions.

Since the blossoming of science, we have found out much about the universe, about life and about the laws that govern natural processes. Thanks to specialized branches of scientific research, such as chemistry, physics, biology and medicine, we have been able to improve both the quality of our lives and our life expectancies. Prior to the scientific revolution, there was little change in these facets of human existence and we bumbled along with only small, though sometimes significant, advances.

In the face of scientific evidence, religious leaders are now beginning to admit that religion is not about answering the "how?"; instead they claim that religion is the only way to answer the "why?". However, one does not need to believe in a specific god or religion to come up with answers to "why?"; nor do answers based on "faith" carry any validity. Adding a god to the answer merely stops one from thinking further, and pre-supposes that the speaker knows that god's mind.

The only way to get people to accept each other as all being basically the same is to eliminate those artificial distinctions that are taught from an early age. Often these barriers are too strong to be easily overcome unless one goes through an entire process of reviewing what one has learned since childhood. If children were never taught anything about the stories behind each religion, how many, as adults, would accept them as the truth? How many people would then choose to believe religious teachings? The stories of each religion are taught to children as facts. If you would not be happy for the stories of a different religion to be taught as facts to your child, why should it be right that the stories of your religion are indoctrinated into them. After all, children are just children worldwide. It is not until parents, or a whole community, teach these myths as facts that problems start.

It is amazing how many people, if granted just one wish, would ask for "world peace". If it is such a common desire, why has it not happened? Is it because we can't visualize what is required for it to occur? Or because we cannot imagine what such a world would look like? Is it that we just don't recognize the major impediments, or is it because those impediments are a part of our long-standing, indoctrinated belief systems and therefore too difficult for us to cast aside?

Progressing towards this goal requires us to use our imagination *and* have the will to question and to make the choices that would enable the relevant important changes to occur. This will necessitate a slow, generation-by-generation shift in thinking, such as has occurred with many other societal issues – for example, with the acceptance of equal rights for women, that all citizens should be able to own land within their own country, that all citizens should be able to vote, and, currently, that any two people should be able to marry.

So much tragedy is created by people acting on what they believe to be true rather than on what they can demonstrate to be true. We should respect all people's rights, but not necessarily their beliefs, as the actions created by beliefs often infringe on other people's rights. Those who adhere to any religion are supporting systems that uphold faith as a virtue – that is, claims without evidence. While this situation is still accepted, anyone can justify any act. This is exactly what allows jihadists, for example, to behave as they do.

Although this book focuses mainly on religious belief systems, it is important to acknowledge that there are many other causes of the world's problems and a few of these will be touched on later, particularly in Chapter 3. Many writers have written excellent books on those other issues, including the conflict and oppression caused by nationalism or by political or financial greed.

Many of these problems, however, do not result from belief systems that are so obviously open to questioning or preach and cause such worldwide division. Without a doubt, tribalism will always be a part of humanity, but when it is based on mythology, falsehoods and bigotry and when it preaches an "us versus them" mentality to the point of causing violence, then not only should these beliefs be questioned, but surely we are morally obligated to do so.

* * *

So, this book mostly looks at the history and validity of religious belief systems and their current relevance to humankind. Why? Because religions are often based on just a few main texts and the default position for their adherents is that any evidence contrary to the teachings in these texts is not as valid as "god's word". They insist that these old books are the best guide to how people should behave. One can see throughout history what tragedies this mindset has led to, with perpetrators being able to use the "Nuremberg Defence" – that they were only following religious rules and orders. Those who commit immoral, bigoted or violent crimes in the name of religion often believe wholeheartedly that they are doing right, that they are just following the commands laid out in their scriptures and that their behaviour is divinely ordained, even if others can see that they are wrong. Religious followers repeatedly state that faith and religious beliefs are central to being a good and moral person. What we commonly see, however, is faith being used as both a rationale and vindication for excluding or treating poorly or differently anyone who does not live according to that particular faith's edicts.

Religions appeal to the narcissistic side of us because they make us feel that we are somehow more special than every other living thing on the planet, that we can interact personally with the creator of the universe and that we may continue to live on after our deaths in a "better place". In contrast, secular thought has at its core the understanding that we have so much more to know and the belief that humanity need not suffer endlessly because of narrow religious views. Instead of looking at the sky and seeing a god, secularists look at the sky and try to understand the almost incomprehensible scale of things and how and why things occur – without the shackles of old belief systems. Secular thinking creates the opportunity to see all other people as just "other people". Religions do not want this; they are happy to have divided and divisive societies.

Religious adherents often do not accept scientific evidence for phenomena because it contradicts the view of history set out in their religious texts. Studies have shown, for example, that a disproportionate percentage of the more religious, who reject the evidence for evolution and the timescales of the universe, also reject the evidence for human-induced climate change.[1] Repeated polling in America shows that between 40 and 45 per cent of the population believe the biblical narratives to be factual and not just metaphorical, and that life on Earth is less than 10,000 years old. Although the figures are lower in most European countries, there is still a substantial percentage of the population there who believe this and make life decisions as if it were true.

This mindset is creeping into politics, especially in the United States, where Christian fundamentalists have recently been elected to and appointed to important government positions. With their anti-scientific views, these people have the potential to cause major global damage by ignoring the research carried out by thousands of scientists from many different disciplines. The appointment of Evangelical Christians to important political posts in the US government does not bode well for the future of the world and alarm bells should be ringing across the globe. We must call out these false beliefs or else the future of all life on Earth may be in peril. When the effects of doing nothing could be catastrophic, it is no longer acceptable for us to simply let people "believe what they want". These are the policy-makers for our planet and their beliefs will affect the entire world.[2]

In the meantime, humans are slowly destroying the planet, and the rate of destruction is increasing as the world population explodes. We reached 1 billion humans around 1804, then 2 billion in 1927, 3 billion in 1960 and we are now at over 7 billion in the year 2017. What humanity and life on Earth needs is a slowdown or reversal of human population growth. Without this, environmental damage will increase, especially habitat destruction. According to the World Wildlife Fund, for example, "Some 46–58 thousand square miles of forest are lost each year – equivalent to 48 football fields every minute."[3] as a result of deforestation.

Pollution of waterways and the atmosphere, and the hunting to extinction of countless species also continue, yet most religious leaders still tell their followers to "go forth and multiply", in a kind of religious arms race. Many religious leaders refuse to educate their followers about, or allow, simple contraceptive measures; hence they are partly to blame for the accelerating problems that our descendants will soon face. Only those with a secular viewpoint have the courage to promote the much-needed benefits of population control. While the Pope talks about caring for our environment, he still preaches against the use of contraceptive measures.

* * *

It is important to forewarn readers that some comments made or concepts raised in this book may offend. Strong, confrontational words are often required to get people to reflect on long-held beliefs. The purpose of this book is not, however, to offend individuals directly, but rather to question belief systems. I want to make readers stop and think, and then ask questions they may never before have thought of asking. I certainly hadn't thought about all of these ideas in any depth until fairly recent times, and it was often the most confronting facts and discussions that created the most thought-provoking moments.

Religions are still so much a part of most societies that we often don't have the mental space to consider all reasonable alternatives. No one should feel any guilt while reading this book if they haven't previously asked some of the questions raised or read many of the religious textual quotes. Most people grow up within the intellectual constraints that their society has placed on them, especially during the formative years of childhood and adolescence. I am sure that many people have had passing questions or thoughts about the issues about to be discussed, but it is hard to think further about them if there are few large public displays of similar views. And most people would prefer not to pursue such thoughts if it means questioning or abandoning the belief systems of their family and community.

To benefit from this book, you have to be altruistic and ask yourself whether, if you gave up certain beliefs, it might improve the world for your descendants, even if it causes you some personal discomfort. Those who have children or grandchildren are perhaps more likely to appreciate the need to make sacrifices to create a better life for later generations, but we are all capable of making this leap. This book asks this of the reader, and it also asks, towards the end: what sort of changes can each individual make to help us and our children have a safer and more equality-based existence?

In this discussion, we must keep in mind that there have been three main stages in the history of humankind, which might be termed the magical, religious and scientific. One would hope that in this scientific phase, using scientific methods, we should be able to make more objective decisions about how we live our daily lives, how we view and can accept all other people, and how we interact with all of the other creatures and environments around us. It really is 11:59pm on the "Age of Religions" clock for humankind. It is time to move on.

To better conceptualize our possible future, however, we must first have an understanding of our past – how we arrived at this point and where we as human beings stand relative to everything else. We cannot begin to investigate or reject religious teachings until we first review and accept the evidence that questions the very foundations of them all. Where do we come from? How long have we been here? Are the stories recounted by religious texts supported by evidence, or are they myths? How do we know this? And how much supporting evidence is there for a secular view of the world?

We have no problem dismissing the creation stories and myths of many indigenous peoples around the world, yet often cannot see past the creation stories and myths that form the backbones of our own and the other prevailing major religions. Given that most religions make claims about the origin of life and humankind, and about the time-frames involved, we must start by investigating these claims.

AUTHOR'S NOTE

For quotes from religious texts, I have mainly used the following sources: www.biblegateway.com for both Old and New Testament quotes, and www.quran.com for quotes from the Koran. The dictionary definitions are from www.merriam-webster.com.

1

OUR HOME: THE UNIVERSE AND THE PLACE WE CALL "EARTH"

Currently, we know of nothing larger or grander than the entity we refer to as "the universe". It is a realm of possibly infinite size, about which we are gradually finding out more and more. Many nations and organizations around the world are working together to contribute to our knowledge of what the universe is made of, its scale and shape, its age, and how it has developed and might continue to change. Space probes and satellites, terrestrial telescopes and scanners, even underground research facilities, are constantly gathering and sharing images and data that might help us better understand what is out there and how it came to be.

At the South Pole in Antarctica there is a complex known as Bicep2, which detects gravitational waves of the early universe and the effects of the "Big Bang". On the high-altitude plains of the Atacama Desert in northern Chile stands a $1.5 billion facility encompassing an array of 66 variously sized radio-telescopes, which was jointly built by scientific teams from Asia, Europe, North America and Chile. Called

ALMA (Atacama Large Millimeter Array), it gathers observations in millimetre and sub-millimetre wavelengths that may provide insights into the birth of stars during the early universe, as well as images of more recent local star and planet formation.

Scientists have been able to estimate the age of the universe using a number of methodologies, which include:

1. determining the ages of very old stars by understanding their life cycles and how quickly or slowly they have been burning up their energy
2. measuring the rate of expansion of the universe by measuring cosmic microwave background fluctuations
3. using radiometric dating techniques
4. utilising cosmological "redshifts" of various radiations.

The current, most widely accepted estimate is approximately 13.78 billion years, with an error margin of about +/–60 million years.

People often respond to such statements by asking, "But what preceded the birth of the universe?" Ongoing investigations in physics and cosmology are leading to a number of possible answers, including the "multiverse theory", which suggests that the universe that we exist in is just one universe in a multitude of universes. These theories are fascinating but too complex to even try to explain here.[1]

> "The singularity at the Big Bang doesn't indicate a beginning to the universe, only the end to our theoretical comprehension"
> – Sean M. Carroll, Cosmologist

Theists – people who believe in a god or gods – often say, "That's all very well, but surely there must have been a divine creator who set it all up in the first place?" On the surface this seems a reasonable question, but in reality all it does is move the responsibility one step further down the road, because as much as we can ask where the complex laws of the universe originated from, so must we ask where the even more complex divine creator came from? Suggesting an even more complex scenario is creating an even greater question, not the opposite. And if one can explain a god without a creator, then one should be able to explain a universe without one. The universe is, in fact, a simpler entity than a god.

Many theists often also argue, "A universe can't come from nothing." But invoking a god does not help because what were the building blocks that a god or gods used to create the universe? If they were something definable then there was always something there; and, if not, then the universe has still come from "nothing". The answer is exactly the same.

Similarly, it is understandable that theists are not happy about the answer to why our universe exists being, "It just does." Yet if you ask them why their god exists, they will provide the same answer: "He just does."

We must accept that at this stage of human intelligence and knowledge there is nothing wrong with simply saying we don't know, rather than creating an even more complex entity than the universe. Some questions may never be answered by *Homo sapiens*, but if science can't answer them, then without doubt religions certainly cannot either.

We must remember that until 100,000 years ago, our brains evolved to survive and avoid predation on the plains in Africa, and it is still only a relatively short time (on the evolutionary scale) since then. Understanding concepts of the extra-large (the universe, galaxies and so on) or the extra small (atoms, quantum mechanics and the like) does not come intuitively to the human brain. For tens of thousands of years, until we began to understand gravity in the late 1600s, it was beyond most people's comprehension that we could live on anything but a "flat earth" – otherwise we would surely fall off. It is still hard to explain this to many people. Take a child or an adult from a less educated background and show them a globe with little people attached and ask how they can all possibly stay on.

There are thought to be over 200 billion galaxies in the universe – galaxies being vast collections of stars and planets – with each one containing maybe 200 billion stars and planets. This figure is based on observations made by the Hubble Space Telescope, which can reveal thousands of galaxies in a single composite picture.

We live in *one* of those 200 billion galaxies, and call ours the "Milky Way". It's a spiral galaxy approximately 100,000–120,000 light years across, which means that if we could travel at the speed of light (which we can't), it would take over 100,000 years just to traverse our own galaxy. And our solar system, with the eight planets whose names are so well known to us, plus our star, the Sun, make up just a speck in our galaxy, located on the edge of one of the concentrations of gas and dust called the Orion Arm.

Hubble Ultra deep field view of distant galaxies
(courtesy NASA and STScI)

We use light years to measure space because it is just too huge to comprehend or explain in kilometres or miles. The speed of light is approximately 300,000 kilometres per second, which equates to 9.5 trillion kilometres in a year. In real terms, this means that the light generated from the Sun takes just over eight minutes to reach us here on Earth; so when we look at the Sun, we see it as it was about 8 minutes ago, not how it is now. This is fascinating, because if intelligent life forms existed on a planet 70 million light years away (which is not that far, relative to the scale of the universe) and those beings were looking at Earth through a super-powerful telescope, they would see the dinosaurs roaming the surface of our planet. The images of *our* existence wouldn't reach them until long after we were gone. Likewise, when we look at very distant stars through a telescope, although we can see them, they may actually no longer exist, because their light has taken such a long time to reach our eyes. And the light we see from distant galaxies via today's advanced telescopes had been travelling for billions of years before it was photographed. So, when we look at things in "outer space", we are actually looking back in time.

How old is Earth?

Okay, so now we have an understanding of what is around our planet, but what about Earth itself?

For the last few thousand years, people have theorized about the age and history of our world, using a variety of approaches. Some early scholars (notably ancient Greek and Middle Eastern thinkers) suggested that as there were no written records prior to a certain time, Earth must have been created then. Religious authorities counted the lifetimes described in the Bible to come up with an age for Earth of approximately 6,000 years.

In 1896, the French chemist Henri Becquerel discovered and began to study and understand the phenomenon of radioactivity, whereby certain elements decay into others by shedding atomic particles. He realized that the ratio of atoms in the original element to the decayed element could be used to determine the age of a substance if you knew the rate of decay of the original element, commonly expressed as its half-life, or the time it takes to shed 50 per cent of its atoms. This led to the development of radiometric dating, which is the most common method of determining the ages of earthly materials.

Through this method and other corroborative techniques, the age of Earth has been determined to be 4.54 billion years old, with a margin of error of 1 per cent. As Earth was formed by an accretion method, whereby it slowly increased to its current size by gravitationally pulling in nearby rocks, dust and debris, there was no single point in time at which Earth could be said to have come into being.

A designed universe?

All of this information should already demonstrate that the notion that humankind was shaped in the "image of god" and that we are the pinnacle of a god's creation is purely egocentric, small-minded, and wishful thinking. The religious viewpoint appears to regard the existence of the rest of our Milky Way galaxy as insignificant, never mind the rest of the universe! And it assumes that the universe was finely tuned for our benefit, while in fact 99.9999999999 per cent of it is at best indifferent to human life and most likely inhospitable to us.

If theists reach the conclusion that the universe must have been designed by a god (by having only a simplistic look at it) what then do these believers think a universe that wasn't designed by a god would look like? I would say: just like this one! Theists have a damn big job ahead of them explaining the purpose of the other 99.9999999999 per cent of the universe if it was created by a god whose primary focus is humankind on earth, whereas without the involvement of a god, the presence of the rest of the universe requires no further explanation.

Despite supposedly having been written or inspired by the creator of the universe, the old religious texts, such as the Torah, the New Testament and the Koran, contain no enlightening comments about the universe, no observations that would not have been visible to the naked eye. Religious thought creates this shallow idea that the universe has no meaning without the presence of humankind, whereas scientific evidence indicates the opposite: that the universe would exist just fine without us. Moreover, it's likely that among the billions of galaxies and billions of planets within each galaxy, there exist other life forms. And given the timescales involved, it's possible that some of these life forms are far more advanced than humans.

2 HOW DID WE GET HERE?

At the outset, we must make it clear that as yet we do not have any definitive evidence as to how the first animate life began on Earth. Four and a half billion years ago, our planet was far different from the world we currently see. There were no water-filled oceans, forests or living things. It was a rocky planet obviously devoid of any life, with atmospheres that would be toxic to current life forms.

It did, however, encompass a suitable, nutrient-rich mix of elements from which the first complex chemicals and, likely, amino acids were able to form. Today, scientists are continually experimenting and assessing data to work out how animate life then developed, in a collaborative process similar to the attempts to understand the scale of the universe.

There is much interest and research into the field known as "abiogenesis" the process by which non-living substances such as simple organic compounds become more complex until they can be considered life forms. Viruses, which we have only become aware of in recent times, are one such interesting form of life. They carry genetic material, reproduce and evolve through natural selection; however, they lack key characteristics (such as cell structure) of more sophisticated life forms. Because they possess some but not all such qualities, viruses have been described as "organisms at the edge of life" or "replicators".

Given the myriad of physical properties that exist in the universe, it was highly likely that such complex chemical interactions would eventually happen somewhere. When science is eventually successful in providing strong evidence that life can form this way, it will finally prove that a god was not required to create life. From that moment on, all of humankind will have to finally accept Nietzsche's famous comment that "God is dead".

For the first few billions of years on Earth, life was extremely simple. Gradually, multicellular life forms came into being, which then begat more and more complex forms of life. This process, evolution, happens on a time-scale that in most cases is imperceptible, spontaneous alterations, or mutations, leading to tiny changes from generation to generation. Evolution does not involve one creature giving birth to a completely different creature; nor are there simplistic "hybrids", where an animal is half one species and half another. The change is so gradual that if you look at only one or two or even a few preceding generations, the differences will not be apparent; however, if you can examine hundreds of generations over thousands of years, you will sometimes start to see distinct physical changes. For example, all of the varieties of dogs that we have as pets, from the large Saint Bernard to the tiny Chihuahua, are derived from a common wolf ancestor that lived just 10,000 years or so ago. Much of this selection process was accelerated by human intervention, but it is still evidence of the changes that can occur on a relatively short evolutionary timescale.

Even if no fossils were ever found (and only an incredibly tiny number of all living things do fossilize), boundless evidence and traces of the evolutionary process could still be identified. They are evident in DNA and the differences between species, in the geographical distribution of plants and animals, and in the embryological development and comparative anatomy of all living things.

For example, present-day humans retain many physical and behavioural attributes that evolved for a particular purpose but are no longer required. These include the appendix, coccyx (tail bone at the base of our spine), wisdom teeth, nipples on males, hair on various parts of the body, the paranasal sinuses, and a variety of redundant muscles, such as those that can move our ears forwards, which originally allowed us to better detect approaching threats. On this erratum list, one of the top contenders for evidence of a change in the evolutionary pathway is the recurrent laryngeal nerve. In many animals, this nerve, the tenth of the twelve cranial nerves, emerges directly from the brain to supply the throat and laryngeal region. The interesting thing about this nerve is that in our ancestors, the tetrapods, from a few hundred million years ago, the nerve travelled along a short path from the brain to the gills, passing around blood vessels from the heart. In modern mammals it was "trapped" below these blood vessels and, as mammalian bodies elongated and the heart moved further from the brain, so too did this nerve have to elongate. As a result, it does a U-turn after descending down into the chest towards the heart and returns back upwards quite a distance to get back to its area of innervation.

This anatomical pathway is especially odd when one then looks at its path in the giraffe. It only needs to travel a distance of 2 feet, yet it commences at the base of the brain, runs down the giraffe's long neck to its heart and then ascends back up the neck to the mouth region, a total of up to 30 feet! If this is "intelligent design" then the designer is certainly not very intelligent. Education is the only way to enlighten people who still deny evolution.

There are also many physiological and behavioural remnants of our ancestry, including "goose bumps". This mechanism of making hairs stand on end evolved to aid heat retention and to make the individual look larger. Today, it is of little use to humans but remains helpful for our mammalian cousins who are far more hirsute than us.

"We are certainly wonderfully developed, but we are not wonderfully made." – Richard Dawkins, Evolutionary Biologist

Design flaws

There is amazing complexity in the natural world, but there is no sign of perfect or intelligent design. There are fish that live at the bottom of the ocean with eyes that are non-functional, since there is no light there. There are birds with token wings that cannot use them to fly. In fact, there are countless features retained by living creatures that are purely remnants of their evolutionary development.

As much as we like to be told that we are "the pinnacle" of creation, we in fact carry many redundant parts in our bodies and a great deal of redundant genetic information, proteins and other chemicals. Much of our DNA contains non-coding base pairs (material in our chromosomes that appears to be completely redundant) and there are well over a thousand genetically-related diseases. If a god created us, why did he create so much waste and so many built-in faults and time-bombs?

We are just a point on a branch that is extending and will continue to grow and change. We are neither an end-point nor a supreme creation. Yes, we are the most powerful and influential creatures currently on the planet, but we are in fact very limited in our abilities. We cannot inhabit the 70 per cent of the planet covered by the oceans, seas, rivers and lakes. On land we can barely exist in the desert or cold regions and we cannot survive at very high altitudes. In fact, we humans can only live comfortably on a very small proportion of our planet's surface.

We do not possess enormous body strength like elephants, or arm strength like gorillas, or jaw strength like crocodiles – we have to cook most of the foods in our diets to soften them for our relatively weak jaw muscles. Our vision is limited to what we call the "visible spectrum", a relatively narrow range of all that can be observed. Bees and many other insects, as well as a number of other animals, can observe the world in the ultraviolet range, beyond the "visible spectrum". Plant species that depend on insect pollination often display colours and patterns that we humans are only able to see with special lighting but that are vivid to certain insects. Many birds can see things in the ultraviolet range and some have markings on their plumage that are only visible in such light. The distance range of our vision is quite limited too. We do not have "eyes like a hawk" and most people by middle age require assistance to see up close or at a distance.

Our sense of smell seems almost feeble when compared to many creatures, such as dogs, which are able to detect what we would call tiny traces of scents. A number of animals utilize senses that we cannot even begin to comprehend. For example, sharks, rays and platypuses have electroreception; bats have echolocation; snakes have infrared detection; and bees and pigeons can sense and utilize Earth's magnetic fields to navigate.

We are also not the only creatures to have an understanding of "self". There have been many experiments that show some sense of self among a number of different species. In the mirror self-recognition test, an animal is habituated to a mirror for a period of time (so that it begins to understand that its reflection is not threatening); then the animal is anaesthetized so that a single or multiple dots can be painted or stuck on its body without it knowing. The animal is then allowed to wake and look in the mirror. A number of animals began to touch the spots or even try to remove them.

This was summarized very well by Professor Marc Bekoff, Professor Emeritus of Ecology and Evolutionary Biology at the University of Colorado, Boulder:

> So, while animals might not ponder life and death the way humans do, they still may have some sense of self ... Not only are some animals self-aware, but also that there are degrees of self-awareness. Combined with studies by my colleagues, it's wholly plausible to suggest that many animals have a sense of "mine-ness" or "body-ness". So, for example, when an experimental treatment, an object, or another individual affects an individual, he or she experiences that "something is happening to this body". Many primates relax when being groomed and individuals of many species actively seek pleasure and avoid pain. There's no need to associate "this body" with "my body" or with "me" (or "I"). Many animals also know the placement in space of parts of their body as they run, jump, perform acrobatics, or move as a coordinated hunting unit or flock without running into one another. They know their body isn't someone else's body ...

> Some people, don't want to acknowledge the possibility of self-awareness in animals because if they do, the borders between humans and other animals become blurred and their narrow, hierarchical, anthropocentric view of the world would

be toppled. But Darwin's ideas about continuity, along with empirical data and common sense, caution against the unyielding claim that humans and perhaps a few other animals such as other great apes and cetaceans are the only species in which some sense of self has evolved.[1]

3 | THE APPEARANCE OF HUMANS

A question that is often asked is, "Who was the first human?" This mindset originates from a number of religious and cultural stories, most notably the story of Adam and Eve. In order to comprehend that there was no sudden or instant point in time when a certain upright creature that we call a human came into being, we need to understand the evolutionary process.

We have little difficulty understanding genetics and the passing of similarities from one generation to the next. We look at either our children or our forebears and we see resemblances. We are also relatively easily and comfortably able to trace back maybe one hundred generations and understand that we are related to someone who existed, say, 2,000 years ago. But try going back 20,000 years and it becomes pretty much impossible to imagine. Try then going back 200,000, or more importantly, 2 million years, and it becomes beyond the limitations of our daily thoughts, much in the same way as the scale of a galaxy, or the universe.

It is essential, though, to understand the longer timeframe, because this is how far back we need to go to understand when the first hominid species existed. They looked in many ways similar to us, no longer like their ape or monkey predecessors. They were walking upright at least 5 million years ago, as evidenced by a number of anatomic features in fossil remains, such as leg and pelvis angles, as well as the position of the foramen magnum, the hole in the base of the skull where the spinal cord connects to the brain stem. Go back further in time and these features are absent, meaning that our ancestors at that time moved in a crouched and more ape-like position.

To attempt to name a precise time when humankind appeared is like trying to pinpoint the point when a person changes from a child to an adult. Although in most countries, we legally and arbitrarily accept that that occurs at 18 years of age, in real terms the child of 17 years and 364 days does not at the stroke of midnight become a different person because they are suddenly 18 years old. It is a gradual change, whereby a child develops physically, emotionally and behaviourally into what we call an adult.

Likewise we adopt specific dates to determine the nomenclature of fossils and appearance of "new species". For taxonomic reasons, fossils may be named as one species when, for example, they hail from 3 million years ago, and named something else if they are from 2 million years ago, if there are significant (though often relatively small) anatomical differences.

One of the most common questions regarding evolution is, "If we are descended from monkeys, why are there still monkeys?" To answer that question, let's have a look at the lineage of some of the modern great ape species, which includes chimpanzees, bonobos (very similar to chimpanzees), gorillas and humans. Approximately 8 million years ago none of these species existed; however, there was a common ancestor, a forest ape. It looked like an ape but not exactly like any of the current aforementioned species.

Over time the genetic diversity of its descendants coupled with movement into different environments led to gradual changes in this creature's genes and hence its appearance. As this continued over thousands of generations, the descendants began to look more and more different from their distant forebears and the other ape species living in different environments. Over millions of years, this branching has given rise to the current range of great apes. As they did not exist millions of years ago, we are not descended from these apes, but are merely distant cousins of them all.

When one looks at the complexity of creatures that exist, it is very difficult to comprehend that all life began from single-celled creatures. When we look at all of the specialized organs of the body and how they interact, it is no wonder ancient humans dreamed that this could only have come about as a result of divine intervention. But we now know that all of the species that we currently see plus the 99 per cent of species that are now extinct came about as a result of evolution over vast periods of time.

Charles Darwin produced an amazing theory for his era, considering that it was based only on observation of existing species and no fossil records or genetic analyses. As science has advanced, more and more data has confirmed evolution to be true. As with all developing theories, science asks that it should be testable and also falsifiable. For evolution to take place, there are three requirements: environmental pressures or competition for resources must force living creatures to adapt to survive; genetic information must be heritable; and changes in genes, known as mutations, must be possible. If these three conditions exist together then evolution simply *must* occur. But if any of these were shown to be absent or false, then the theory would be flawed.

Consequently, any of the following would destroy the theory:

- if it could be shown that organisms with identical DNA have different genetic traits
- if it could be shown that mutations do not occur.
- if it could be shown that when mutations do occur, they are not passed down through the generations
- if it could be shown that although mutations are passed down, no mutation could produce the sort of phenotypic changes that drive natural selection
- if it could be shown that selection or environmental pressures do not favour the reproductive success of better adapted individuals
- if it could be shown that the genetic makeup of these better

    adapted individuals does not begin to vary from their ancestors
    with a concomitant change in their phenotype/appearance
- if it could be shown that the timescales required for evolution
do not exist.

None of these have been proved and, hence, evolution is considered to
be a fact by those who understand it.

The renowned scientist J.B.S. (Jack) Haldane made a couple of
famous comments on this topic that help put these ideas into perspective. The first was a response to an evolution sceptic:

> *Evolution skeptic*: Professor Haldane, even given the billions of
> years that you say were available for evolution, I simply cannot
> believe it is possible to go from a single cell to a complicated
> human body, with its trillions of cells organized into bones and
> muscles and nerves, a heart that pumps without ceasing for
> decades, miles and miles of blood vessels and kidney tubules,
> and a brain capable of thinking and talking and feeling.

> *Professor Haldane*: But madam, you did it yourself, and it only
> took you nine months!

Another time Haldane was asked if there was anything that might
cause him to question his understanding of evolution. He thought for
a second and responded, "The presence of a fossil rabbit in pre-Cam-
brian rock." What he was referring to here was that despite there being
millions of fossils of all varieties of creatures, not one has been dated to
a period that does not match the appropriate evolutionary timescale.
The layering of the fossil record clearly shows the increasing complexity of organisms over time and advancement of creatures towards those
that exist today.

Even if no more fossils of the pre-modern human species were found,
new and at times more accurate information could still be obtained
from molecular biology and genetic analyses. Through mathematical
modelling of these analyses, we can calculate when "branching" of the
evolutionary tree occurred and when certain anatomical and biochemical changes took place.

A common catch-cry of those who don't (or refuse to) understand evolution is "It's only a theory." But the common usage of the term "theory" is a little different from the way the term is used by scientists. In scientific circles, "theory" refers to a comprehensive explanation that is supported by a vast body of evidence. Many scientific theories are so well established that no new evidence is likely to arise to alter them substantially. For example, no new evidence will demonstrate that Earth does not orbit around the Sun (heliocentric theory), or that living things are not made up of tiny building blocks called cells (cell theory).

In reality, it is no longer justifiable to ask whether one believes in evolution, only whether or not one accepts it. The only "evidence" against it are several old texts written hundreds or thousands of years ago. No other credible evidence supports the contrary view.

Even the Vatican has begun to accept evolution (though it still claims it had a divine source and is guided by their god which is not the scientific view). Pope Francis has said, "Evolution in nature is not in contrast with the notion of divine creation because evolution requires the creation of the beings that evolve."

Science and society

It was the Greek civilization of 2,500 years ago that brought science into everyday life, to the benefit of the broader community. The Greeks realized that knowledge could be acquired through observation, and that there were immutable laws governing the natural world, which were often at odds with the myths and superstitions of their ancestors. Understanding these laws allowed them to predict future events and outcomes, something that had previously been the prerogative of soothsayers and gods. It also became evident that human laws were mutable and could be agreed upon without the approval of the gods. This newfound freedom of thought allowed for the creation of the first democratic society, in which anyone was allowed to be heard and could have a say in the laws that governed the people. This was a great advance on having to live by fixed laws derived from sacred texts, and it allowed humans to devise laws that were relevant to their times and circumstances.

4

THE HISTORY OF DEITY BELIEFS

Homo sapiens has always been a curious creature and ancient people needed something to explain nature and to help them understand what was going on around them and to them. They comprehended little of cause and effect, and myth became a binding tool that kept tribes together, allowing for a structured sharing of information that could be of benefit to the group.

Believing in a higher power may have started when an action occurred that was then followed by a positive outcome. The fact that the outcome, such as a food source wandering by or rains falling, was going to occur anyway was beyond the grasp of ancient peoples, as they could not see far, either physically or into the future. Actions that seemed to lead to successful outcomes probably then became rituals, which were subsequently passed down through the generations.

Discussions of historical events may have led to certain historical figures becoming revered as fonts of wisdom or cultural heroes, and myths may have sprung up around them. Then, going a step further along this pathway, a particular historical or mythical figure may have been cited as the original creator of the rituals and rules of the tribe. Stories may then have been told about misfortunes that befell those who did not follow the tribe's rules.

Archaeologist Henri Frankfort said: "It is essential that true myth be distinguished from legend, saga, fable and fairy tale. All these may retain the elements of myth ... But true myth presents its images and its imaginary actors, not with the playfulness of fantasy, but with a compelling authority. It perpetuates the revelation of a 'Thou'."

Many myths slowly became more elaborate over the generations, with additional heroes coming into existence, and the narratives becoming epics in which triumphs and failures were interwoven. Over generations, people would sit around and swap stories and, as in the childhood game of Chinese whispers, these stories would be continually altered and added to, both in length and complexity.

Such stories also reflected attempts to understand other creatures, particularly animals that were a food source, and identify patterns and meanings in natural phenomena. These included the great mystery of the fertility of women and the creation of new life. The connection of procreation to the appearance of a new life nine months later is an understanding that we take for granted, but to early humans who had not yet made the connection, the birth of a new individual from a woman must have seemed both mysterious and miraculous. Even nowadays we use the term "the miracle of birth", even though we understand both the cause and the process. This is also probably why early art forms often portrayed "Mother Gods" and why "Mother Nature" and "Mother Earth" are feminine terms. Early humans may have thought that women received some spirit from an external source to become pregnant and create new life. Very few male figurines and gods existed in the early stages of art and sculpture, because the male's role in this incredible event was not fully comprehended.

This idea of a possible spiritual source of life encouraged people to seek to appease and gratify creator gods. Humans throughout time have worshipped nearly everything, be it from the earth, on the earth (either plant or animal) or above the earth. But in the last few millennia, most beliefs have focused on the idea of a being superior to and far removed from normal life, often existing up in the sky, from where the god can see all that is going on below. A likely origin of the sky-god belief was the mystery of the sun "dying" in the evening and being "reborn" in the morning. Also linked to this was the observation that in the night sky the Moon, a nighttime guiding light, mysteriously waxed and waned. The patterns of the stars, which in some cultures are thought to depict zodiacal signs and mythical creatures or symbols, would also have contributed to this idea that supernatural power resided in the heavens.

Sacrifice was also a common way to appease a deity, be it the offering of plants, animals or humans, a practice that nowadays happens only in "primitive cultures", even though, as will soon be shown, it was supposedly practised and requested by the god of the Old Testament.

Creation of the Stories

Primitive humans came up with many long, complex creation stories that were passed down through the generations. The Aboriginal peoples of Australia, who have lived there approximately 50,000 years, have many Dreamtime or Dreaming stories that explain creation, and the conversion of a formless land into one rich in geographical features and sacred sites. They include stories related to climate, food and water sources and the creation of particular landforms.

Aboriginal stories tell of ancestral figures that often had supernatural powers, but these beings were not seen as gods to be propitiated. At the same time, much worldly knowledge was accumulated and transmitted through these stories, which were shared via the spoken word, dance or paintings. Aboriginal stories demonstrate that such accounts can date back tens of thousands of years, become remarkably complex and play an important role in communities, in this case helping people to survive in a harsh continent.

In Europe and North Africa, many creation stories were linked with female creation figures, which were often depicted in carved stones, dating possibly as far back as 200,000 years ago. These include the famous Venus of Berekhat Ram, found in northern Israel, and the Venus of Tan-Tan, from Morocco. A preponderance of such carvings appeared throughout Africa, the Middle East and Europe about 25,000 years ago.

In Ancient Egypt, deities were first recorded in texts approximately

5,000 years ago and they generally represented the natural forces and phenomena that needed to be supported and appeased through rituals and offerings. Hundreds of gods existed at any one time, and the stories of each god encompassed many myths. This polytheistic view lasted for an extremely long time, though it seems that certain gods gradually came to be seen as more powerful than others. Divine behaviour was believed to govern all of nature, and Egyptians prayed at temples and shrines for divine help. Some gods were human figures, some were animals, while others were a combination of the two.

Ancient Greek religion was likely based on even older Mycenaean and Minoan religions. Its sects, though varied, shared many traits and beliefs. They were mainly polytheistic, with Zeus being the king of the gods while other gods had separate but important roles. For example, Poseidon ruled over the seas, Helios controlled the Sun and Aphrodite was the goddess of love. Greek religion developed an extensive mythology, mainly describing how the deities interacted with and affected humankind. Many religious festivals were devised, moral codes were created, sacred texts were compiled and temples were constructed for worship, including sacrificial services.

It has been suggested that across the whole of history humans have created over 3,000 gods, spanning various timespans, regions and cultures. All have been revered for an extended period of time, but none have been written about as much as the gods of the three main monotheistic religions. It may be that the existence of extensive written texts and only a single god makes it more difficult to "disown" or "disprove" the deity – hence their greater longevity.

In addition, Christianity adopted the Jewish Old Testament god and then Islam drew on stories and characters from both the Old and New Testaments. By building on top of existing stories, these religions may have acquired greater authority and, subsequently, more loyal adherents. After all, it is much harder to argue down Christianity without first showing that the Old Testament is false; and to disprove Islam, one would have to argue against both the Old and the New Testaments before one could even start on its own stories.

For example, in Judaism, Christianity and Islam, the Adam and Eve story starts things off. Christians believe that Adam and Eve's mistake created the premise of "original sin", one of the main reasons why Jesus sacrificed himself. In the Koran, Mohammed meets with Adam in the heavens on his famous "night journey" and Adam is also mentioned on a number of other occasions.

The stories that form the backbones of the many current religious texts did not suddenly "pop" into existence. They were devised, developed and added to until they could be written down, and then they were further modified and reworked many times over into the forms that we currently read today.

The earliest major written hero or deity story is a collection commonly called The Epic of Gilgamesh, which dates from 3,000–4,000 years ago. Many stone tablets have been found in Mesopotamia that relate various chapters of this tale. The story, of great length and detail, recounts the life of Gilgamesh, a part god, part human character, as well as Utnapishtim, Enkidu and other characters. Intriguingly, many of these stories have parallels with those later recounted in the Old Testament. In both, for example, a man is created from the earth by a god, and he is introduced to a woman who tempts him into accepting a food, and is then banished and unable to return. Utnapishtim is told by the gods to build a large boat to allow him and his family to survive a flood, and to take animals on board with him. He sets forth three different birds to determine whether or not there is dry land. This is very similar to the later but better-known story of Noah in the Old Testament books (which most historians would say was based on the Gilgamesh story).

The books that form the backbone of the main surviving monotheistic religions were written at a time when people had only an inkling of what was going on around them. They had no understanding of the scale of the greater world, let alone the extent of the universe or, conversely that microscopic bacteria, viruses and other invisible entities caused diseases. So stories were created to help explain what was then still unexplainable – except by invoking gods, whose imagined supernatural powers could be used to explain just about anything.

Whereas today we can see weather patterns and cyclones building and can predict weather more than a week ahead, in the distant past, storms were seen as signs that the gods had been angered. Nowadays, we can prevent diseases through immunization or control them using a variety of methods, but in earlier times outbreaks of diseases were thought to be divine retribution for human sins.

On every continent, native peoples have invented their own gods, rituals and beliefs about creation, as well as ways to appease and appeal to their gods. Most of these religions are older than the current major religions, and magic and miracles exist in them all. God is and always has been simply a name for a lack of understanding about something. Humans, like most creatures, are pattern-seeking. If we cannot understand the cause of something, many people would rather find comfort in a false theory than have no answer at all.

5 THE CURRENT MAIN MONOTHEISTIC RELIGIONS

All three of the main monotheistic religions – Christianity, Judaism and Islam – developed stories and teachings purporting to provide definitive answers to all the major philosophical questions. However, when one reads the books of these religions, it is evident that they were written by people who had never travelled far, let alone experienced the great variety of peoples and other natural phenomena that existed across Earth. As with all prior religions, their writings interweave myths with accounts of real places and events.

Adherents believe, however, that these writings are not just stories *about* the gods but the words *of* the one true god. Yet there is not one shred of evidence that they are the actual words of a deity. There is not a single sentence that could *not* have been written by the peoples of that time; there is not one single comment or prediction that would demonstrate that the texts and stories should be attributed to an all-knowing supernatural being. There is never any mention, for example, of the causes of diseases, cures for cancers or sub-atomic particles;

no predictions about electricity, cars, the Internet, and so on. They are all merely the words of men of the time. When adherents are asked to point to evidence within the texts that they are divinely inspired, they cannot identify even one sentence that is not consistent with human beliefs at that time or one comment that categorically shows that they are words that could only have come from a god.

This is exceedingly difficult, but try to imagine that you have come to this point in the reading of this book and that you know nothing about the religious stories and cultures in which you were raised. Erase all information that has become ingrained in your thoughts pertaining to your beliefs. If you cannot take a step back and clear your views and opinions, then it is likely you will find this next part of the book thought-provoking but confronting to read. We must remove the bias that allows us to happily and comfortably look at other religions and think, "Their views are incorrect; mine are the correct ones." Only then will you be able to continue reading and show as much scepticism for the stories, cultures and practices of your own religion as you show for those of other religions.

Consider the following:

- If you are Christian, Jewish or Hindu, you do not believe that Mohammed was the prophet of Allah, the god of Islam, and that, using his superpowers, he flew to heaven on a winged horse; or that the stories and laws of the Koran are an accurate representation of what happened 1,500 years ago or prescribe the correct way for *all humans* to live their lives.
- If you are Christian, Muslim or Hindu, you do not believe that the Jews are the special or chosen people of Yahweh, the god of Judaism, or that the stories and laws in the Old Testament are an accurate representation of what happened 4,000–6,000 years ago or prescribe the correct way for *all humans* to live their lives.
- If you are Muslim, Hindu or Jewish, you do not believe that Jesus had supernatural powers and is the son of some sort of trinity of a god, or that the stories and laws of the New Testament are an accurate representation of what happened 2,000 years ago or prescribe the correct way for *all humans* to live their lives.
- If you are Christian, Jewish or Muslim, you do not believe

that the various Hindu gods and many associated sacred texts are an accurate representation of how the world was created or prescribe the correct way for *all humans* to live their lives.

What are the implications of this? If Muslim beliefs are correct, then 1.6 billion are right and 5.4 billion people are wrong. If Jewish beliefs are correct, then 14 million people are right and 7 billion people are wrong. If Christian beliefs are correct, then 2.2 billion people are right and nearly 5 billion people are wrong. And if Hindu beliefs are correct, then 1 billion people are right and 6 billion people are wrong.

As is commonly said, "They can't all be right but they can certainly all be wrong." Many people respond to this with a hypocritical but magnanimously generous statement along the lines of "Well, they are all entitled to their own beliefs" – in other words, "I am right and they are wrong." This mindset often hides the subtext that if a person says this too vehemently, then maybe they will actually have to reflect more deeply and justify their own beliefs to the world. Maybe better to keep quiet so that others too will keep quiet and then none of us will have to ask "impolite" questions. This situation has led to people being too shy to ask not only "Which god is real?" but also "Are any gods real?"

With over 3,000 gods in human history to choose from, how did we come to believe in the ones that we do believe in? This is where most people say, "Well, that's just what I choose to believe." But where did that belief come from? Did it come from a rational assessment of the many options available to us? In reality, most people have never given themselves, or been given, the opportunity or time to reflect on this question. The reality is that religious belief nearly always derives from childhood teachings. Had you as a child been adopted by another society or country and brought up with a different religious belief, then you would just as vehemently be arguing that that religion or god is the true and correct one and that you have the book to "prove" it. So many of us have never thought about it that way. How can it possibly be that the belief system you have adopted is correct and all the others are false, yet if you – the same walking, living existing being – were "switched" to another culture then you would be arguing against yourself?

This is *the* most important headspace that we need to give ourselves: time to ask ourselves honestly if we can substantiate and validate our choices and actions. For the world can only progress if everyone on the planet eventually goes through this assessment process. To say that one believes such and such or simply has "faith" is, in reality, intellectual laziness. Faith is not a virtue, it is the absence of reason; it is a term often used when people simply don't know or understand something, and its use is not to be admired. It is far better to say simply "I don't know, but let's try to find out" than to be guided by falsehoods and mysticisms.

There is absolutely nothing wrong with admitting that we don't know, and it is certainly the most honest response we can give. As human beings, we certainly do not have all of the answers; there are innumerable things that we don't understand. But to choose to ignore evidence or choose not to think about the validity of our beliefs (and, remember, beliefs lead to actions) is the kind of thinking we need to eliminate in order to achieve greater harmony in the world.

The Beginnings of Monotheism

Judaism

Judaism was not the first monotheistic belief system, but it is the oldest surviving of the currently defined religions and it formed the backbone of the two largest current religions, Christianity and Islam. Its rules and guidance are based largely on the five books known as the "Torah" or "Old Testament" with additions and layering of interpretations added in the years since its inception.

Today most academic scholars say that the Torah had multiple authors, and that its composition took place over centuries. This hypothesis, sometimes called the Wellhausen Hypothesis, theorizes that the Old Testament was derived from originally independent, parallel and complete narratives, which were subsequently combined into the book's current form by a series of redactors (editors).

The proposition was developed in the 18th and 19th centuries from an attempt to reconcile inconsistencies in the biblical text. By the end of the 19th century it was generally agreed that there were four main sources, which had been combined into their final form by a series of redactors. These four sources came to be known as the Yahwist, or Jahwist; the Elohist; the Deuteronomist, (from the Book of Deuteronomy) and the Priestly Writer.

The analysis suggests that the dates and places of compilation for each of these sources were as follows:

- Yahwist source: written c. 950 BCE in the southern Kingdom of Judah
- Elohist source: written c. 850 BCE in the northern Kingdom of Israel
- Deuteronomist: written c. 600 BCE in Jerusalem during a period of religious reform
- Priestly source: written c. 500 BCE by Kohanim (Jewish priests) in exile in Babylon.

Although there have been some modifications to the theory in recent times, the basics have remained the same, in that the Torah is believed to have been collated from a variety of sources.

Jews believe that the Torah is the word of Yahweh, as dictated to Moses approximately 4,000 years ago. However, there is not one mention of any of the characters in the Torah in any document from Egypt, Babylonia or Israel of that era. Nor is there any evidence of the Pharaoh as described in the Old Testament or the enslavement of the Hebrew nation or a mass exodus as described therein – something which, had it been true, would have undoubtedly been mentioned somewhere in the millions of Egyptian documents, for instance. Nor is there a single archeological site or artefact from the region that strongly corroborates any of the stories of the Old Testament.

A sentence at the end of the Old Testament that talks about Moses' death and burial includes the statement "but to this day no-one knows where his grave is". This suggests that the stories were written long after Moses supposedly lived. There are many other passages that point to the text having been written much more recently than claimed, and there exist many excellent books that work through the evidence for this sentence by sentence.

Another interesting aspect of the development of Judaism is the archeological and Biblical evidence for a goddess called Asherah, who was Yahweh's partner in the early days. She appears in a number of texts, including a sentence in Exodus and in the Book of Kings, and on a number of inscriptions, including one found in the Sinai desert, which refers to "Yahweh and his Asherah".

> **Exodus 34:13–14** Break down their altars, smash their sacred stones and cut down their Asherah poles. Do not worship any other god, for the Lord, whose name is Jealous, is a jealous God.

> **2 Kings 21:7** Then he set the carved image of Asherah that he had made, in the house of which the LORD said to David and to his son Solomon, "In this house and in Jerusalem, which I have chosen from all the tribes of Israel, I will put My name forever."

> **1 Kings 15:13** He even deposed his grandmother Maakah from her position as queen mother, because she had made a repulsive image for the worship of Asherah. Asa cut it down and burned it in the Kidron Valley.

Although modern Judaism asserts that Judaism since the Old Testament has been following only Yahweh, evidence suggests that, up until possibly even the last few centuries BCE, polytheism was still a common part of Jewish theology. Indeed, Judaism has been constantly evolving in terms of what and whom it believes in. Discussions relating to Asherah have been ignored, however, likely in an attempt to corroborate the assumption that only a single god has long been the mainstay of the religion. Two commonly ignored passages in the book of Genesis show that the authors of the Torah were polytheists and were just starting to promote Yahweh as the most important god amongst other gods.

> **Genesis 1:26** Then God said, "Let us make mankind in our image, in our likeness, so that they may rule over the fish in the sea and the birds in the sky, over the livestock and all the wild animals, and over all the creatures that move along the ground."

Use of both words "us" and "our" show that Yahweh was apparently working in concert with other deities, and this continues a bit later when again arises the plural term "us" as if Yahweh is speaking to the other gods off camera.

Genesis 3:21–22 The Lord God made garments of skin for Adam and his wife and clothed them. And the Lord God said, "The man has now become like one of us, knowing good and evil. He must not be allowed to reach out his hand and take also from the tree of life and eat, and live forever."

In fact the religion and its stories had been developing up until the time the writings were collated to form the Torah, and this is why there are still so many mistakes and oddities in the book. They are purely a reflection of human understanding at that time, rather than the words of an all-knowing deity.

For example, on the first day of creation, apparently God created light:

Genesis 1:1–5 In the beginning God created the heavens and the earth. Now the earth was formless and empty, darkness was over the surface of the deep, and the spirit of God was hovering over the waters. And God said, "Let there be light" and there was light. God saw that the light was good, and he separated the light from the darkness. God called the light "day" and the darkness he called "night". And there was evening and there was morning – the first day.

Then on days two and three the land and the seas were made and all plants and vegetation. It was not until day four that the Sun and the Moon were created. So how could there have been light on day one, and night and day, without the Sun?

Genesis 1:16–19 God made two great lights – the greater light to govern the day and the lesser light to govern the night. He also made the stars. God set them in the vault of the sky to give light on the earth, to govern the day and the night, and to separate light from darkness. And God saw that it was good. And there was evening, and there was morning – the fourth day.

What normally follows from questioning this and many other soon-to-be-discussed stories is a re-interpretation of the texts to fit with what modern science now shows us. We take it for granted that the

Sun is the source of all of the bright light that we see in our solar system, but it was obviously not so clear-cut back then.

Another of the many interesting details relates to the Adam and Eve story, in which the snake is punished for deceiving humanity.

> **Genesis 3:14** You will crawl on your belly and you will eat dust all the days of your life.

As historical zoology shows us, snakes never had legs or wings so punishing a snake by making it crawl on its belly was not really much of a punishment! It must be assumed that the authors thought the mythologies that pervade the Old Testament would never be read and believed as facts, but were merely metaphors. Hence the authors were not concerned about the stories being scientifically accurate. Unfortunately, too many people have taken the words literally in the three millennia since they were compiled.

Another example relates to the story about Noah. He is advised to choose seven pairs of kosher animals and only a single pair of all other animals to take on the ark:

> **Genesis 7:1–4** The Lord then said to Noah, "Go into the ark, you and your whole family, because I have found you righteous in this generation. Take with you seven pairs of every kind of clean animal, a male and its mate, and one pair of every kind of unclean animal, a male and its mate, and also seven pairs of every kind of bird, male and female, to keep their various kinds alive throughout the earth. Seven days from now I will send rain on the earth for forty days and forty nights, and I will wipe from the face of the earth every living creature I have made."

Yet the kosher rules are not created until much later in the Torah. It's also interesting that there were supposedly *seven* pairs of all of the kosher animals on the ark, making the numbers of animals aboard even more far-fetched than most people realize.

What believing in the Old Testament means is that for all of the 150,000-plus years of human existence God chose to speak to only a few Middle Eastern nomads, and then only for a very short period of time, and has never had any communication in the 4,000 years since.

If you believe that the stories in the Old Testament are true, then you believe that an all-knowing and all-powerful god created human-kind instantly and as is. It follows then that the first generation was responsible for the fall of humankind and the reason why we are now all born sinners, and that the second generation was responsible for the first murder (Adam and Eve's son Cain killed his brother Abel) soon after stating that he had made mankind in his image

Only a few generations later, this all-knowing God suddenly decided that he had made such flawed creatures that he now had to wipe them all out with a flood, except for *one* family. How there were so many wicked people after only a few generations is never explained, nor the fact that the second generation, consisting of only two males, Cain and Abel, created future generations… somehow. It is also odd that God then re-populated the earth with the same flawed species that he had just wiped out!

In addition, if you believe that the stories in the Old Testament are true, you also accept that all life on earth was created in just a few days. This includes the myriad insects, mammals, birds, reptiles and amphibians, as well as the many millions of microscopic bacteria, viruses and so on.

You also believe that humans were assembled from dust, an inert material with no genetic information, into living things with the full complement of genes and strands of double-helix DNA in every cell, all organelles and intracellular chemicals, all formed into complete organs working synchronously together. And yet creationists say that abiogenesis, a much slower process of inanimate chemicals gradually becoming more complex, is impossible!

Were Neanderthals also the progeny of Adam and Eve? Were the other *Homo* species, such as *Homo erectus* and *Homo habilis*, also their descendants, who then evolved into different species, which then became extinct?

Which is more likely, the instant appearance of millions of different animal species, or the gradual formation of all of these species over a billion years of evolution?

If you believe the Old Testament to be true, then you believe that all these species fitted into Noah's ark and lived on board for a year (not 40 days, it rained for the first 40 days) after which they spread out across the globe to Europe, Asia, Africa, North and South America, Australia, Antarctica and the North Pole over a short period of time after the flood receded. This includes desert creatures such as camels, and cold-habitat creatures such as polar bears and penguins. All had supposedly been housed together on a boat; somehow carnivores and their prey had been kept separate, perhaps with fish in tanks and terrariums, filled with freshwater for freshwater fish and saltwater for saltwater species.

WHENEVER SCIENCE DISPROVES SOMETHING IN THE BIBLE, SUDDENLY IT WAS...

"ONLY A METAPHOR"

There are estimated to be 950,000 different insects, 10,000 different bird species, 10,000 different reptiles, 5,000 different mammals and 7,000 amphibians. What foods did they eat in the early days after they got off the ark when there would have been no living vegetation? The carnivores would have had to eat only one of a species for it to instantly become extinct!

Science can and has explained the diversity of nature and how each species came to exist in each ecosystem, while the Old Testament requires you to believe that a pair of each species was able to repopulate the earth, even though many species have only one offspring at a time and other genetic issues would make this feat impossible.

It is ironic, also, that proponents of the Noah's ark story who ignore evolution query "missing links" in the millions-of-years-old fossil records, yet cannot produce fossils of penguins, kangaroos, polar bears and the like in the Middle East, from where they supposedly originated.

Is it not just a trifle backward to believe that koalas, which sleep 18 hours a day, slowly made their way to Australia, swimming across many seas to reach the island continent 6,000 years ago? Considering that they only eat a very few species of eucalyptus leaves and none of those trees exist anywhere but Australia, what did the koalas eat and how did they survive over the hundreds of years the journey would have taken? If, on the other hand, you comprehend evolution, continental drift and the timescales involved, you can understand that millions of years ago the ancestors of these animals (who were not the same as present-day koalas) were able to reach Australia via land connections and that they then evolved into the creatures that exist today. This is also why there are no fossils or bones of any species along their supposed paths of migration from where Noah's ark landed (Mount Ararat) to where they currently reside.

It is an indictment of critical thinking that there are still *any* adults who actually believe the story of Noah's ark when it is so obviously mythology and a rip-off of the *Epic of Gilgamesh*, a story that pre-dated it and was simply a local legend, and other similar Middle Eastern flood stories. This is why it is not present in any of the many other cultures that existed around the world at that time. This is why it is not mentioned in Asian mythology, African mythology, Australian Aboriginal mythology, or indigenous North or South American mythology. It was solely a folkloric story of the Middle East.

If this god really wanted to start again with humankind but was happy for the animals to continue, why not just eliminate man alone, why kill all of the innocent animals? Not only does it make no sense, it is nonsense.

If you believe the stories in the Bible, then you believe that the variety of languages came about because people decided to build a tower (the Tower of Babel) that reached up to the sky, and that because the god of the Bible wasn't too keen on that idea he gave them all different languages so that they couldn't understand each other, and then spread those languages across the globe.

Genesis 11:1–9 Now the whole world had one language and a common speech. As people moved eastward, they found a plain in Shinar and settled there. They said to each other, "Come, let's make bricks and bake them thoroughly." They used brick instead of stone, and tar for mortar. Then they said, "Come, let us build ourselves a city, with a tower that reaches to the heavens, so that we may make a name for ourselves; otherwise we will be scattered over the face of the whole earth." But the Lord came down to see the city and the tower the people were building. The Lord said, "If as one people speaking the same language they have begun to do this, then nothing they plan to do will be impossible for them. Come, let us go down and confuse their language so they will not understand each other." So the Lord scattered them from there over all the earth, and they stopped building the city. That is why it was called Babel – because there the Lord confused the language of the whole world. From there the Lord scattered them over the face of the whole earth.

Is this the way the range of languages in the world came about or is this just a poor attempt by unworldly Bronze Age men to explain the origin of languages? If it were true, why has god not destroyed the International Space station, a collaborative effort of humanity showing that "nothing that they plan to do will be impossible for them"? And if the god of the Old Testament is concerned about what humanity could achieve working together with common goals, then he obviously wants a divided world rather than a united one.

Is Yahweh against a global effort to manage climate change? Is he against the eradication of viruses, bacteria and diseases that he supposedly created? And if he was upset about a tower being built "to the heavens", what are his views of aeroplanes, humans landing on the Moon or the search for life in other parts of the universe? Or does he just not want humankind to understand him or have contact with him?

If you believe the stories in the Bible then you believe that the god of the Old Testament promised the land now called Israel to the Jewish people forever. In the approximately 3,000 years since this episode, the Jews have not "owned" the land for most of this time but have been living all over the world. Considering he told them that the land would be theirs if they circumcised their children in an "everlasting deal", one could certainly argue that he did not deliver on his side of the bargain.

> **Genesis 17:7–8** I will establish my covenant as an everlasting covenant between me and you and your descendants after you for the generations to come, to be your God and the God of your descendants after you. The whole land of Canaan, where you now reside as a foreigner, I will give as an everlasting possession to you and your descendants after you; and I will be their God.

If you believe in the stories in the Bible, then you believe that an entire nation of people "wandered" in the desert for 40 years, in a tiny strip of land between the Red Sea and Israel. According to the story, after departing Egypt and miraculously crossing the Red Sea, the Hebrew nation was not allowed into the land of Israel for two generations. If an entire nation had lived there that long, surely there would be some archaeological evidence of their settlement, especially since they had apparently just finished building the "great cities of Pithom and Rameses"? Surely there would at least be piles of bones in a cemetery?

If you consider another view, that they didn't settle because they were "wandering", it must be made clear that this area is at its maximum 200 kilometres wide. Most people can comfortably walk more than 20 kilometres in a day, so even if the Hebrews were constantly moving, within a fortnight they would have been in Israel, unless they were just going around in circles. Furthermore, there are no great permanent water supplies in the desert to maintain an entire stationary nation and its livestock. So, again, is this likely to have been a real situation, or simply part of a mythology?

If you believe the stories in the Bible, then you believe that sheep can spontaneously give birth to variegated sheep by mating in front of magical sticks.

> **Genesis 30:37–39** Then Jacob took fresh sticks of poplar and almond and plane trees, and peeled white streaks in them, exposing the white of the sticks. He set the sticks that he had peeled in front of the flocks in the troughs, that is, the watering

places, where the flocks came to drink. And since they bred when they came to drink, the flocks bred in front of the sticks and so the flocks brought forth striped, speckled, and spotted.

If you believe the stories in the Bible then you believe that God spoke to a human being (who must have been super-important to God yet no-one at the time had really heard of) via a donkey.

Numbers 22:26–30 Then the angel of the Lord moved on ahead and stood in a narrow place where there was no room to turn, either to the right or to the left. When the donkey saw the angel of the Lord, it lay down under Balaam, and he was angry and beat it with his staff. Then the Lord opened the donkey's mouth, and it said to Balaam, "What have I done to you to make you beat me these three times?" Balaam answered the donkey, "You have made a fool of me! If only I had a sword in my hand, I would kill you right now." The donkey said to Balaam, "Am I not your own donkey, which you have always ridden, to this day? Have I been in the habit of doing this to you?" "No," he said.

If you believe the stories in the Bible, then you believe that tying one's child down and holding a knife above them as if you are about to kill them is an acceptable action. Can you imagine the sheer terror a child would feel being betrayed by a parent like this? Yet the person who is said to have done this, Abraham, is considered a great figure, one of the patriarchal heroes of the Bible. In modern times, such a person would be placed into an asylum or imprisoned.

If you believe that the words of the Bible are the words of God rather than Bronze Age men, then you have to accept that God didn't look closely enough at the number of legs on the insects that he had created.

Leviticus 11: 20–23 All flying insects that creep on all fours shall be an abomination to you. Yet these you may eat of every flying insect that creeps on all fours: those which have jointed legs above their feet with which to leap on the earth. These you may eat: the locust after its kind, the destroying locust after its kind, the cricket after its kind, and the grasshopper after its kind. But all other flying insects which have four feet shall be an abomination to you.

Insects have six legs, not four.

You also have to accept that he had a poor knowledge of bats, which are of course mammals and not part of the bird family. The writers of the Torah obviously did not hold degrees in basic biology.

Leviticus 11:13–19 These are the birds you are to regard as unclean and not eat because they are unclean: the eagle, the vulture, the black vulture, the red kite, any kind of black kite, any kind of raven, the horned owl, the screech owl, the gull, any kind of hawk, the little owl, the cormorant, the great owl, the white owl, the desert owl, the osprey, the stork, any kind of heron, the hoopoe and the bat.

If you believe the stories in the Bible, then you accept the following as a god's cure for leprosy (rather than just the ramblings of Bronze Age men):

Leviticus 14:1–7 The Lord said to Moses, "These are the regulations for any diseased person at the time of their ceremonial cleansing, when they are brought to the priest: The priest is to go outside the camp and examine them. If they have been healed of their defiling skin disease, the priest shall order that two live clean birds and some cedar wood, scarlet yarn and hyssop be brought for the person to be cleansed. Then the priest shall order that one of the birds be killed over fresh water in a clay pot. He is then to take the live bird and dip it, together with the cedar wood, the scarlet yarn and the hyssop, into the blood of the bird that was killed over the fresh water. Seven times he shall sprinkle the one to be cleansed of the defiling disease, and then pronounce them clean."

If you believe the stories in the Bible, then you believe an all-knowing god needed the Hebrew people to paint sheep blood on their doorways so that when he went to kill all first-born sons he would not go to the wrong house.

> **Exodus 12:12–13** On that same night I will pass through Egypt and strike down every firstborn of both people and animals, and I will bring judgment on all the gods of Egypt. I am the Lord. The blood will be a sign for you on the houses where you are, and when I see the blood, I will pass over you. No destructive plague will touch you when I strike Egypt.

If the god of the Old Testament is all-knowing and all-powerful, why the need for ten plagues, assuming he knew in advance that the first nine plagues were going to achieve nothing yet would affect the entire Egyptian populace, most of whom were probably nice people going about their daily lives? Was this a creative embellishment made by the writers to add more drama to the story? And how could killing all first-born infants, who had done no wrong, be the right thing to do when God could have killed the pharaoh and thus solved the problem simply and rapidly? Was the god of the Old Testament looking for dramatic build-up and crescendo? How can one condone widespread infanticide?

If you believe the stories in the Bible, then you have to accept that the god of the Old Testament didn't always make correct decisions, and could be talked around to more reasonable positions. And had Moses kept quiet then God would have killed many people.

> **Exodus 32:9–14** "I have seen these people," the Lord said to Moses, "and they are a stiff-necked people. Now leave me alone so that my anger may burn against them and that I may destroy them. Then I will make you into a great nation." But Moses sought the favour of the Lord his God. "Lord," he said, "why should your anger burn against your people, whom you brought out of Egypt with great power and a mighty hand? Why should the Egyptians say, 'It was with evil intent that he brought them out, to kill them in the mountains and to wipe them off the face of the earth'? Turn from your fierce anger; relent and do not bring disaster on your people. Remember your servants Abraham, Isaac and Israel, to whom you swore by your own self: 'I

will make your descendants as numerous as the stars in the sky and I will give your descendants all this land I promised them, and it will be their inheritance forever.'" Then the Lord relented and did not bring on his people the disaster he had threatened.

If you believe the stories in the Bible, then you believe that they are the words of an all-knowing and all-powerful being, as dictated to Moses, and not the words of Bronze Age men. This seems a little odd, though, when one reads the final sentences of the Old Testament, which appear to have been written by someone looking back in time and trying to create a dramatic closing scene, in the manner of a Hollywood blockbuster.

> **Deuteronomy 34:5–12** And Moses the servant of the Lord died there in Moab, as the Lord had said. He buried him in Moab, in the valley opposite Beth Peor, but to this day no one knows where his grave is. Moses was a hundred and twenty years old when he died, yet his eyes were not weak nor his strength gone. The Israelites grieved for Moses in the plains of Moab for thirty days, until the time of weeping and mourning was over. Now Joshua son of Nun was filled with the spirit of wisdom because Moses had laid his hands on him. So the Israelites listened to him and did what the Lord had commanded Moses. Since then, no prophet has risen in Israel like Moses, whom the Lord knew face to face, who did all those signs and wonders the Lord sent him to do in Egypt—to Pharaoh and to all his officials and to his whole land. For no one has ever shown the mighty power or performed the awesome deeds that Moses did in the sight of all Israel.

And if you believe the Bible, then you believe that, just before he died, Moses sat down in a quiet spot away from his nation of people, while God dictated and he slowly wrote down, over a number of weeks, all of the words now contained in the Old Testament. Did he use 80 goat skins and an ink stylus to write it as per the currently used versions? If so then this means the god of the Old Testament dictated as facts the Genesis story, as well as all of the above and every other "explanation" that science has since proven to be the common false beliefs of the time. Did Moses get toilet breaks? Did he get writer's cramp? Did he ever say to Yahweh, "Hey, I didn't say it like that!"?

In reality, the Old Testament is similar to Homer's *Iliad* and *Odyssey* in that it is a well-constructed work of fiction that includes descriptions of some places and people who really existed (though the pharaohs, for example, are never named) and reflects commonly held views of the time.

* * *

Nine-year-old Joey was asked by his mother what he had learned in Sunday School.

"Well, Mum, our teacher told us how God sent Moses behind enemy lines on a rescue mission to lead the Israelites out of Egypt. When he got to the Red Sea, he had his army build a pontoon bridge and all the people walked across safely. Then he radioed headquarters for reinforcements. They sent bombers to blow up the bridge and all the Israelites were saved."

"Now, Joey, is that really what your teacher taught you?" his Mother asked.

"Well, no, Mum, but, if I told it the way the teacher did, you'd never believe it!"

* * *

Christianity

In the world today, Christianity has the greatest number of adherents of all religions, with estimated followers of approximately 2.2 billion, though practices and levels of adherence vary greatly, with a large proportion of Christians only vaguely believing in the religious stories or considering themselves religious. There are possibly 40,000 different denominations of Christianity worldwide, with many countries having their own congregational names and rules. Whichever denomination one belongs to, preaching is based mostly on the 27 books that form the New Testament. Christians regard both the Old and New Testaments to be a part of the sacred texts that form the core of their religion. Christianity is based on the belief in the teachings of Jesus and that he is a son of God and a part of God.

As with the discussion of the evidence (or lack thereof) for the characters in the Old Testament, so we must look at the current academic views and evidence regarding the foundations of Christianity.

There is much scholarly questioning and doubt as to whether or not Jesus was a real person, or a creation of the times subsequent to when he supposedly existed. Again we must start from the position of assuming nothing and questioning everything. The word "Christ" comes from the Greek word *khristos*, meaning "the anointed one". It was not Jesus' surname, as it is used in current times, and he would have been known only as Jesus of Nazareth or Jesus, son of Joseph, during his lifetime; the title was created later, to mean "Jesus the anointed". Whether or not Jesus truly existed is beyond the scope of this brief overview, except in general terms, to allow the reader to begin to question the basic validity of the text and stories that form the New Testament.

The documents that form the New Testament are believed to have been written in an old version of Greek; however, as will be discussed, none of the original documents have ever been found. All of the texts that are read today have been collated, translated and edited throughout the ages by a great variety of authors over many centuries. So, when someone believes that they are quoting the words of Jesus, what they must realize is that those words were not written down when the events supposedly happened or the comments were supposedly made, nor was it in English, and that the texts have in fact been edited and re-edited numerous times.

Most biblical scholars believe the following about the main writings of the New Testament:

- We have no known documents from the first century CE that corroborate any of the stories of the New Testament (more details below). Christian followers of the first few centuries CE were the ones who wrote these texts, and the oldest surviving manuscripts that exist are those that were written hundreds of years after the supposed events.

- Two of the oldest copies of the New Testament that we have, the Codex Sinaiticus (major parts of which are on display in the British Museum) and the Codex Vaticanus (kept at the Vatican Library) are believed to be from the 4th century. When one compares the two texts, it is easier to find verses that differ from one another than it is to find consecutive verses that entirely agree with each other. According to Herman Hoskier, a renowned biblical scholar, there are over 3,000 textual differences between the Codex Sinaiticus and the Codex Vaticanus in the Gospels alone. And if one was to compare either of these texts with the current King James Bible, the further variations would also be in the thousands!

- There are over 8,000 old manuscripts that form the basis of the New Testament and no two are identical. There were many revisions, language changes and sources throughout time. The compilation of the King James Bible, the source for most Christian readings, was commenced in 1604 and completed in 1611. It was the third translation into English to be approved by the English Church authorities, and was instigated in response to perceived problems in earlier translations.

- The King James Bible was written by 47 men and by the 1700s had become the most common version used in Anglican and Protestant churches; it is now the most printed book in history. To compile it, the men worked in six groups with 40 unbound copies of the 1602 edition of the Bishops' Bible, specially printed so that the agreed changes of each committee could be recorded in the margins. The groups worked on certain parts separately and the drafts produced by each group were then compared and revised to make them more consistent.

So, in fact, the "word of god" is a book compiled in the 17th century from pre-existing translations of thousands of contradictory 4th-century scrolls that are said to be copies of documents written in the first century that in fact have never been found.

As with the Old Testament then, the stories and miracles described in the New Testament must be regarded with a great deal of scepticism. Imagine someone quoting you decades after you said something, and before it was written down by anyone else, and then claiming that their record is 100 per cent accurate. Most people find it difficult enough to remember verbatim what was said in a conversation last week, let alone many, many years afterwards.

There are no authors' names on the Gospels. In the process of recopying, different regional manuscripts emerged, in which different corrections and adjustments were made for theological reasons or to iron out inconsistencies between the different versions, as well as errors made during translation to the local language. The editions of the New Testament that we read today were established by collating all major surviving manuscripts, as well as information from citations by other writers. They are works of consensus.

Most New Testament scholars believe what is known as the "Marcan Priority" or "Marcan Hypothesis". It asserts that the authors of the Gospels of Luke and Matthew used the Gospel of Mark as their source. In addition, many scholars believe that Luke and Matthew also drew on what is commonly called the "Q source" (from the German word *Quelle*, meaning "source"), a hypothetical collection of documents drawn from early Christian followers' oral traditions.

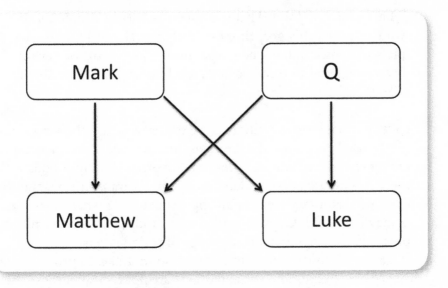

The Marcan Priority

The Gospels are the main source for our understanding of Jesus. The following is a summary of the scholarly consensus with regards to the periods when the Gospels were likely written:

The Gospel of Matthew This is the first text of the New Testament and, the background suggests that it recounts events that took place during the years 80–90 CE.

The Gospel of Mark This was probably the first of the texts to be written and it recounts events which took place around 65–70 CE.

The Gospel of Luke This is listed and read as the third of the Gospels; the background suggests it recounts events that took place around 80–100 CE. The earliest partial manuscripts found that make up Luke's Gospel are five 3rd-century papyrus fragments; the earliest complete versions are 4th and 5th century; however, the authors of these documents were never named.

The Gospel of John There is much scholarly debate as to who authored this gospel; most likely it was not Jesus' disciple and apostle John. The gospel itself shows signs of having been composed in three "layers", reaching its final form about 90–100 CE.

Despite having been rewritten over the centuries, all four of the currently used forms of the Gospels include many contradictions, including stories and chronologies that are often entirely at odds with each other. The texts have undergone a complex transmission, and the versions we read today are only an approximation of what the original texts may have said. Copyists added and dropped words in order to accommodate changing understandings of previous versions.

It has been pointed out that the names John, Luke, Matthew, Peter, James, Mark, Phillip, Thomas and others are not typical of those used in Israel 2,000 years ago. A likely explanation for this, as many Biblical scholars assert, is that the Gospels were not written by people who ever met Jesus but by early Christians who historicized mythology or mythologized historical events.

Christians often cite Old Testament "prophecies" that were fulfilled by Jesus. But it's really not surprising that these prophecies came true – the authors of the New Testament would have had the Old Testament by their side as they wrote. Given that, it's almost embarrassing that most of these so-called prophecies are about as precise as a horoscope in your daily tabloid.

If you believe in the stories that make up the New Testament then you believe that particles of pure hydrogen and oxygen in the molecular form of water defied all laws of physics and instantly transformed into much more complex chemicals containing many more elements than hydrogen and oxygen, to suddenly become wine.

John 2 On the third day a wedding took place at Cana in Galilee. Jesus' mother was there, and Jesus and his disciples had also been invited to the wedding. When the wine was gone, Jesus' mother said to him, "They have no more wine." "Woman, why do you involve me?" Jesus replied. "My hour has not yet come." His mother said to the servants, "Do whatever he tells you." Nearby stood six stone water jars, the kind used by the Jews for ceremonial washing, each holding from twenty to thirty gallons. Jesus said to the servants, "Fill the jars with water"; so they filled them to the brim. Then he told them, "Now draw some out and take it to the master of the banquet."

They did so, and the master of the banquet tasted the water that had been turned into wine. He did not realize where it had come from, though the servants who had drawn the water knew. Then he called the bridegroom aside and said, "Everyone brings out the choice wine first and then the cheaper wine after the guests have had too much to drink; but you have saved the best till now." What Jesus did here in Cana of Galilee was the first of the signs through which he revealed his glory; and his disciples believed in him.

You also believe that Jesus healed a number of people in a variety of ways, including making a magic potion of saliva and dirt.

> **John 9** As he walked along, he saw a man blind from birth. His disciples asked him, "Rabbi, who sinned, this man or his parents, that he was born blind?" Jesus answered, "Neither this man nor his parents sinned; he was born blind so that God's works might be revealed in him. We must work the works of him who sent me while it is day; night is coming when no one can work. As long as I am in the world, I am the light of the world." When he had said this, he spat on the ground and made mud with the saliva and spread the mud on the man's eyes, saying to him, "Go, wash in the pool of Siloam" (which means Sent). Then he went and washed and came back able to see.

He supposedly also healed lepers, a woman who had been suffering from haemorrhages, someone who was paralysed, and even someone who was deaf and mute, by touching their ears then spitting and touching his tongue (Mark 7:13)!

It is no surprise that many fundamentalist Christian churches have faith healers who claim to cure the ailments of their congregants by drawing on the powers of Jesus. The question must be asked whether or not rational people really believe these modern-day faith healings and, if not, do they really believe in those from 2,000-year-old stories?

Other interesting miracles attributed to Jesus include that of using a few loaves of bread and a couple of fish to feed 5,000 people – somehow cloning of the DNA, organs, and flesh of the fish occurred instantaneously and the raw fish were also converted into nice bite-sized fillets ready to be passed around.

Jesus was supposedly able to perform these miracles, yet he was unable to escape crucifixion. Christians would argue that the reason that he didn't avoid crucifixion was to show humans that they had erred, and to forgive their sins yet the ridiculousness of the "original sin"/Adam and Eve story (now that we know that there was no Adam or Eve or even a first human being) makes the premise of self-sacrifice absurd.

And why would the death of an eternal being have any inherent value? After all, Jesus' followers believed that he was the son of a god and at one with that god. Why, therefore, would they be concerned about the death of the human form of an all-powerful being who is able to create life at a whim? Why would it be overwhelmingly sad that he died, if he can be recreated whenever?

The absurdity of Christianity reaches a crescendo with the crucifixion story. If you had been there and saved Jesus, then Christianity would not exist, for without Jesus dying on the cross "for the sins of humanity" and the subsequent resurrection, one would be left with only some sermons and anecdotes from a Middle Eastern philosopher. He would have lived a normal life and died normally, and a religion would not have been created around him.

Continuing this logic, those who supposedly brought about the crucifixion or gave Jesus up should in fact be lauded as the unwitting creators of Christianity. They should be the protagonists of a parable of life, an example of how sometimes a negative can become a positive. Theologians are, however, excellent at re-interpreting stories to create whatever life lessons they wish.

And why did Jesus not use his superpowers to avoid crucifixion when surely the best scenario would have been for him to continue to preach and teach humankind how to live? Had he not been crucified, would he have lived to age 70 and then died of natural causes, or would he have remained eternally present?

Christianity has used the crucifixion story to control believers by saying that Jesus "died for their sins", but, had he not been crucified, wouldn't we be better off because he would still be around to interact eternally with humankind? Why did he pass on his teachings only to a small group of people and for such a short period of time? The past 2,000 years show how unsuccessful that method was.

Why didn't Jesus just point out the mistakes people were making and say, "Please learn from this; it is not how you should be acting towards others. Now I'm going back to my sky cloud and will be watching you from there." The self-sacrifice and dying limited his achievements to an ineffectually short period of time and, significantly, resembled a number of previous life–death–birth deities (for example, Osiris, Dionysis, Tammuz).

And if Jesus' father was God, then he was not very caring about innocent children because, according to the book of Matthew, he let Herod kill all the babies in the region.

> **Matthew 2:16–18** When Herod realized that he had been out-witted by the Magi, he was furious, and he gave orders to kill all the boys in Bethlehem and its vicinity who were two years old and under, in accordance with the time he had learned from the Magi. Then what was said through the prophet Jeremiah was fulfilled: "A voice is heard in Ramah, weeping and great mourning, Rachel weeping for her children and refusing to be comforted, because they are no more."

If you believe in the stories of the New Testament, you also believe in a list of very interesting creatures. The New Testament does not have as malevolent a god as that of the Old Testament, but its authors had much more vivid imaginations with respect to devils and other fantastical creatures, even though these life forms were never seen or recorded by any other historian of the time, nor were they seen at any time before or since. There are mentions of:

Dragons
Revelation 12:9 The great dragon was hurled down – that ancient serpent called the devil, or Satan, who leads the whole world astray. He was hurled to the earth, and his angels with him.

Leviathans
Job 41 His snorting throws out flashes of light; his eyes are like the rays of dawn. Firebrands stream from his mouth; sparks of fire shoot out. Smoke pours from his nostrils as from a boiling pot over a fire of reeds. His breath sets coals ablaze, and flames dart from his mouth. Strength resides in his neck; dismay goes before him.

Unicorns
Job 39 Will the unicorn be willing to serve thee, or abide by thy crib? Canst thou bind the unicorn with his band in the furrow? Or will he harrow the valleys after thee?

Behemoth
Job 40:15–24 Look at Behemoth, which I made along with you and which feeds on grass like an ox. What strength it has in its loins, what power in the muscles of its belly! Its tail sways like a cedar; the sinews of its thighs are close-knit. Its bones are tubes of bronze, its limbs like rods of iron. It ranks first among the works of God, yet its Maker can approach it with his sword. The hills bring it their produce, and all the wild animals play nearby. Under the lotus plants it lies, hidden among the reeds in the marsh. The lotuses conceal it in their shadow; the poplars by the stream surround it. A raging river does not alarm it; it is secure, though the Jordan should surge against its mouth. Can anyone capture it by the eyes, or trap it and pierce its nose?

Devils – mentioned many times, notably in
Luke 8:30–33 And Jesus asked him, saying, "What is thy name?" And he said, Legion: because many devils were entered into him. And they besought him that he would not command them to go out into the deep. And there a herd of many swine feeding on the mountain: and they besought him that he would suffer them to enter into them. And he suffered them. Then went the devils out of the man, and entered into the swine: and the herd ran violently down a steep place into the lake, and were choked.

If you believe in the stories in the New Testament, then you believe that for 100,000-plus years human existence continued according to the laws of nature, with babies dying of starvation and disease, and murders, rapes and adultery taking place as usual, and then, all of a sudden, the Judaeo-Christian deity sent his son into a Bronze-Age Middle-Eastern backwater to save the world? Prior to this, this god had been happily sitting back watching and waiting until he thought, "Now is about the right time to appear and clarify the moral rules for humanity, but I'll only say it to a few people in a lightly populated part of the world."

Contradictions in the Gospels

There are numerous contradictions in the Gospels and many books have listed and discussed them. Here are some brief examples just to reinforce the point that the "Chinese whispers" of biblical compilation have played havoc with the content:

- The gospels of Luke and Matthew talk about Jesus being born when Herod was still ruler, yet Herod died in 4 BCE. Later the Gospel of Luke talks about Jesus being born during the Census of Quirinis, which actually occurred in 6–7 CE. Most mainstream scholars do not see the Luke and Matthew nativity stories as historically factual, and for this reason they do not consider them a reliable method for determining Jesus' date of birth. Or maybe the "final" writers of the Bible just got the story plain wrong.
- Matthew 1 lists Jesus' lineage, all the way back to King David

via his son Solomon, in 28 generations. But in Luke 3, the lineage is traced back to King David via his son Nathan, in 43 generations. Furthermore, in Matthew, Joseph's father was Jacob, while in Luke, Joseph's father was Heli.

- In John 9:39, Jesus says, "For judgment I have come into this world, so that the blind will see and those who see will become blind." Soon after, in John 12:47–48, he says, "If anyone hears my words but does not keep them, I do not judge that person. For I did not come to judge the world, but to save the world."
- In Mark 1:13–14, Jesus begins his ministry after John's arrest, whereas in John 3:22–25 Jesus begins his ministry before John's arrest.
- In Matthew 4:1–2 and Mark 1:10–13, immediately after the baptism story, Jesus spends 40 days in the wilderness, while in John 2:1, three days after the baptism story, Jesus attends a wedding.
- In Matthew 8:1–5, Jesus cures Simon Peter's mother-in-law *after* he cleanses the leper, but Jesus cures Simon Peter's mother-in-law *before* he cleanses the leper in Mark 1:30–42 and Luke 4:38–5:13.
- After walking on water, Jesus goes to Gennesaret in Mark 6, whereas he goes to Capernaum in John 6.
- Jesus says to honour your mother and father in Matthew 15, Matthew 19, Mark 7, Mark 10 and Luke 18, but in Matthew 10, Luke 12 and Luke 14 he says that he has come to set people against their parents.
- The "sermon on the mount" takes place up a mountain in Matthew 5, but in Luke 16 Jesus goes down to the flatlands to deliver it.
- In Matthew 6, Jesus teaches the "Lord's prayer" to many at the "sermon on the mount", but in Luke 11 he teaches it only to his disciples, on a different day.
- Jesus says to love your enemies in Matthew 5, but in Luke 19 he says to "kill the enemies in front of me".
- When leaving Jericho, Jesus heals two unnamed blind men in Matthew 20, but in Mark 10, when leaving Jericho, he heals one named blind man.

- In Matthew 26, Jesus tells Peter that he will deny him three times while at the Mount of Olives, but in Luke 22 he tells Peter that he will deny him three times when they are at the Passover meal.
- When Jesus is before Pilate he says nothing in Matthew 27 and Luke 23, whereas he gives some answers in Mark 14 and many answers in John 18.
- Upon being crucified, Jesus is offered: vinegar and gall, which he tastes but refuses to drink in Matthew 27; vinegar, which he drinks, in John 19; and wine and myrrh, which he doesn't drink, in Mark 15.
- It is light when Mary goes to the tomb of Jesus in Matthew 28 and Mark 16, but it is dark when she goes there in John 20.
- In Matthew 28, when Mary visits the tomb of Jesus, the stone is still in position until an angel moves it, but the stone has already been moved when she arrives in Mark 16, Luke 24 and John 20.
- Mary first sees the risen Jesus at the tomb in John 20 but in Matthew 28 she first sees him when she is on her way home.
- There is a violent earthquake at the tomb in Matthew 28, but there is no mention of this in Mark 16, Luke 24 or John 20.
- In John 20, Jesus' first appearance after the resurrection is to Mary Magdalene at the tomb, but in Luke 24 it is to two men walking to Emmaus who have been advised that he has not been seen previously.
- The ascension to heaven occurs in Mark 16 while Jesus is with the disciples seated at a table, but in Luke 24 it takes place outdoors at Bethany.

This list is by no means exhaustive – it is not too difficult to compile a list of 150–200 contradictions from online sources. Clearly, as a result of rewrites at various times in history, very different descriptions of the same events abound in the Gospels. Is it therefore likely that the events of the New Testament, as quoted by current-day preachers and adherents, actually occurred? Or is it more likely that they are fables that were added to and modified over time by the early creators and followers of Christian belief, and later collated into written stories and then, later still, presented as facts rather than stories? We will never know. It does, however, seem most likely that if there was a historical Jesus, he was mythicized by his followers (as happens with many famous people over time), or a mythical Jesus was historicized by early Christians, as happens in nearly all religions.

It is fascinating that the supposed parents of Jesus, Mary and Joseph (if one can call them parents if it was a virgin birth), are barely mentioned in the New Testament, apart from a few fleeting comments. And is it not bizarre that there is not much discussion of the virgin birth, when it was such a miraculous, and indeed the only, sign of Jesus' divine origins in the entire first 30 years of his life? Or is it possible that in the early times of Christianity the virgin birth story did not stand out as "miraculous" because the concept was merely borrowed from previous deity legends? Many other previous gods had claimed to have come into existence as a result of virgin births, including Horus, from his mother Isis (Ancient Egypt); Krishna, from his mother Devaki (9th century BCE); Buddha, from his mother Maya (6th century BCE); Mercury, the son of Maia (5th century BCE); and Perseus, the son of Danae (Ancient Greece). So the story of a virgin birth leading to the creation of a god was not new. For creators of a new cult or religion it probably seemed that if one was going to have a prophet, it was best that he was said to have come into the world via a virgin birth.

And what was God in the form of Jesus doing for the first 25–30 years of his life? Did he use any of his superpowers when other children were mean to him or took his toys? Was he a troublesome teenager who played pranks? Would he have ever suffered from diseases or even simple ailments such as food poisoning? Did he go out with his friends and try alcohol and ogle women? What was God/Jesus doing during all of this time that made up almost his whole life?

One wonders what the world would be like if the Roman Emperor Constantine had not embraced Christianity. It is not known exactly why he did so, because until then Christians had been persecuted under the Roman Empire. Constantine's conversion was the catalyst for the transformation of Christianity from a local cult to a widespread religion. Had this event not occurred, it is possible that Christianity may have fizzled out like so many religions of the time, or just continued quietly as a minority religion, as was the case with Judaism. However, there was quite a difference between the two religions in that Judaism was insular whereas Christianity urged its followers to spread the words of the Gospels, as Christian missionaries have done in recent times. Indeed, had Christian Europeans not been such successful explorers and conquerors, North and South America might today be populated by adherents of other religions or even native belief systems, rather than the 1 billion Christians who now predominate the two continents and make up almost half of Christendom. And, of course, the many military excursions over hundreds of years that later became known as the Crusades, as well as the Inquisitions, all of which helped both spread and solidify Christianity through the Western world, may never have occurred.

> "Christianity did not become a major religion by the quality of its truth but by the quantity of its violence." – Michael Sherlock

Islam

The word *Islam* means "surrender" or "prostration" in Arabic and this idea is the major tenet of the religion. Most non-Muslims consider that Islam began at the time of Mohammed around the 6th and 7th centuries; however, Muslims believe that Islam has been present since the beginning of existence. Islam begins with Adam and claims that Noah, Abraham, Moses and Jesus were also Islamic prophets, and that Mohammed is the last in that line. He is therefore not seen as the founder or author of Islam but as a prophet who received and disseminated revelations described to him by Allah, the God of Islam, via the angel Gabriel.

According to Muslim tradition, this commenced at a cave outside Mecca, in present-day Saudi Arabia, on the night that has become known as "the Night of Power and Excellence" in the year 610 CE. Gabriel appeared to Mohammed again in a second revelation, a period of time later, saying,

> When I was midway on the mountain, I heard a voice from heaven saying "O Mohammed! You are the apostle of Allah

and I am Gabriel." I raised my head towards heaven to see who was speaking, and Gabriel in the form of a man with feet astride the horizon, saying, "O Mohammed! You are the apostle of Allah and I am Gabriel." I stood gazing at him moving neither forward nor backward, then I began to turn my face away from him, but towards whatever region of the sky I looked, I saw him as before.

The revelations that came to form the entire Koran were passed on over a very lengthy period – approximately 23 years. They were initially committed to memory by Mohammed's followers and later written down by scribes (Mohammed himself was illiterate) who feared the words might be lost as the followers died off or were killed in battle. The present-day version of the Koran was in fact compiled well after Mohammed's death. One version of the story says it was first put together by Zaid ibn Thabit just after Mohammed's passing and then rewritten and organized into the structure that is seen today. Another recounts that various collections were initially compiled, and then a definitive version was created by a committee appointed by Caliph Uthman, also in the 600s CE, after which the other versions were declared null and void.

Unlike the Old and New Testaments, the Koran is not told as a chronological story but is a compilation of all the revelations that Mohammed told his followers. The Koran frequently asserts that the text is divinely ordained and is therefore to be treated with reverence and cannot be questioned. Whereas the events in the Old and New Testaments were mostly seen as stories about a god compiled by scholars, albeit including some words directly from that god, the whole of the Koran was said to be as Allah had said it. This claim implies that all other religions are less significant than Islam and that if one wants to be a true god-follower, one must be a Muslim and live by the Koran.

Intermingling with Jews who lived in the regions that Mohammed visited had a profound influence on the Koranic stories, and a number of the characters and events from the Old Testament appear in the Koran. However, as in a game of Chinese whispers the stories often differ.

For example, the story of Adam and Eve appears early in the Koran, but with some changes. Adam and Eve eat the fruit from the "tree of immortality" and Satan inspires them, whereas in the Old Testament they eat from the "tree of knowledge" and a snake inspires them. Muslims will say that their versions of the stories are correct because they are the words as spoken by Allah; Old Testament followers will argue that their text is correct and that Muslim scribes introduced the errors.

Going hand-in-hand with the Koran are the Hadith, collections of tales, teachings and sayings of Mohammed which, when combined, help followers interpret the Koran. Different sects of Islam, such as the Sunni and Shia, base their belief systems on different Hadith.

Some of the stories about Mohammed in the Hadith are worth scrutinizing with regard to whether they can be said to portray real events. One well-known story concerns what is called "Isra and Mi'raj" or the "Night Journey", when Mohammed was taken on a flying horse from Mecca to Jerusalem and up to the heavens before being dropped back off at Mecca. As with the Old Testament, if certain characters never existed (as science has shown) and certain events could never have taken place, then the validity of the whole work must be open to question.

To counter this idea, the Koran proclaims, early on, that everything in it is true:

> **Koran 2:2** This is the Book about which there is no doubt, a guidance for those conscious of Allah.

Imagine reading this type of introduction in any other book. Would it convince you that it must therefore be 100 per cent true, or would it, more likely, immediately seed an element of doubt as to its authenticity?

Another fascinating claim made by Muslims is that the Koran must be the word of God because it is written so well and so poetically that no human being could possibly have written it. Conveniently, very few people today speak the Classical Arabic of the Koran fluently enough to be able to validate this indoctrinated belief. And of course just saying that a work is more beautiful than any other – as non-Muslim scholars might say of a work by Shakespeare, Wordsworth or Mozart – is hardly a strong argument.

In 1972 a version of the Koran dating from the beginning of Islam was found in Sana'a, Yemen. It contained many minor differences to the version read today. This suggests that there were in fact various versions of the stories, which in turn means that the Koran cannot be Allah's unaltered words.

The Koran appears to be defending itself against such accusations when it says:

> **Koran 2:23–24** And if you are in doubt what we have sent down upon Our Servant Mohammed, then produce a surah [chapter] the like thereof and call upon your witnesses other than Allah, if you should be truthful. But if you do not – and you will never be able to – then fear the Fire, whose fuel is men and stones, prepared for the disbelievers.

So in other words, you can try to write your version of the Koran but it won't be true and you will therefore burn in hell. Just a slight Catch 22?

If you believe in the teachings of Islam, then you believe that a mortal being, Mohammed, was sliced open, washed internally and somehow magically put back together, leaving no scars. You also believe in a magical horse (similar to the Greek Pegasus, which interestingly also happened to be white and able to fly) and that Mohammed met with the "other prophets", including Adam, Abraham, Moses and Jesus, up in the "seven heavens". And that, going back and forth between Moses and Allah, he negotiated to have the requisite number of daily prayer rituals reduced from 50 to five – the number of times Muslims must pray today.

> **Sahih al-Bukhari, volume 4, Book 54, Hadith number 429**
> The Prophet said, "While I was at the House in a state midway between sleep and wakefulness (an angel recognized me), as the man lying between two men. A golden tray full of wisdom and belief was brought to me and my body was cut open from the throat to the lower part of the abdomen and then my abdomen was washed with Zam-zam water and (my heart was) filled with wisdom and belief.

> Al-Buraq, a white animal, smaller than a mule and bigger than a donkey, was brought to me and I set out with Gabriel. When I reached the nearest heaven, Gabriel said to the heaven

gatekeeper, 'Open the gate.' The gatekeeper asked, 'Who is it?' He said, 'Gabriel.' The gatekeeper asked, 'Who is accompanying you?' Gabriel said, 'Mohammed.' The gatekeeper said, 'Has he been called?' Gabriel said, 'Yes.' Then it was said, 'He is welcomed. What a wonderful visit his is!' Then I met Adam and greeted him and he said, 'You are welcomed O son and Prophet.'

Then we ascended to the second heaven. It was asked, 'Who is it?' Gabriel said, 'Gabriel.' It was said, 'Who is with you?' He said, 'Mohammed' It was asked, 'Has he been sent for?' He said, 'Yes.' It was said, 'He is welcomed. What a wonderful visit his is!' Then I met Isa (Jesus) and Yahya (John the Baptist) who said, 'You are welcomed, O brother and a Prophet.'

Then we ascended to the third heaven. It was asked, 'Who is it?' Gabriel said, 'Gabriel.' It was asked, 'Who is with you?' Gabriel said, 'Mohammed.' It was asked, 'Has he been sent for?' 'Yes,' said Gabriel. 'He is welcomed. What a wonderful visit his is!' (The Prophet added:) There I met Joseph and greeted him, and he replied, 'You are welcomed, O brother and a Prophet!'

Then we ascended to the 4th heaven and again the same questions and answers were exchanged as in the previous heavens. There I met Idris and greeted him. He said, 'You are welcomed O brother and Prophet.'

Then we ascended to the 5th heaven and again the same questions and answers were exchanged as in previous heavens. There I met and greeted Aaron who said, 'You are welcomed O brother and a Prophet.'

Then we ascended to the 6th heaven and again the same questions and answers were exchanged as in the previous heavens. There I met and greeted Moses who said, 'You are welcomed O brother and a Prophet.' When I proceeded on, he started weeping and on being asked why he was weeping, he said, 'O

Lord! Followers of this youth who was sent after me will enter Paradise in greater number than my followers.'

Then we ascended to the seventh heaven and again the same questions and answers were exchanged as in the previous heavens. There I met and greeted Ibrahim who said, 'You are welcomed O son and a Prophet.'

Then I was shown Al-Bait-al-Ma'mur (Allah's House). I asked Gabriel about it and he said, 'This is Al Bait-ul-Ma'mur where 70,000 angels perform prayers daily and when they leave they never return to it (but always a fresh batch comes into it daily).'

Then I was shown Sidrat al-Muntaha (a tree in the seventh heaven) and I saw its Nabk fruits which resembled the clay jugs of Hajr (a town in Arabia), and its leaves were like the ears of elephants, and four rivers originated at its root, two of them were apparent and two were hidden. I asked Gabriel about those rivers and he said, 'The two hidden rivers are in Paradise, and the apparent ones are the Nile and the Euphrates.'

Then fifty prayers were enjoined on me. I descended till I met Moses who asked me, 'What have you done?' I said, 'Fifty prayers have been enjoined on me.' He said, 'I know the people better than you, because I had the hardest experience to bring Bani Israel to obedience. Your followers cannot put up with such obligation. So, return to your Lord and request Him (to reduce the number of prayers.' I returned and requested Allah (for reduction) and He made it forty. I returned and (met Moses) and had a similar discussion, and then returned again to Allah for reduction and He made it thirty, then twenty, then ten, and then I came to Moses who repeated the same advice. Ultimately Allah reduced it to five. When I came to Moses again, he said, 'What have you done?' I said, 'Allah has made it five only.' He repeated the same advice but I said that I surrendered (to Allah's Final Order). Allah's Apostle was addressed by Allah, 'I have decreed My Obligation and have reduced the burden on My servants, and I shall reward a single good deed as if it were ten good deeds.'"

We must now start to look at and assess the Koran and the Hadith for inconsistencies. Remember, the Koran is supposedly the actual words of god. It therefore should contain no errors. But again, science has uncovered a number of these errors in the time since these texts were written.

Sahih al-Bukhari 3329 – Narrated Anas: When Abdullah bin Salam heard the arrival of the Prophet at Medina, he came to him and said, "I am going to ask you about three things which nobody knows except a prophet: What is the first portent of the Hour? What will be the first meal taken by the people of Paradise? Why does a child resemble its father, and why does it resemble its maternal uncle." Allah's Messenger said, "Gabriel has just now told me of their answers." Abdullah said, "He [i.e. Gabriel] from amongst all the angels, is the enemy of the Jews." Allah's Messenger said, "The first portent of the Hour will be a fire that will bring together the people from the east to the west; the first meal of the people of Paradise will be Extralobe (caudate lobe) of fish-liver. As for the resemblance of the child to its parents: If a man has sexual intercourse with his wife and gets discharge first, the child will resemble the father, and if the woman gets discharge first, the child will resemble her." On that Abdullah bin Salam said, "I testify that you are the Messenger of Allah."

Regarding the first two points, any answer could have been made up and been correct, but with regards to the third question, it required a scientifically correct answer. It is, however, straight-out wrong; there is no scientific support for the appearance of a foetus being determined by whoever orgasmed first. These are obviously just the words of 7th-century humans with limited scientific knowledge.

Another sign of poor understanding relates to exactly where sperm are made within the human body.

Koran 86:5–7 So let man observe from what he was created.

He was created from a fluid ejected, emerging from between the backbone and the ribs.

If the Koran is the words of Allah, an all-knowing god, then he obviously didn't understand human anatomy. Interestingly, though, this view of the source of sperm was commonly held in the Bronze Age Middle East.

Also Allah was apparently unable to foresee scientific advances in weather prediction, 3D ultrasounds and foetal genetic analyses.

Koran 31:34 Indeed, Allah alone has knowledge of the hour and sends down rain and knows what is in wombs.

The Koran again shows that it is derived from the Old Testament and prevailing Middle Eastern views on creation, rather than from science and an all-knowing deity, when it repeats the six-days creation myth.

Koran 50:38 And we did certainly create the heavens and earth and what is between them in six days, and there touched us no weariness.

And, again, with the repetition of the story of Adam and Eve being formed from the ground: there is zero discussion of evolution or the timescales of life on earth.

Koran 15:26 And we did certainly create man out of clay from an altered black mud.

Koran 7:189 It is He who created you from one soul and created from it its mate that he might dwell in security with her.

Many statements in the Koran reflect the era's geocentric view of the solar system – the idea that the Sun and Moon revolve around Earth (as opposed to the truth, that Earth and the other seven planets in our solar system revolve around the Sun).

Koran 36:40 It is not for the sun to overtake the moon, nor doth the night outstrip the day. They float each in an orbit.

Koran 91:1–2 By the sun and his (glorious) splendour; by the moon as she follows him.

Koran 21:33 And He it is Who created the night and the day, and the sun and the moon. They float, each in an orbit.

And speaking of not understanding and knowing all that was out there, Allah says that Adam (yes, him again) knew all the creatures on Earth by name, and he asked him to name them, which Adam supposedly then did. Of course, given that there are millions of species of creatures on Earth, this would have taken an eternity.

Koran 2:31–33 And he taught Adam the names – all of them. Then he showed them to the angels and said "Inform me of the names of these, if you are truthful." They said, "Exalted are You, we have no knowledge except what you have taught us. Indeed, it is You who is the knowing, the Wise." He said, "O Adam, inform them of their names" and when he had informed them of their names, he said "Did I not tell you that I know the unseen aspects of the heavens and the earth? And I know what you reveal and what you have concealed."

And now to another fantastical story about nature. Apparently, King Solomon had the ability to speak in human language to ants and the ants had the ability to speak perfectly to Solomon in the dialect that he spoke, and they had a nice conversation together!

Koran 27:17–19 And gathered for Solomon were his soldiers of the jinn and men and birds, and they were marching in rows. Until, when they came upon the valley of the ants, an ant said, "O ants, enter your dwellings that you not be crushed by Solomon and his soldiers while they perceive not." So Solomon smiled, amused at her speech and said, "My Lord, enable me to be grateful for your favour which you have bestowed upon me and upon my parents and to do righteousness of which you approve. And admit me by your mercy into the ranks of Your righteous servants."

And birds were supposedly able to kill a herd of elephants by dropping stones onto them.

> **Koran 105:1–5** Have you not considered, (O Mohammed), how your Lord dealt with the companions of the elephant? Did he not make their plan into misguidance? And he sent against them birds in flocks, striking them with stones of hard clay, and he made them like eaten straw.

The Koran is also supposed to be an eternal document, and Mohammed merely a transmitter of the message from Allah. How convenient is it then that a number of provisions were made only for the benefit of Mohammed? For instance, while every other Muslim male was allowed to have up to four wives, if Mohammed wanted more he could have them.

> **Koran 33:50** O Prophet, indeed We have made lawful to you your wives to whom you have given their due compensation and those your right hand possesses from what Allah has returned to you of captives and the daughters of your paternal uncles and the daughters of your paternal aunts and the daughters of your maternal uncles and the daughters of your maternal aunts who emigrated with you and a believing woman if she gives herself to the Prophet and if the Prophet wishes to marry her, this is only for you, excluding the other believers. We certainly know what We have made obligatory upon them concerning their wives and those their right hands possess, but this is for you in order that there will be upon you no discomfort.

When Mohammed then wanted to marry the ex-wife of his adopted son but worried that the people would not look upon this action well, lo and behold Allah made it all okay.

> **Koran 33:37** And you feared the people, while Allah has more

right that you fear Him. So when Zayd had no longer any need for her, We married her to you in order that there not be upon the believers any discomfort concerning the wives of their adopted sons when they no longer have need of them.

And when Mohammed had a dispute with one of his wives about him having slept with a slave, Allah conveniently allowed him to get away with it and not feel any guilt about it.

Koran 66:1 O Prophet, why do you prohibit yourself from what Allah has made lawful for you, seeking the approval of your wives? And Allah is Forgiving and Merciful.

When you start to accept that many of the events and characters that make up the Old Testament are mythical, it becomes clear that Mohammed simply based his accounts on stories he gleaned from his meetings with local Jews and Christians during his travels. It is no surprise that he never refers to anything from outside his sphere of existence of no more than a few hundred kilometres in any direction from Mecca – there's no mention of Africa, Europe, the Americas, the rest of Asia, Australia, the Arctic or Antarctica, nor the myriad of people or animals that lived in those places. He was simply another of many false prophets who kept coming back with ideas over two to three decades, trying to establish an alternative belief system that benefitted him and his growing group of followers. When one reads the Koran, it reads exactly as if it were written by someone who had heard the stories of the Old and New Testaments, plagiarized them (poorly) and combined them with some of his own tales.

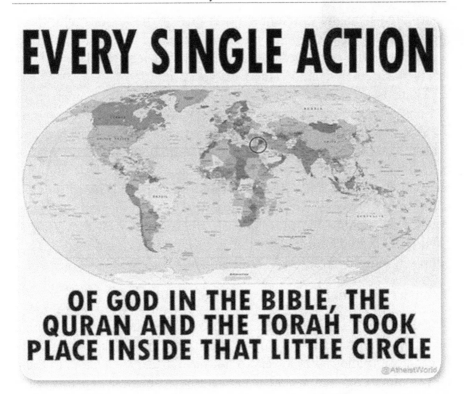

Interpreting the texts

It must be admitted that there are many pearls of wisdom that can be gleaned from religious texts – there are, however, also many pearls of wisdom in the complete works of Shakespeare. And like Shakespeare, the abovementioned religious texts are works of fiction. They may be based on places that exist, or existed, and even some people who truly lived; however, they are still undoubtedly fanciful. They may contain some interesting life lessons, but, as we will see in the next chapter, they also include many poor teachings which adherents can, and often do, use to support their own bigotry and violence.

Alongside the main texts that form the backbone of each of the monotheistic religions exist countless commentaries by sages and scholars. Often, these consist of interpretations of the texts or guides to applying their rules and teachings in everyday life. They can and do lead to many interesting discussions, but the fact that they can be interpreted in many different ways is one of the reasons why there are so many sects within each religion. If the god of each religion had wanted the rules to be clear, he should have made them clear and not left it to extremely fallible humans to sort out!

There is a vast gulf between any empirical/historical analysis of the texts and the theological analyses of the texts. Most Bible scholars (those who study its historicity) agree with the above views, and science also shows that many of the stories are both false and fantastical. Given this, it should today be made clear in secular teaching that the Old Testament, New Testament and Koran are all based on false creation mythologies, similar to those that many other cultures have devised throughout the ages, and that there is no such thing as the "Word of God". There are only the words of humans, and religions are simply systems of structured obscurantism.

What's in a name? The advantages of monotheism

There are many ways in which religions market the concepts of their own gods and the switch from polytheism to monotheism was a brilliant move. It allowed followers to not have to ascribe a name to their deity, something that would otherwise be required when following multiple deities. This, in turn, made deity constructs appear even further removed from humanity, and allowed for the creation of a single, nameless, all-knowing and all-powerful "supreme being", to be given the most powerful title of all, just "God".

Even though the Old Testament names the god of its stories Yahweh, as well as a few other titles, Jews are not allowed to say this name nor write the word "god" without a hyphen, as in "G-d". Uttering "God said" instead of, say, "Yahweh said" is also much more powerful and it makes both the speaker and the listener forget that the deity was created by humans.

The simple title "God" (or "Allah") helps elevate and enthrone the deity and create an image and persona that is more difficult to question. Most people from a monotheistic background seem to see clearly that polytheistic religions with their many named gods are mythical, yet cannot see it with their own religion because their deity has been named as the one and only "God". If the Judaeo-Christian world reverted to calling its god Yahweh, without a doubt more people would question the idea that he is the all-powerful creator. (And it would be even more the case if he were called Fred, John or Rupert!)

A very brief overview of Hinduism

Approximately 1 billion people on this planet classify themselves as Hindus. Hinduism is, however, not truly one religion but rather a family of faiths and beliefs that outsiders lumped together under this umbrella term to create a convenient grouping. In fact, among most adherents the term Sanatana Dharma is used, meaning a "right/eternal way of life and thought". There was no founder of Hinduism, so there was no specific time of commencement; it is rather a continuum of development of ancient beliefs. Hinduism is therefore difficult to define, in Western terms, as "a religion".

There is no set clerical structure or governing body of Hinduism, no prophet or single binding book, or even a unified system of laws or rules. The deity beliefs can be polytheistic, monotheistic, atheistic or any other option that one decides upon. Unlike the three major monotheistic religions, which are based on a main text and some related stories, Hindu beliefs are based on a variety of texts with quite different mythologies, each of which is the mainstay of a slightly different belief system.

Many devotees of Hinduism see its variety of gods as manifestations of an ultimate god or force, while others believe each god has a separate role or even that there are no gods at all. Often the Hindu gods are seen as forces of nature or as representative of particular moral values. The main gods include Vishnu, Shiva, Brahma, Ganesha, Kartikeya, Parvati, Lakshmi, Kali and others.

There are many ideas that are common to all branches of Hinduism, including that all living creatures have an eternal soul, plus a number of central concepts, such as dharma (ethics/duties), karma (action and consequences), kama (pleasure, especially through love), artha (power and substance) and moksha (release or liberation from this life or all lives).

Most religious rituals take place in the home, often around a family shrine. The widely used term "puja" refers to an act of worship made to honour or praise a deity or to spiritually celebrate an event. It may be accompanied by a recitation from a favourite script, the lighting of lamps, singing devotional songs, or meditating.

A very brief overview of Buddhism

Approximately 500 million people in the world today classify themselves as Buddhists. Buddhism is different again from the other major religions in that followers often do not worship a deity; it is therefore open to question whether it is a true religion or simply a philosophy. Like Hinduism, Buddhism encompasses a great variety of beliefs, traditions and practices. The majority are, however, based on the teachings and moral injunctions of a man, Siddhartha Gautama, who later became known as the Buddha or "enlightened one".

He is believed to have been born in the year 623 BCE in Nepal and lived most of his life in northern India. His chief concern was to solve both the physical and metaphysical problems of self, and he believed that appeasing a deity in the hope of altering one's circumstances was misguided. His teachings were more about achieving salvation through true knowledge, self-discipline, self-purification, meditation and concentration, and ending suffering through the elimination of ignorance and craving.

There are no strict, ancient, dogmatic rules in Buddhism and therefore followers are never made to feel guilty by being labelled a "sinner". It is more about encouraging individuals to try to find enlightenment.

The Dalai Lama once said: "From one viewpoint, Buddhism is a religion, from another viewpoint Buddhism is a science of mind and not a religion. Buddhism can be a bridge between these two sides. Therefore, with this conviction, I try to have closer ties with scientists, mainly in the fields of cosmology, psychology, neurobiology and physics. In these fields there are insights to share, and to a certain extent we can work together."

"People often claim to hunger for truth, but seldom like the taste when it's served up." – George R.R. Martin

6

MORALS AND ETHICS: WHAT ARE THEY AND WHO "OWNS" THEM?

As defined by the *Merriam-Webster Dictionary*, morals are

- concerned or related to what is right and wrong in human behaviour
- based on what you think is right and good
- considered right and good by most people: agreeing with a standard of right behaviour,

while ethics are:

- the principles of conduct governing an individual or a group.

Although the words have slightly different meanings, to simplify things the word "morals" will be used here to refer to both.

Homo sapiens is not the only species to exhibit moral behaviour. We can see it in other species, including chimpanzees, other apes and monkeys and a number of other mammalian species. What is interesting, however, is the ever-increasing significance of morals in day-to-day life as humans have evolved..

Some will argue that evolution is a selfish process and why, therefore, should morals play such a significant part in an individual's life? There are many ways to answer this, but we must be cognizant of the huge difference in the way humans now live – in large communal groups, towns, cities and countries – compared to how they lived thousands of years ago.

Until less than 10,000 years ago, few moral rules would have been required, as people still lived in small groups. With the advent of societies came the need for order, without which a community could not survive. So, although morals are often about the acts of individuals, in order for a group (and hence individuals and their offspring) to thrive and compete against other groups, a set of core values is required. The same applies to groups of many animals.

Morals are the backbone of a good society. They are one of the defining traits of humanity, in that only humans can, as a group, decide and explain what they are. They may shift throughout time as new situations arise and, hence, the views within a society change.

The great majority of people in a society need to accept the same moral values for them to work. To create a better world, all barriers between subgroups of humans would have to continue to dissolve, until, ultimately, there would be a single set of morals for all of humanity. Until we as an entire human race can decide on the majority of them together, there will never be worldwide unity; and until religious and other superstitious myths, teachings and rules are eradicated, this can never happen.

But how do we choose our moral rules? As will be shown, that process should most definitely not be based on old texts that contain too many poor and outdated rules. Morals should be secular and relevant to the current state of a society. They are far too complex to be determined by ancient religious writings. Modern life encompasses an infinite variety of moral dilemmas whose solutions depend partly on a society's stage of development as well as far too many background issues to be defined in a few religious books.

As an example, one of the Ten Commandments says, "Thou shalt not kill." That is a great ideal and should be one of the central tenets by which we should live. It is in fact self-evident that, for a society to function, we need to follow this doctrine. However, well-known thought experiments such as the "trolley problem" and its variations highlight the complexities of dealing with such issues.[1]

This is precisely why most people and most countries abide by a secular and ever-changing legal justice system. Religious apologists see this as the wrong way to create rules, as they believe it relies on fallible human thought processes instead of what they see as the infallibility of the teachings of their deity (despite the fact, as we have seen, that these are based on multiple human interpretations of texts anyway). But modern moral and ethical dilemmas require contemporary thinking and perspectives to find the most equitable solutions. And yet other approaches will be needed 100 or 500 years from now. We cannot rely on texts written thousands of years ago for entirely different circumstances and entirely different societies. They should be studied to provide insights into the times in which they were written, but that's all. To have our morals defined by ancient texts and have religious adherents offering "eternal godly truths" to support a particular, outmoded viewpoint is the antithesis of what is required to improve the world. That simply allows too many people to believe that their actions, even the endorsement of slavery or displays of bigotry and hatred towards other groups, are divinely approved and, therefore, justifiable.

It is often said in support of religions that they instituted the first morals. But, as has already been shown, these texts do not date as far back as was once assumed. Furthermore, there were a number of earlier secular texts that attempted to codify laws for societal living. For example, the Code of Hammurabi, a Babylonian king who lived almost 4,000 years ago, included almost 300 laws. These were carved into a seven-and-a-half-foot tall stone stele, which is now on display at the Louvre in Paris; copies are on display in a few other museums around the world. Pre-dating that is the Code of Ur-Nammu, which is over 4,000 years old.

In comparison, the writings of the Old Testament, the New Testament and the Koran are, respectively, 3,000, 2,000 and 1,400 years old. It was when these later religions and their leaders started claiming initiation and ownership of morals that things started to go wrong. As a result, modern adherents of these texts still follow many of their very arcane, unchanged laws, even though societies have changed and despite the fact that most of their followers have never actually read the texts and base their understanding solely on the cherry-picked sections that they have been taught.

For too long, the monotheistic religions, especially, have claimed to "own" morals and claimed that without belief in a god we have an immoral society because there is then no higher being to whom you are duty-bound and who can punish you if you do not behave according to those rules. This is an extremely poor supporting argument, as the subtext of this is that without a person's belief in whichever deity they follow, or if their deity were shown not to exist, they would commit crimes freely.

As political commentator Amanda Marcotte has said:

> Atheists are routinely asked how people will know not to rape and murder without religion telling them not to do it, especially a religion that backs up the orders with threats of hell. Believers listen to me carefully when I say this: when you use this argument, you terrify atheists. We hear you saying that the only thing standing between you and Ted Bundy is a flimsy belief in a supernatural being made up by pre-literate people trying to figure out where the rain came from. This is not very reassuring if you're trying to argue from a position of moral superiority.

Morals are in fact inherent within us, and we don't require a deity to create them. A non-deity-based belief system such as Buddhism teaches morals, and somehow Buddhists are able to accept and endorse moral behaviour without the need for guidance from a deity or threats of punishment.

One only has to ask a religious person if they would kill their child if their god told them to. At this point, most will avoid answering the question, because answering 'yes' would indicate what most would consider a dangerous mindset and a questioning of one's faculties, whereas answering 'no' would mean that they have to admit that they have an inherent sense of morality independent of their religion. As will be shown, morality does not come from religion; it pre-dates it and will continue to be a part of humanity well after the current religions go the same way as all previous ones.

I have been drawn into many discussions by adherents on the following textual quotes relating to morals, mostly about their interpretation (or re-interpretation). However, they tend to miss the fundamental points I am usually making, namely:

- Is it possible to have world peace while the various current religions exist?
- Is it possible for all people to have the same opportunities and the same rights, irrespective of gender, sexuality or different beliefs while religions exist?
- Can we create better life teachings and philosophies than those that existing religions offer? (After all, I keep being asked, "What will replace religions?")

Morals from The Old Testament

So what are the moral teachings of the Old Testament, for example? The Ten Commandments are often said to have been a great starting point for a moral framework for humanity. But when you actually read them, you realize they aren't quite as helpful as you might have imagined. The first three all relate to the Old Testament god rather than humans (which suggests Yahweh was an insecure character), and the fourth simply aims to reinforce the creation story by reminding everyone to rest on the Sabbath, just as God did. So that leaves only six that can be applied to human morals, and those six would already have been a part of everyday Bronze Age societies prior to the time they were written.

Here are the full ten, as per the Old Testament:

1. You shall have no other gods before me.
2. You shall not make for yourself a carved image, or any likeness of anything that is in heaven above, or that is in the earth beneath, or that is in the water under the earth. You shall not

bow down to them or serve them, for I the Lord your God am a jealous God, visiting the iniquity of the fathers on the children to the third and the fourth generation of those who hate me, but showing steadfast love to thousands of those who love me and keep my commandments.

3. You shall not take the name of the Lord your God in vain, for the Lord will not hold him guiltless who takes his name in vain.

4. Remember the Sabbath day, to keep it holy. Six days you shall labour, and do all your work, but the seventh day is a Sabbath to the Lord your God. On it you shall not do any work, you, or your son, or your daughter, your male servant, or your female servant, or your livestock, or the sojourner who is within your gates. For in six days the Lord made heaven and earth, the sea, and all that is in them, and rested on the seventh day. Therefore the Lord blessed the Sabbath day and made it holy.

5. Honour your father and your mother, that your days may be long in the land that the Lord your God is giving you.

6. You shall not murder.

7. You shall not commit adultery.

8. You shall not steal.

9. You shall not bear false witness against your neighbour.

10. You shall not covet your neighbour's house; you shall not covet your neighbour's wife, or his male servant, or his female servant, or his ox, or his donkey, or anything that is your neighbour's.

I'm fairly confident that most people have not read the second commandment in its entirety, and its moral teaching is lamentable to say the least. Yahweh will punish innocent future generations for the sins of their ancestors? Is this really a great moral lesson? Imagine presenting this to children as a good and fair moral code. Fairness and suffering become very difficult to explain when this commandment is discussed.

As Christopher Hitchens once said:

Is it really to be believed that until they got to the foot of Mount Sinai, the followers of Moses believed up until then that adultery, murder, theft and perjury were OK? They are suddenly told, oh hey, we've got some new ideas for you. I don't think so. I think that our ancestors were smarter than that and even if they weren't, they wouldn't have got that far if they were under the contrary impression. The golden rule is something that you don't have to teach a child. There's no need to say, "And if you don't follow this rule, you'll burn in hell forever." That is immoral teaching.

Aside from this, the last of the Ten Commandments enshrines the view that women are simply chattel, or the property of men. It sees wives as being on the same level as slaves, animals or the property of a neighbour. Is this really a great moral lesson?

It is also amazing that some of the worst things a human being can do to another human being are not mentioned, such as rape and slavery. In fact, as we will see, the Old Testament does not regard these as major crimes at all; indeed, it suggests that only minor punishments are appropriate for these acts or even none at all if it involves killing/enslaving/raping enemies of Yahweh. In fact, most times it is considered a crime against the husband (his property) than a crime against the woman involved.

One of the most common claims made by adherents of most religions is that their god is "all-loving". They say it because it has been repeated to them over and over by religious leaders and in schools. But have these people actually read the Bible? In reality, it seems that most of them have only read a few carefully selected sections they have been directed to. For many of them, it's a lot like reading a disclosure statement or the terms of a software upgrade: at best, they skim-read and simply click "AGREE" without actually reading what they have signed up for. They just trust the source.

You would think, for example, that loyal adherents would want to know what the god of the Old Testament will do to them if they don't follow his rules. Yet how many people have read the passages below from Deuteronomy? I have included the entire lengthy section because it isn't just a short idle threat; it is a no-holds-barred, malevolent, psychotic attack, not only on people who don't follow the commandments, but also on their families and their possessions. And I have yet to come across a human being who could keep to all of the mandated rules, or has seen any evidence of such punishments having been enforced.

After reading this, please pause to consider whether: (1) this is a loving god, (2) this is a reasonable list of punishments, (3) these punishments have ever been handed out, despite the occurrence throughout history of abhorrent acts and the evident existence of abominably wicked people, and (4) you would really want to venerate this character. Also, make sure you read verses 53–57, as for me they typify the character of the god of the Old Testament. Finally, and most importantly, having pondered all of this, consider whether or not it is likely that this god actually exists.

Deuteronomy 28:15–55, on the consequences of disobedience: 15 But it shall come about, if you do not obey the Lord your God, to observe to do all His commandments and His statutes with which I charge you today, that all these curses will come upon you and overtake you: 16 Cursed shall you be in the city, and cursed shall you be in the country. 17 Cursed shall be your basket and your kneading bowl. 18 Cursed shall be the offspring of your body and the produce of your ground, the increase of your herd and the young of your flock. 19 Cursed shall you be when you come in, and cursed shall you be when you go out. 20 The Lord will send upon you curses, confusion, and rebuke, in all you undertake to do, until you are destroyed and until you perish quickly, on account of the evil of your deeds, because you have forsaken Me. 21 The Lord will make the pestilence cling to you until He has consumed you from the land where you are entering to possess it. 22 The Lord will smite you with consumption and with fever and with inflammation and with fiery heat and with the sword and with blight and with mildew, and they will pursue you until you perish 23The heaven which is over your head shall be bronze, and the earth which is under you, iron. 24 The Lord will make the rain of your land powder and dust; from heaven it shall come down on you until you are destroyed. 25 The Lord shall cause you to be defeated before your enemies; you will go out one way against them, but you will flee seven ways before them, and you will be an example of terror to all the kingdoms of the earth. 26 Your carcasses will be food to all birds of the sky and to the beasts of the earth, and there will be no one to frighten them away. 27 The Lord will smite you with the boils of Egypt and with tumours and with the scab and with the itch, from which you cannot be healed. 28 The Lord will smite you with madness and with blindness and with bewilderment of heart; 29 and you will grope at noon, as the blind man gropes in darkness, and you will not prosper in your ways; but you shall only be oppressed and robbed continually, with none to save you. 30 You shall betroth a wife, but another man will violate her; you shall build a house, but you will not live in it; you shall plant a vineyard, but you will not use its fruit. 31 Your ox shall be slaughtered before your eyes, but you will not eat of it; your donkey shall be torn away from you, and will not be restored to you; your sheep shall be given to your enemies, and you will have none to save you. 32 Your sons and your daughters shall be given to another people, while your eyes look on and yearn for them continually; but there will be nothing you can do. 33 A people whom you do not know shall eat up the produce of your ground and all your labours, and you will never be anything but oppressed and crushed continually. 34 You shall be driven mad by the sight of what you see. 35 The Lord will strike you on the knees and legs with sore boils, from which you cannot be healed, from the sole of your foot to the crown of your head. 36 The Lord will bring you and your king, whom you set over you, to a nation which neither you nor your fathers have known, and there you shall serve other gods, wood and stone. 37 You shall become a horror, a proverb, and a taunt among all the people where the Lord drives you. 38 You shall bring out much seed to the field but you will gather in little, for the locust will consume it. 39 You shall plant and cultivate vineyards, but you will neither drink of the wine nor gather the grapes, for the worm will devour them. 40 You shall have olive trees throughout your territory but you will not anoint yourself with the oil, for your olives will drop off. 41 You shall have sons and daughters but they will not be yours, for they will go into captivity. 42 The cricket shall possess all your trees and the produce of your ground. 43 The alien who is among you shall rise above you higher and higher, but you will go down lower and lower. 44 He shall lend to you, but you will not lend to him; he shall be the head, and you will be the tail. 45 So all these curses shall come on you and pursue you and overtake you until you are destroyed, because you would not obey the Lord your God by keeping His commandments and His statutes which He commanded you. 46 They shall become a sign and a wonder on you and your descendants forever. 47 Because you did not serve the Lord your God with joy and a glad heart, for the abundance of all things; 48 therefore you shall serve your enemies whom the Lord will send against you, in hunger, in thirst, in nakedness, and in the lack of all things; and He will put an iron yoke on your neck until He has destroyed you. 49 The Lord will bring a nation against you from afar, from the end of the earth, as the eagle swoops down, a nation whose language you shall not understand, 50 a nation of fierce countenance who will have no respect for the old, nor show favour to the young. 51 Moreover, it shall eat the offspring of your herd and the produce of your ground until you are destroyed, who also leaves you no grain, new wine, or oil, nor the increase of your herd or the young of your flock until they have caused you to perish. 52 It shall besiege you in all your towns until your high and fortified walls in which you trusted come down throughout your land, and it shall besiege you in all your towns throughout your land which the Lord your God has given you. 53 Then you shall eat the offspring of your own body, the flesh of your sons and of your daughters whom the Lord your God has given you, during the siege and the distress by which your enemy will oppress you. 54 The man who is refined and very delicate among you shall be hostile toward his brother and toward the wife he cherishes and toward the rest of his children who remain, 55 so that he will not give even one of them any of the flesh of his children which he will eat, since he has nothing else left, during the siege and the distress by which your enemy will oppress you in all your towns. 56 The most gentle and sensitive woman among you – so sensitive and gentle that she would not venture to touch the ground with the sole of her foot – will begrudge the husband she loves and her own son or daughter 57 the afterbirth from her womb and the children she bears. For in her dire need she intends to eat them secretly because of the suffering your enemy will inflict on you during the siege of your cities. 58 If you do not carefully follow all the words of this law, which are written in this book, and do not revere this glorious and awesome name – the Lord your God – 59 the Lord will send fearful plagues on you and your descendants, harsh and prolonged disasters, and severe and lingering illnesses. 60 He will bring on you all the diseases of Egypt that you dreaded, and they will cling to you. 61 The Lord will also bring on you every kind of sickness and disaster not recorded in this Book of the Law, until you are destroyed. 62 You who were as numerous as the stars in the sky will be left but few in number, because you did not obey the Lord your God. 63 Just as it pleased the Lord to make you prosper and increase in number, so it will please him to ruin and destroy you. You will be uprooted from the land you are entering to possess.

On rape

Rape is one of the most awful crimes that can be committed, often leaving an individual in lifelong torment, and most modern secular judicial systems rightly impose heavy sentences for this crime. Yet the Old Testament not only accepts rape, but actually endorses it.

Genesis 19:5–8 They called to Lot, "Where are the men who came to you tonight? Bring them out to us so that we may know them" Lot went outside to meet them and shut the door behind him and said, "No, my friends. Don't do this wicked thing. Look, I have two daughters who have never slept with a man. Let me bring them out to you, and you can do what you like with them. But don't do anything to these men, for they have come under the protection of my roof."

These are the words of the apparently righteous Lot of Sodom – the man Yahweh decided to save and highlight as an example of a person with sound morals – as he gives away his daughters for rape!

Deuteronomy 20:10–14 When you march up to attack a city, make its people an offer of peace. If they accept and open their gates, all the people in it shall be subject to forced labour and shall work for you. If they refuse to make peace and they engage you in battle, lay siege to that city. When the Lord your God delivers it into your hand, put to the sword all the men in it. As for the women, the children, the livestock and everything else in the city, you may take these as plunder for yourselves. And you may use the plunder the Lord your God gives you from your enemies.

Numbers 31:15–18 "Have you allowed all the women to live?" he asked them. "They were the ones who followed Balaam's advice and enticed the Israelites to be unfaithful to the Lord in the Peor incident, so that a plague struck the Lord's people. Now kill all the boys. And kill every woman who has slept with a man, but save for yourselves every girl who has never slept with a man."

So here Yahweh is saying that when it comes to punishing your enemies it's okay to seize and rape virgins.

Deuteronomy 22:28–29 If a man happens to meet a virgin who is not pledged to be married and rapes her and they are discovered, he shall pay her father fifty shekels of silver. He must marry the young woman, for he has violated her. He can never divorce her as long as he lives.

In this case, women are merely property that can be paid for. And note the very important qualification "and they are discovered". So if they are not discovered, it is not then a crime requiring compensation? Note also that the rapist must marry her because no longer being a virgin she is not as valuable to her father. What sort of moral teaching is this by Yahweh, to force a victim of rape to marry her attacker?

> **Deuteronomy 22:23–24** If a man happens to meet in a town a virgin pledged to be married and he sleeps with her, you shall take both of them to the gate of that town and stone them to death – the young woman because she was in a town and did not scream for help, and the man because he violated another man's wife. You must purge the evil from among you.

This one is even more horrifying because the god of the Old Testament doesn't care about the victim of the rape; her sin is that of not yelling out – never mind that she was likely prevented from doing so under threat of violence.

In summary, it appears that, according to the Old Testament, it is perfectly fine to rape people not of your belief system, and in most instances only a minor offence to rape someone of the same belief system. It is only a problem if the victim happens to be a virgin, of the same belief system and is about to be married off to another man. Rape in the bible was more of a property crime against a man than an awful deed to a woman.

On slavery

Aside from murder and rape, enslaving another human must be one of the most immoral acts a person can perpetrate – to take control of another person as if they are not human at all but merely property. So, is the Old Testament against slavery or does it actually endorse such behaviour and even value slaves as property? And do the words suggest that a loving god wrote them, or just a bunch of racist, sexist men who believed that some peoples (and women) were lesser citizens?

> **Leviticus 25:44–46** Your male and female slaves are to come from the nations around you; from them you may buy slaves. You may also buy some of the temporary residents living among you and members of their clans born in your country, and they

will become your property. You can bequeath them to your children as inherited property and can make them slaves for life, but you must not rule over your fellow Israelites ruthlessly.

So Yahweh is here endorsing the idea of buying people and thereafter considering them your property.

> **Exodus 21:2–4** If you buy a Hebrew servant, he is to serve you for six years. But in the seventh year, he shall go free, without paying anything. If he comes alone, he is to go free alone; but if he has a wife when he comes, she is to go with him. If his master gives him a wife and she bears him sons or daughters, the woman and her children shall belong to her master, and only the man shall go free.

Freedom for the men, but not for the women and children?

> **Exodus 21:7–11** If a man sells his daughter as a servant, she is not to go free as male servants do. If she does not please the master who has selected her for himself, he must let her be redeemed. He has no right to sell her to foreigners, because he has broken faith with her. If he selects her for his son, he must grant her the rights of a daughter. If he marries another woman, he must not deprive the first one of her food, clothing and marital rights. If he does not provide her with these three things, she is to go free, without any payment of money.

Selling your offspring? What fantastic parental morals to advocate.

> **Exodus 21:20–21** Anyone who beats their male or female slave with a rod must be punished if the slave dies as a direct result, but they are not to be punished if the slave recovers after a day or two, since the slave is their property.

So here is a double whammy: an endorsement of slavery as well as approval of beating another human being, as long as they are back up and working in a day or two. Again, does this sound like moral guidance from an eternal deity or self-interested rules from the patri-archs of the time?

> **Exodus 21:32** If the bull gores a male or female slave, the owner must pay thirty shekels of silver to the master of the slave, and the bull is to be stoned to death.

Here is an endorsement of slavery and of the killing of an enslaved animal for acting out its natural instincts.

On genocide and killing

Numerous times in the Old Testament Yahweh tells his followers to kill all their enemies, and not just those who are fighting, but women and children too. Can you imagine our world if humankind actively encouraged and endorsed such atrocities today?

> **Deuteronomy 2:32–34** When Sihon and all his army came out to meet us in battle at Jahaz, the Lord our God delivered him over to us and we struck him down, together with his sons and his whole army. At that time we took all his towns and com-pletely destroyed them – men, women and children. We left no survivors.

> **Deuteronomy 3:4–6** At that time we took all his cities. There was not one of the sixty cities that we did not take from them – the whole region of Argob, Og's kingdom in Bashan. All these cities were fortified with high walls and with gates and bars, and there were also a great many unwalled villages. We completely destroyed them, as we had done with Sihon king of Heshbon, destroying every city –men, women and children.

> **Deuteronomy 7:1–2** When the Lord your God brings you into the land you are entering to possess and drives out before you many nations – the Hittites, Girgashites, Amorites, Canaan-ites, Perizzites, Hivites and Jebusites, seven nations larger and stronger than you – and when the Lord your God has delivered them over to you and you have defeated them, then you must

destroy them totally. Make no treaty with them, and show them no mercy.

Deuteronomy 13:12–15 If you hear it said about one of the towns the Lord your God is giving you to live in that trouble-makers have arisen among you and have led the people of their town astray, saying, "Let us go and worship other gods" (gods you have not known), then you must inquire, probe and inves-tigate it thoroughly. And if it is true and it has been proved that this detestable thing has been done among you, you must certainly put to the sword all who live in that town. You must destroy it completely, both its people and its livestock.

Deuteronomy 20:16–17 However, in the cities of the nations the Lord your God is giving you as an inheritance, do not leave alive anything that breathes. Completely destroy them – the Hittites, Amorites, Canaanites, Perizzites, Hivites and Jebusi-tes – as the Lord your God has commanded you.

On homosexuality

Non-heterosexuals have been treated poorly by all religions and it probably all began with the teachings in the Old Testament, as it was the precursor to the texts of Christianity and Islam. It is interesting to note that only male homosexual sex is mentioned. Is the god of the Old Testament accepting of lesbian sex? Or is it more likely that the male writers only found male homosexual sex too unpleasant for them?

Leviticus 18:22 Do not have sexual relations with a man as one does with a woman; that is detestable.

Leviticus 20:13 If a man has sexual relations with a man as one does with a woman, both of them have done what is detesta-ble. They are to be put to death; their blood will be on their own heads.

Have there ever been a few sentences that have condemned a whole section of society as brutally as these lines? In the 3,000 years since this was written, hundreds of thousands of gay people have been killed and nearly all have been persecuted their entire lives. So much so that to this day many gay people are still too afraid to "come out" when they are aware of their feelings. Interestingly, in current times, most Jewish preachers do not openly condemn homosexuals (who are, however, not usually allowed to hold clerical positions) in the same way that most Christian leaders have and still do. In most religions, it is still very difficult for gay people to be open about their sexuality.

What is often not understood or known is that at least 500 other animal species engage in homosexual behaviour. Most farmers of sheep, cattle and horses witness males mounting other males in the paddocks. In fact a large percentage of rams do not mate with ewes but mate with other rams and form long-term bonds with other males. Our closest living relatives, the bonobos (similar to chimpanzees) engage in a full range of homosexual activities, male to male and female to female. Homosexual behaviour is natural and may even have evolutionary benefits.

Often in animal societies, males are required to fight other males for the right to mate with a female, which frequently results in injury or death for one or both of the combatants. And if a female is not satisfied with a male mate, she may kill or consume him. A number of species even die after mating heterosexually or soon after giving birth. This is not exactly a ringing endorsement for an exclusively heterosexual lifestyle. And, in fact, there may be certain advantages for some groups in accepting homosexuality. For example, it might be considered "safer" to leave a homosexual male to protect females, as then there is no concern that he will mate with them while the other males are absent.

A number of studies of the evolutionary advantages of homosexuality are currently being undertaken; fortunately, in this more scientific age, these studies can proceed without the scrutiny and impediment of religious organizations. Studies have shown a genetic predisposition for homosexuality, just as there is for being left-handed.

If religious adherents want to have a discussion about unnatural sexual behaviour, they should consider mandated abstinence from sex. The recent uncovering of decades and likely centuries of paedophilia and other aberrant sexual acts (and their cover-ups) carried out by religious people who live this way underlines that it is a pressing and hugely significant issue. Given that celibacy is a lifestyle choice (rather than a genetic predisposition), and unnatural for most people, it's perhaps not so surprising that it has led to widespread abuse.

The treatment and value of women

Nowhere is it more evident that the Bible was written by men rather than by a god than in the many comments about the treatment and value of women. As seen above, they are viewed as property and not as equal human beings; rape is barely seen as a crime; and women are valued much lower than men. Polygamy is embraced, as are concubines. So why are we not highlighting and exalting these biblical moral doctrines to our children and telling them that this is how they should live their lives? Maybe the Old Testament is not such a great moral guide after all?

> **Genesis 3:16** To the woman he said, "I will make your pains in childbearing very severe; with painful labour you will give birth to children. Your desire will be for your husband, and he will rule over you."

This is said after Eve eats the forbidden fruit in the Garden of Eden. God has decided not only that men will rule over women eternally, but also that the pain and suffering of childbirth will have to be borne by all future mothers. Any woman who has an epidural or general anaesthetic to help them through childbirth is presumably therefore a sinner.

> **Exodus 22:16–17** If a man seduces a virgin who is not pledged to be married and sleeps with her, he must pay the bride-price, and she shall be his wife. If her father absolutely refuses to give her to him, he must still pay the bride-price for virgins.

Again, women are mere property to be purchased at an appropriate price, and women must be virgins, but the sexual status of men is irrelevant.

Leviticus 12:1–5 The Lord said to Moses, "Say to the Israelites: 'A woman who becomes pregnant and gives birth to a son will be ceremonially unclean for seven days, just as she is unclean during her monthly period. On the eighth day the boy is to be circumcised. Then the woman must wait thirty-three days to be purified from her bleeding. She must not touch anything sacred or go to the sanctuary until the days of her purification are over. If she gives birth to a daughter, for two weeks the woman will be unclean, as during her period. Then she must wait sixty-six days to be purified from her bleeding.'"

So, according to the god of the Old Testament, giving birth to a girl makes a woman twice as unclean as when she gives birth to a boy.

Leviticus 27:1–7 The Lord said to Moses, "Speak to the Israelites and say to them: 'If anyone makes a special vow to dedicate a person to the Lord by giving the equivalent value, set the value of a male between the ages of twenty and sixty at fifty shekels of silver, according to the sanctuary shekel; for a female, set her value at thirty shekels for a person between the ages of five and twenty, set the value of a male at twenty shekels and of a female at ten shekels; for a person between one month and five years, set the value of a male at five shekels of silver and that of a female at three shekels of silver; for a person sixty years old or more, set the value of a male at fifteen shekels and of a female at ten shekels."

Here, women are only worth about half the value of men.

Deuteronomy 22:20–21 If, however, the charge is true and no proof of the young woman's virginity can be found, she shall be brought to the door of her father's house and there the men of her town shall stone her to death. She has done an outrageous thing in Israel by being promiscuous while still in her father's house. You must purge the evil from among you.

As is typical of the Old Testament, women must be virgins, but the status of men is irrelevant. Imagine how we would have to treat women in Western society if this view was still in place. It must also have been a very unpleasant exercise for a woman to have to prove her virginity.

> **Deuteronomy 25:11–12** If two men are fighting and the wife of one of them comes to rescue her husband from his assailant, and she reaches out and seizes him by his private parts, you shall cut off her hand. Show her no pity.

Even though the wife in this scenario is actually trying to rescue her husband, instead of being rewarded for being supportive and helpful she is to be brutally and forever punished.

> **Deuteronomy 21:10–14** When you go to war against your enemies and the Lord your God delivers them into your hands and you take captives, if you notice among the captives a beautiful woman and are attracted to her, you may take her as your wife. Bring her into your home and have her shave her head, trim her nails and put aside the clothes she was wearing when captured. After she has lived in your house and mourned her father and mother for a full month, then you may go to her and be her husband and she shall be your wife. If you are not pleased with her, let her go wherever she wishes. You must not sell her or treat her as a slave, since you have dishonoured her.

Again, women are simply spoils of war, to be treated as property, but in this case the Old Testament also rates women by their appearance.

Once again, do these sound like the words of a benevolent all-loving God who sees women as equal, or are they the words of sexist men of the Bronze Age who saw women as property? Why do people keep saying that the Bible is a great moral guide? Most likely because they have only read or been taught the least offensive parts of the texts.

Scriptures like the ones quoted above have led to practices that have for millennia treated women subordinately and excluded them from the full range of opportunities that men have available to them. In Judaism, for example, only recently and only in certain branches of the religion have women been permitted to fully participate in religious services; more often they have to sit separately, usually upstairs (most synagogues are built on two levels) or behind a curtain. They are also supposed to wear wigs to cover their hair and must wear "modest" clothes. Men are not dictated to in the same ways.

Circumcision and genital mutilation

What kind of moral and loving deity would require eight-day-old babies to have an operation in an age when dying as a result of a simple infection or botched procedures was common? And surely an act can only be morally correct if you choose to do it yourself, rather than having it forced upon you before you are old enough to say whether you agree with it or not? The god of the Old Testament ignores such concerns.

> **Genesis 17:10–13** Every male among you shall be circumcised. You are to undergo circumcision, and it will be the sign of the covenant between me and you. For the generations to come every male among you who is eight days old must be circumcised, including those born in your household or bought with money from a foreigner – those who are not your offspring. Whether born in your household or bought with your money, they must be circumcised. My covenant in your flesh is to be an everlasting covenant.

Note that, at the same time, Yahweh again endorses the enslavement and sale of humans.

Human and animal sacrifices

Are you aware that Yahweh called for human sacrifices? In fact, in the Old Testament he calls for the sacrifice of 32 female virgins, as well as many animals.

> **Numbers 31:25–40** The Lord said to Moses, "You and Eleazar the priest and the family heads of the community are to count all the people and animals that were captured. Divide the spoils equally between the soldiers who took part in the battle and

the rest of the community. From the soldiers who fought in the battle, set apart as tribute for the Lord one out of every five hundred, whether people, cattle, donkeys or sheep. Take this tribute from their half share and give it to Eleazar the priest as the Lord's part. From the Israelites' half, select one out of every fifty, whether people, cattle, donkeys, sheep or other animals. Give them to the Levites, who are responsible for the care of the Lord's tabernacle."

So Moses and Eleazar the priest did as the Lord commanded Moses. The plunder remaining from the spoils that the soldiers took was 675,000 sheep, 72,000 cattle, 61,000 donkeys and 32,000 women who had never slept with a man.

The half share of those who fought in the battle was:

337,500 sheep, of which the tribute for the Lord was 675;
36,000 cattle, of which the tribute for the Lord was 72;
30,500 donkeys, of which the tribute for the Lord was 61;
16,000 people, of whom the tribute for the Lord was 32.

Other crimes with suitable punishments

Many other harmless acts are considered to be "reprehensible" in the Old Testament. Those that offend Yahweh include:

- wearing clothes of mixed fabrics
- eating fruit from a tree before it is five years old
- planting two different types of seed in your field
- shaving the hair on the side of your head or the edges of your beard
- when you build a new house, making a parapet around your roof
- ploughing with an ox and a donkey yoked together
- wearing the clothing of the opposite sex (apparently the Lord your God detests anyone who does this. I'm not sure how many school plays would work at same-sex schools.)
- picking up sticks for firewood on Sabbath day, even if it is just

to keep one's family warm; punishment is a slow and painful stoning to death

- owning and displaying pictures or sculptures that may be deemed to be idolatrous; today this would include pictures of sports stars, actors or singers in the bedrooms of teenagers.

Numbers 15:32–36 Now while the sons of Israel were in the wilderness, they found a man gathering wood on the Sabbath day. And those who found him gathering wood brought him to Moses and Aaron, and to all the congregation; and they put him in custody because it had not been declared what should be done to him. Then the Lord said to Moses, "The man shall surely be put to death; all the congregation shall stone him with stones outside the camp." So all the congregation brought him outside the camp, and stoned him to death with stones, just as the Lord had commanded Moses.

How about reasonable protection of freedom of speech, the cornerstone of creating a free, just and open society? If we had to obey the following rules, not many of us would make it through our teenage years.

Leviticus 20:9 For every one that curseth his father or his mother shall be surely put to death: he hath cursed his father or his mother; his blood shall be upon him.

Leviticus 24:16 Anyone who blasphemes the name of the Lord is to be put to death. The entire assembly must stone them. Whether foreigner or native-born, when they blaspheme the Name they are to be put to death.

Does it not seem strange that an all-powerful deity would be offended simply by someone using his name in an inappropriate manner? Thankfully in modern times Yahweh ignores his rule and lets you get away with texting or saying 'OMG'!

Leviticus 24:11–14 The son of the Israelite woman blasphemed the Name with a curse; so they brought him to Moses. (His mother's name was Shelomith, the daughter of Dibri the Danite.) They put him in custody until the will of the Lord should be made clear to them. Then the Lord said to Moses: "Take the blasphemer outside the camp. All those who heard him are to lay their hands on his head, and the entire assembly is to stone him."

Coveting is another matter, though.

> **Exodus 20:17 and repeated in Deuteronomy 5:21** The Tenth Commandment says, "You shall not covet your neighbour's house; you shall not covet your neighbour's wife, nor his male servant, nor his female servant, nor his ox, nor his donkey, nor anything that is your neighbour's."

Apart from condoning the treatment of wives as chattel, this places the act of coveting your neighbour's possessions – a more or less harmless thought crime – at the same level as more serious crimes. The reality is that comparing and competing is a natural part of all of us, and for evolutionary reasons has been so for a billion years, so to adopt this attitude is quite absurd. For example, working harder because you have seen what may be possible with extra work should not be criticized; "envy" can occasionally be a great motivational tool when used appropriately.

Fortune-tellers and those who claim to be able to communicate with "the spirits" are also intolerable according to Yahweh.

> **Leviticus 20:27** A man or woman who is a medium or spiritist among you must be put to death. You are to stone them; their blood will be on their own heads.

Yahweh was also very picky about who should offer him sacrifices and offerings.

> **Leviticus 21:18–22** No man who has any defect may come near: no man who is blind or lame, disfigured or deformed; no

man with a crippled foot or hand, or who is a hunchback or a dwarf, or who has any eye defect, or who has festering or running sores or damaged testicles. No descendant of Aaron the priest who has any defect is to come near to present the food offerings to the Lord. He has a defect; he must not come near to offer the food of his God.

How strange that the people born with these defects must have been made this way by Yahweh himself.

Even the above small sampling of rules and laws makes it clear that we cannot possibly accept the Old Testament as a valid guide to morality, as most devout Jews and Christians claim we should. And a more in-depth assessment of all of the Old Testament is likely to lead most unbiased readers to a conclusion similar to the one reached by Richard Dawkins:

> The God of the Old Testament is arguably the most unpleasant character in all fiction: jealous and proud of it; a petty, unjust, unforgiving control-freak; a vindictive, bloodthirsty ethnic cleanser; a misogynistic, homophobic, racist, infanticidal, genocidal, filicidal, pestilential, megalomaniacal, sadomasochistic, capriciously malevolent bully.

Biblical Morality Test

According to the Bible, which of the following crimes is NOT punishable by death according to Yahweh?

1. Belonging to a nation that is already living in "The Promised Land"
2. Picking up sticks on a Saturday
3. Not being a virgin on your wedding night
4. Raping a woman
5. Saying god's name inappropriately

If you said #4, then by most standards, you are more moral than the Old Testament god. According to its teachings, you can commit rape and be OK but you can be killed for any of the others.

Having read a selection of teachings from the Old Testament, it is a rewarding challenge to come up with one's own "new and improved" Ten Commandments. Here are mine:

1. Do to others as you would like done to you.
2. Do not do to others as you would not like done to you.
3. Promote the greater good versus one's own desires as often as possible.
4. Treat all other human beings as equals.
5. Respect the environment and all other living things. Leave the world a better place.
6. Be mindful of your actions and always prepared to take responsibility for them.
7. Try to understand other people and the world using logic and thinking for yourself rather than just accepting what you are told. Always feel free to question.

8. Do not automatically place ideas or beliefs ahead of people.
9. Always allow other people the right to disagree with you and endeavour to overcome any disagreements with discussion and not by violence.
10. Strive to help everyone attain the greatest possible levels of freedom, rights and opportunities.

Morals from the New Testament

Nowadays, many people accept that the Old Testament, written approximately 3,000 years ago, may not be an ideal source of moral guidelines, but what about the New Testament? Where does it stand on many similarly important issues, especially since so many of us are used to hearing the words "not a very Christian thing to do"?

As a starting point, it's notable that the New Testament iterates in the Book of Matthew that Jesus not only agrees with the laws and prophets of the Old Testament but also that he will make sure that they are enforced.

> **Matthew 5:17** Think not that I am come to destroy the law, or the prophets: I am not come to destroy, but to fulfill.

So how tolerant and moral are the teachings in the New Testament? The following is, again, just a small sample.

On the acceptance of others

Here are some of the teachings of the supposedly peaceful Jesus, advising his followers how to act in certain situations or how he will act on their behalf.

> **Matthew 10:14–15** If anyone will not welcome you or listen to your words, leave that home or town and shake the dust off your feet. Truly I tell you, it will be more bearable for Sodom and Gomorrah on the day of judgment than for that town.

Here Jesus is saying that unless the locals accept you, they will be destroyed in a way even worse than what happened to the inhabitants of Sodom and Gomorrah in the Old Testament story – God wiped them out in one fell swoop.

> **Matthew 10:21–22** Brother will betray brother to death, and a father his child; children will rebel against their parents and have them put to death. You will be hated by everyone because of me, but the one who stands firm to the end will be saved.

Teaching people to kill family members if they don't agree? I guess a round-table discussion was out of the question?

> **Matthew 10:33–37** But whoever disowns me before others, I will disown before my Father in heaven. Do not suppose that I have come to bring peace to the earth. I did not come to bring peace, but a sword. For I have come to turn a man against his father, a daughter against her mother, a daughter-in-law against her mother-in-law, a man's enemies will be the members of his own household. Anyone who loves their father or mother more than me is not worthy of me; anyone who loves their son or daughter more than me is not worthy of me.

What an awful expectation that prospective followers must love a being they never have met more than their own children. What sort of god would require such extreme loyalty? One should not demand automatic respect and love; it must be earned for it to be true.

> **Matthew 13:41–42** The Son of Man will send out his angels, and they will weed out of his kingdom everything that causes sin and all who do evil. They will throw them into the blazing furnace, where there will be weeping and gnashing of teeth.

> **Matthew 18:6** But whoso shall offend one of these little ones which believe in me, it were better for him that a millstone were hanged about his neck, and that he were drowned in the depth of the sea.

Again, believe in Jesus or you shall die a horrible and tortured death. Imagine the uproar if these threats or methods were used nowadays in the Western world.

> **Matthew 18:8–9** If your hand or your foot causes you to stumble, cut it off and throw it away. It is better for you to enter life maimed or crippled than to have two hands or two feet and be thrown into eternal fire. And if your eye causes you to stumble, gouge it out and throw it away. It is better for you to enter life with one eye than to have two eyes and be thrown into the fire of hell.

We are fortunate that few people actually do this in modern times. Maybe most Christians don't truly believe in these stories or the need to obey them.

Jesus goes on to describe the "End Times", which will be full of murdering, famines and earthquakes, but will be followed by his glorious return. He states that this will all happen with no notice, but that it will take place in the very near future. Two thousand years later, that prediction does not appear too accurate.

> **Matthew 24:34** Truly I tell you, this generation will certainly not pass away until all these things have happened.

> **Matthew 25:41–46** Then he will say to those on his left, "Depart from me, you who are cursed, into the eternal fire prepared for the devil and his angels. For I was hungry and you gave me nothing to eat, I was thirsty and you gave me nothing to drink, I was a stranger and you did not invite me in, I needed clothes and you did not clothe me, I was sick and in prison and you did not look after me." They also will answer, "Lord, when did we see you hungry or thirsty or a stranger or needing clothes or sick or in prison, and did not help you?" He will reply, "Truly I tell you, whatever you did not do for one of the least of these, you did not do for me." Then they will go away to eternal punishment, but the righteous to eternal life.

Although we should always do what we can to help others, nobody has been murdered, raped or enslaved as a result of the actions described above. How many of us have at times walked past someone in the street in need and not stopped to help? It looks like we may all end up burning in an "everlasting fire".

> **Luke 3:16–17** John answered them all, "I baptize you with water. But one who is more powerful than I will come, the straps of whose sandals I am not worthy to untie. He will baptize you with the Holy Spirit and fire. His winnowing fork is in his hand to clear his threshing floor and to gather the wheat into his barn, but he will burn up the chaff with unquenchable fire."

Again, straight to burning people who do not follow him. One would think most people deserve a second chance or re-education from an all-loving creator, especially given that he created them flawed.

> **Luke 12:5** But I will forewarn you whom ye shall fear: Fear him, which after he hath killed hath power to cast into hell; yea, I say unto you, Fear him.

Psychological games. Fear God or else suffer in the next life.

> **Luke 12:47** And that servant, which knew his lord's will, and prepared not himself, neither did according to his will, shall be beaten with many stripes.

Again, fear God or else.

> **Luke 19:27** But those mine enemies, which would not that I should reign over them, bring hither, and slay them before me.

This incites people to commit genocide against others just because they did not follow God's words. You can just feel Jesus' love in these words!

Luke 22:36 Then said he unto them, "But now, he that hath a purse, let him take it, and likewise his scrip: and he that hath no sword, let him sell his garment, and buy one."

So. swap your clothes for weapons and prepare to kill. Jesus is not as much a preacher of peace as he is made out to be.

Luke 12: 51–53 Suppose ye that I am come to give peace on earth? I tell you, Nay; but rather division: For from henceforth there shall be five in one house divided, three against two, and two against three. The father shall be divided against the son, and the son against the father; the mother against the daughter, and the daughter against the mother; the mother in law against her daughter in law, and the daughter in law against her mother in law.

John 3:18 He that believeth in him is not condemned: but he that believeth not is condemned already, because he hath not believed in the name of the only begotten Son of God.

Believe in Jesus or else.

John 3:36 He that believeth in the Son hath everlasting life: and he that believeth not the Son shall not see life; but the wrath of God abideth on him.

Believe in Jesus or else.

John 15:6 If a man abide not in me, he is cast forth as a branch, and is withered; and men gather them, and cast them into the fire, and they are burned.

Believe in Jesus or else.

Acts 3:23 And it shall come to pass, that every soul, which will not hear that prophet, shall be destroyed from among the people.

Believe in Jesus or else.

Christianity teaches its followers that even a child who hasn't accepted Jesus will burn in hell for eternity. This is one of the reasons that adherents feel they have to teach religious practice and doctrine to their children. They fear that if they don't, their children could possibly be sent to a place called hell. This is a disturbing subtext to have hanging over one's head. Again, control via fear.

How do religious people justify the banishment of people who may be otherwise great contributors to the real world, who may spend their life doing charity work and helping people in many ways, simply because they don't accept the Jesus story? Christianity advises that if you don't follow its belief systems then you will be tortured eternally. Can Christian adherents say they will be happy to be in heaven while multitudes of otherwise good or innocent people are tortured eternally just because they didn't believe in Jesus? How can this be a morally superior position?

> **Romans 5:12** Wherefore, as by one man sin entered into the world, and death by sin: and so death passed upon all men, for that all have sinned.

So because fictional Adam sinned, everyone must die? Had Adam not sinned would we all live eternally? How about every other living creature that also dies, is it because Adam sinned or is death in fact just a natural part of life and nothing to do with the Adam and Eve story?

> **2 Thessalonians 1:8–9** In flaming fire taking vengeance on them that know not God, and that obey not the gospel of our Lord Jesus Christ: Who shall be punished with everlasting destruction from the presence of the Lord, and from the glory of his power.

Romans 1: 26–32 For this cause God gave them up unto vile affections: for even their women did change the natural use into that which is against nature: And likewise also the men, leaving the natural use of the woman, burned in their lust one toward another; men with men working that which is unseemly, and receiving in themselves that recompense of their error which was meet. And even as they did not like to retain God in their knowledge, God gave them over to a reprobate mind, to do those things which are not convenient; Being filled with all unrighteousness, fornication, wickedness, covetousness, maliciousness; full of envy, murder, debate, deceit, malignity; whisperers, backbiters, haters of God, despiteful, proud, boasters, inventors of evil things, disobedient to parents, Without understanding, covenant breakers, without natural affection, implacable, unmerciful: Who knowing the judgment of God, that they which commit such things are worthy of death, not only do the same, but have pleasure in them that do them.

According to this long-winded rant, homosexuals, people who gossip, children disobedient of parents, and so on, should die. If this were actually carried out, there would not be many people left on Earth.

On the equality of women

1 Timothy:2 A woman should learn in quietness and full submission. I do not permit a woman to teach or to assume authority over a man; she must be quiet. For Adam was formed first, then Eve. And Adam was not the one deceived; it was the woman who was deceived and became a sinner.

1 Corinthians 11:8–9 For man did not come from woman, but woman from man; neither was man created for woman, but woman for man.

Matthew 5:32 ... and whoever marries a divorced woman commits adultery.

In the stories of the miracle of the feeding of the multitude, 5,000 men are mentioned, but the women are just an aside – they aren't seen as equals.

> **Matthew 14: 20–21** They all ate and were satisfied, and the disciples picked up twelve basketfuls of broken pieces that were left over. The number of those who ate was about five thousand men, besides women and children.

And in the Gospel of Mark version of this story, women aren't mentioned at all!

In practice, the Old and New Testament views and narratives have meant that women play a lesser role in the religion. In most churches, women have had little to no presence in services or in senior roles. Conversely, where societies are becoming more secular, there are vigorous attempts at attaining equal opportunities for women in the workplace and in daily life (although there is, of course, still a way to go). There are now many female CEOs and women in government, there have been and are female presidents and prime ministers, and in many more situations women are enjoying the same opportunities afforded to men.

Meanwhile in religion the wheels of change move very slowly, if at all, and there is still much opposition to the idea of equality, with the church's male leadership often still claiming divine support for inequality. When will there be a female Pope? If the answer is "never", then religion is still tied down by the shackles of bigotry, as endorsed and reinforced by those old texts.

On slavery

One would have hoped that by the time of the New Testament, God, his followers and the authors of the Gospels would have realized that slavery was an affront to human dignity; but no, the practice is still endorsed.

> **Ephesians 6:5** Slaves, obey your earthly masters with respect and fear, and with sincerity of heart, just as you would obey Christ.

> **Colossians 3:22** Slaves, obey your earthly masters in everything;

and do it, not only when their eye is on you and to curry their favour, but with sincerity of heart and reverence for the Lord.

1 Timothy 6:1–2 Christians who are slaves should give their masters full respect so that the name of God and his teaching will not be shamed. If your master is a Christian, that is no excuse for being disrespectful. You should work all the harder because you are helping another believer by your efforts. Teach these truths, Timothy, and encourage everyone to obey them.

In the following passage, Jesus clearly approves of the beating of slaves, with the severity of the beating depending on whether or not they believed in him.

Luke 12:47–48 The servant who knows the master's will and does not get ready or does not do what the master wants will be beaten with many blows. But the one who does not know and does things deserving punishment will be beaten with few blows. From everyone who has been given much, much will be demanded; and from the one who has been entrusted with much, much more will be asked.

These and other biblical quotations have been used to justify and perpetuate the practice of slavery through the ages, especially in the developing United States, where slavery was only made illegal in 1865. Most modern Christians are unaware of these biblical endorsements or, if they are, prefer not to discuss those sections of the Bible.

Thought crimes

Christianity certainly upped the ante when it came to controlling its followers' thought processes. Even today, it uses threats of eternal physical pain and suffering in hell to steer people away from "sin", and the promise of endless pleasure in heaven to entice believers to keep the faith. But living with these ideas is rather like living the Orwellian life of *1984*, where people are being watched all the time and are never truly free. Whenever a government tries to control its citizens, it will label what it considers dissent as "thought crime"; however, since in most situations a government has no real access to an individual's thoughts, it resorts to training people to oppress themselves by internalizing what is seen as disapproved thought. The same occurs with religious teachings: self-flagellation and self-hatred are common traits of adherents.

> **Matthew 5:21–22** You have heard that the ancients were told, "YOU SHALL NOT COMMIT MURDER" and "Whoever commits murder shall be liable to the court." But I say to you that everyone who is angry with his brother shall be guilty before the court; and whoever says to his brother, "You good-for-nothing", shall be guilty before the supreme court; and whoever says, "You fool", shall be guilty enough to go into the fiery hell.

> **1 John 2:15** Do not love the world or anything in the world. If anyone loves the world, love for the Father is not in them.

> **Matthew 5:27–28** But I say unto you, That whosoever looketh on a woman to lust after her hath committed adultery with her already in his heart. And if thy right eye offend thee, pluck it out and cast it from thee, for it is profitable for thee that one of thy members should perish, and not that thy whole body should be cast into hell.

Oh, and to finish off, make sure that you completely understand the subtext of all of Jesus' stories, otherwise he will ridicule you.

> **Matthew 15: 15–16** Peter said, "Explain the parable to us." "Are you still so dull?" Jesus asked them.

Theft

> **Matthew 21:1-3** As they approached Jerusalem and came to Bethphage on the Mount of Olives, Jesus sent two disciples, saying to them, "Go to the village ahead of you, and at once you will find a donkey tied there, with her colt by her. Untie them

and bring them to me. If anyone says anything to you, say that the Lord needs them, and he will send them right away.

So not only is he condoning theft for his own benefit without mention of recompense but also if he were an all-knowing god then surely he wouldn't have said "if anyone" but instead "when anyone". It appears to be written by the hand of mankind and not a deity.

A statement full of irony

It is an important teaching to respect people rather than material goods, and this is at least touched upon in Christian texts.

> **1 Timothy 6:10** For the love of money is a root of all kinds of evil.

This is a reasonable comment reflecting many societal truths, especially given our modern consumerist lifestyles. The irony, however, is that religious bodies are among the wealthiest organizations, collectively owning the most property on the planet and the most expensive buildings on the planet. They possess diamonds and jewels set in gold, expensive artworks, private planes, and much, much more. Yet they demand money at most services, either directly or via donation boxes; encourage their congregations to pay for honours or give them a percentage of their incomes; and ask outright for presents. The idiom of "the pot calling the kettle black" pops into mind with regards the church's views on material goods.

Two millennia of preaching hatred

Until 1965, the Catholic Church preached that the Jewish people as an entirety, past and present, were responsible for deicide, the killing of their god in the form of Jesus. This led to the Inquisition, pogroms and massacres, the Holocaust and other regular political, economic, religious and social prejudices. Much of Christendom only decided that it was no longer a reasonable and acceptable view to espouse late in the 20th century, well after the perpetrators of the Holocaust had been tried in secular courts. How can the church claim moral superiority, as it has done for 2,000 years, when it was and still is lagging behind what ordinary people would regard as common moral and ethical standards?

Even to this day, many within religious institutions continue to preach homophobia and do not allow gay people to hold high positions within their organizations. If this were a policy in any other business, it would be brought before the courts and the offending party would be publically shamed and forced to change its policies. So why do we allow religious "businesses" to behave in this way?

For too long bigotry has not only been accepted by religions but also endorsed by them. Until recent times, when these issues have been more openly discussed, this bigotry resulted in suicides, murders and people ostracizing their own family members and friends. The teaching that gay people are not normal or are an "abomination" is nothing more than hate speech. Church leaders have always maintained that they are condemning gay people only for what they do, but if they had any understanding of homosexuality they would realize that their criticisms condemn gay people for *who they are* – a huge difference. They are not merely providing an interpretation of scripture; they are actively spreading prejudice, bigotry and injustice.

By preaching that although AIDS is bad, the use of condoms is worse, the church has been directly responsible for the preventable suffering and deaths of millions of people. It is time that the church moved on from a few sentences in an old fable and admitted that it would be far better to use a condom and thereby prevent infected bodily fluids from killing or harming another person. It is especially ironic when churches and believers set up "right to life" campaigns for foetuses but allow others to die of preventable diseases, or children to be born with HIV.

There is also a poor understanding of morals in Jesus' pronouncements on forgiveness. Throughout the New Testament Jesus forgives sins, yet never consults with the victims of those sins. He behaves like he is the affected party while ignoring the real victim. One of the foundations of morality should be that you accept blame and, if possible, make peace with those you have harmed – not pray to someone else for absolution. The belief that real-world actions can be passed off through vicarious redemption rather than true redemption has been perpetuated by the Christian churches throughout history and continues today. Until this idea is eliminated, people will never take full responsibility for their actions.

Partly because religion relies on an abstract notion of forgiveness, societies need secular legal systems that make sure offenders are appropriately punished and make victims feel that justice has been correctly served. It is ironic that religious adherents often pray to their deity that someone will be punished for a crime, but then rely on a secular judiciary system to determine and implement a true punishment. Surely if their deity was really all-seeing and all-powerful, he would mete out punishment himself? After all, the god of the Old and New Testaments supposedly punished sinners and enemies repeatedly thousands of years ago.

Morals from the Koran

The first and most important requirement in understanding the Islamic mindset is that the Koran, being, supposedly, the very words of God/ Allah, is held in even higher regard by its believers than the Old or New Testament. It therefore cannot and must not be questioned, and to do so can be considered a form of apostasy in Islam. This is quite different to Judaism and Christianity, where robust questioning of the texts is common and not seen as a religious crime. With the Koran, the content has to be accepted as 100 per cent accurate and as the only possible guide to correct behaviour. There is no "wriggle space".

So is the Koran a reasonable moral guide for the modern world? Does it merit its status as a positive belief system, currently being used to indoctrinate millions of children every day, worldwide?

Fearing Allah

"Fear Allah" is a command regularly repeated throughout the Koran and is one of the major tenets and teachings of Islam. The best way to control large numbers of people, it seems, is through fear, as politicians of all stripes have demonstrated, or tried to demonstrate, over the centuries. There is probably no other document or belief system that uses (and abuses) this mindset more than the Koran. Muslims live in fear more than any other religious group and, as will be seen, this prevents those brought up in the religion from questioning or leaving it.

A few typical examples are cited below, but the order to fear Allah is repeated over and over throughout the Koran in an endless cycle, as is the idea that he is always watching everything you do.

Koran 2:74 And Allah is not unaware of what you do.

Koran 2:165 And if only they who have wronged would consider that when they see the punishment, they will be certain that all power belongs to Allah and that Allah is severe in punishment.

Koran 2:197 And whatever good you do – Allah knows it. And take provisions, but indeed, the best provision is fear of Allah. And fear Me, O you of understanding.

Koran 2:203 There is no sin upon him – for him who fears Allah. And fear Allah and know that unto Him you will be gathered.

Koran 2:278 O you who have believed, fear Allah and give up what remains due to you of interest, if you should be believers.

Koran 3:16 Those who say, "Our Lord, indeed we have believed, so forgive us our sins and protect us from the punishment of the Fire."

Koran 3:200 O you who have believed, persevere and endure and remain stationed and fear Allah that you may be successful.

To counter this and make Muslims feel like there is at least a glimmer of light at the end of the tunnel, they are also told repeatedly that Allah is a nice god.

Koran 2:218 Indeed, those who have believed and those who have emigrated and fought in the cause of Allah – those expect the mercy of Allah. And Allah is Forgiving and Merciful.

Koran 5:3 This day I have perfected for you your religion and completed My favour upon you and have approved for you Islam as religion. But whoever is forced by severe hunger with no inclination to sin – then indeed, Allah is Forgiving and Merciful.

And even a combination of the above: fear him, plus he loves you.

Koran 5:93 There is not upon those who believe and do righteousness any blame concerning what they have eaten in the past if they now fear Allah and believe and do righteous deeds, and then fear Allah and believe, and then fear Allah and do good; and Allah loves the doers of good.

On the treatment and value of women

Like the other two monotheistic religions, the Koran is a text that was given to a man or men but not to women. And just like the other two religions, unsurprisingly, the rules and stories are all about men being able to treat women as far less valuable human beings, possessions to be owned and used as men see fit.

Koran 2:223 Your wives are a place of sowing of seed for you, so come to your place of cultivation however you wish and put forth righteousness for yourselves.

Here not only do men own women but they can also insist on sex whenever and however they want it; and because these are the words of their god, this is not only permitted but seen as a righteous act.

Koran 2:228 And their husbands have more right to take them back in this period if they want reconciliation. And due to the wives is similar to what is expected of them, according to what is reasonable. But the men have a degree over them in responsibility and authority. And Allah is Exalted in Might and Wise.

Essentially, this is saying that men own their women and have more rights than their wives.

Koran 2:282 And bring to witness two witnesses from among your men. And if there are not two men available, then a man and two women from those whom you accept as witnesses – so that if one of the women errs, then the other can remind her.

In other words, women may be too stupid to act as witnesses and they only count as half a man.

Koran 4:3 And if you fear that you will not deal justly with the orphan girls – then marry those that please you of other women, two or three or four. But if you fear that you will not be just, then marry only one or those your right hand possesses. That is more suitable that you may not incline to injustice.

Men are allowed three or four wives (and only the men have the power of choosing their spouse, and only if the women "please them"). On top of that, men have to be reminded that if they are incapable of being just people, then maybe they should consider "possessing" only one woman.

Koran 4:11 Allah instructs you concerning your children: for the male, what is equal to the share of two females. But if there are only daughters, two or more, for them is two thirds of one's estate. And if there is only one, for her is half. And for one's parents, to each one of them is a sixth of his estate if he left children. But if he had no children and the parents alone inherit from him, then for his mother is one third. And if he had brothers or sisters, for his mother is a sixth, after any bequest he may have made or debt.

Women merit only half of what a man should receive. Are these the words of an all-loving god or, more likely, of Middle Eastern men trying to maintain a male-dominated society?

Koran 4:15–16 Those who commit unlawful sexual intercourse of your women – bring against them four witnesses from among you. And if they testify, confine the guilty women to houses until death takes them or Allah ordains for them another way.

So, men may be forgiven for having an affair but women are to be either held under house arrest for the rest of their lives or murdered in a manner that will be conveyed to the men by Allah.

> **Koran 4:20** But if you want to replace one wife with another and you have given one of them a great amount in gifts, do not take back from it anything. Would you take it in injustice and manifest sin?

Replace one wife with another? What, are they cars or some other form of chattel?

> **Koran 4:34** Men are in charge of women by right of what Allah has given one over the other and what they spend for maintenance from their wealth. So righteous women are devoutly obedient, guarding in the husband's absence what Allah would have them guard. But those wives from whom you fear arrogance – first advise them; then if they persist, forsake them in bed; and finally, strike them.

Here, not only are we told that men are superior to women and in charge of them but also that if women do not obey, men may give them no love or may even beat them. Wife beating is divinely sanctioned. Why is there never once a mention of women being able to have any superior rights, value or retribution in the Koran?

> **Koran 4:176** If there are both brothers and sisters, the male will have the share of two females. Allah makes clear to you His law, lest you go astray. And Allah is Knowing of all things.

Except maybe Allah is unaware of the concept of the morality of equality?

> **Koran 33:30** O wives of the Prophet, whoever of you should commit a clear immorality – for her the punishment would be doubled twofold, and ever is that, for Allah, easy.

The above is merely a selection of the many Koranic teachings on the lesser value of women relative to men. What is very clear is that either Allah is a misogynist or the writers of the Koran were. Take your pick. And whichever you choose, if you still regard the Koran as a good guide to life then you are supporting a system that wants to oppress 50 per cent of the world's population. How on earth can this be seen as a good moral guide? How can parents be happy that their children will be treated totally differently throughout their lives if one is a daughter and one is a son?

Probably one of the worst stories about Mohammed is that of his marriage and sexual relations with one of his wives, Aisha. He married her at the age of six and had sexual intercourse with her at the age of nine, when he was almost 50. One should go to a local primary school to see how innocent a six-year-old or a nine-year-old girl is. Girls of this age should be separated from old men, not forced to be with them. The endorsement of such behaviour in Islamic teaching is thankfully banned under modern, Western secular laws.

Sahih Bukhari volume 5, book 58, number 234–236 The Prophet engaged me when I was a girl of six years. We went to Medina and stayed at the home of Bani-al-Harith bin Khazraj. Then I got ill and my hair fell down. Later on my hair grew again and my mother, Um Ruman, came to me while I was playing in a swing with some of my girlfriends. She called me, and I went to her, not knowing what she wanted to do to me. She caught me by the hand and made me stand at the door of the house. I was breathless then, and when my breathing became alright, she took some water and rubbed my face and head with it. Then she took me into the house. There in the house I saw some Ansari women who said, "Best wishes and Allah's Blessing and a good luck." Then she entrusted me to them and they prepared me (for the marriage). Unexpectedly Allah's Apostle came to me in the forenoon and my mother handed me over to him, and at that time I was a girl of nine years of age.

That the Prophet said to her, "You have been shown to me twice in my dream. I saw you pictured on a piece of silk and someone said to me, 'This is your wife.' When I uncovered the picture, I saw that it was yours. I said, 'If this is from Allah, it will be done.'"

Khadija died three years before the Prophet departed to Medina. He stayed there for two years or so and then he married Aisha when she was a girl of six years of age, and he consumed that marriage when she was nine years old.

There are many Muslims nowadays who dispute the true age of Aisha, but others argue forcefully that the words of the story must be accepted as the truth.

The implications of this are significant, as in many Muslim countries it is not seen as wrong by adherents to marry off daughters at a very young age. This of course deprives the girls of a proper childhood and leads to increased death rates from giving birth when too young.

Many Islamic nations do not allow men to marry child brides under their civil code of laws, but at the same time recognize that Sharia religious laws and courts have the power to override the civil code, which they often do. UNICEF reports that the top five nations in the world with highest observed child marriage rates – Niger (75 per cent), Chad (72 per cent), Mali (71 per cent), Bangladesh (64 per cent) and Guinea (63 per cent) – are all Islamic majority countries.

Female virginity is also held in high regard in Islamic teaching. Brides are expected to be virgins. Meanwhile, male believers are told that in heaven they will be able to consort with virgins. But what about women who want to commit to the pathway to heaven? Are they offered men who do a fair share of the housework and remember to put the toilet seat down? No, there are no such great rewards and entitlements for Muslim women.

What does all of this suggest will be the likely outcome for both men and women brought up under Islamic teaching? What sort of human beings are being moulded when they are raised under this belief system? Over and over, the Koran nearly always talks only to men.

Koran 2:187 It has been made permissible for you the night preceding fasting to go to your wives for sexual relations. They are clothing for you and you are clothing for them. Allah knows that you used to deceive yourselves, so He accepted your repentance and forgave you. So now, have relations with them and seek that which Allah has decreed for you.

And what about the Koran's understanding of the menstrual cycle? Bizarrely, we are told that it can cause "harm" and that women must subsequently be purified.

> **Koran 2:222** And they ask you about menstruation. Say, "It is harm, so keep away from wives during menstruation." And do not approach them until they are pure. And when they have purified themselves, then come to them from where Allah has ordained for you. Indeed, Allah loves those who are constantly repentant and loves those who purify themselves.

Are men impure if they have cut themselves shaving or have open wounds?

> **Koran 2:231** And when you divorce women and they have nearly fulfilled their term, either retain them according to acceptable terms or release them according to acceptable terms, and do not keep them, intending harm, to transgress against them. And whoever does that has certainly wronged himself. And do not take the verses of Allah in jest.

Again, women are your possessions, and men (not women) get to choose to divorce and, by the way, Allah doesn't have a sense of humour, so you'd better follow his rules – he's serious.

Tolerance of others

The Western media and politicians continue to spout that it is "un-Islamic" for Muslims to show intolerance of and carry out violent acts on adherents of other religions, especially of the kind we see on the news on a regular basis. In fact, if you take the Koran at its word, it is "un-Islamic" and a failure to follow the book's teachings *not* to behave the way many "extremists" do.

There are over 100 different verses in the Koran that either encourage or directly call on Muslims to fight against non-believers or "infidels". As we have seen, Yahweh, the god of the Old Testament, was sometimes said to have called for the killing of people of other faiths, but these pronouncements related to particular historical events. They were more descriptive than prescriptive. The Koranic calls, on the other hand, are more open-ended and could apply to any time period, including the present and future. And there are very few opposing comments in the Koran to balance or offset these prescriptions. So, although the vast majority of today's Muslims do not despise or harm people of other faiths, in doing so they are in fact following their own sense of morality and rejecting Koranic teaching.

When it is said that Islam is a religion of peace, this can only be in spite of Koranic teaching rather than as a result of it. Indeed, it is far easier for a Muslim to justify intolerance of others with Koranic verses than to justify acceptance or love of non-Muslims using the same sources.

It is therefore important to realize that although it is only certain people who choose to follow the often violent and intolerant Koranic commands, Islamic teaching is in fact an intolerant ideology full of recommendations that extremists, and particularly jihadists, can and do use to justify some horrendous acts. It is incorrect to state that extremists have corrupted aspects of Islam; the fact is that modern moderate Muslims are (wisely) choosing to ignore some of teachings, and are thereby going against the Koran. The extremists are not the problem; in medical terms, they are merely the signs and symptoms. The problem is the Koran, and it needs to be called out as such.

The reality is that Muslims feel they are able to espouse intolerance for other people's religions because it is divinely mandated in the Koran, yet at the same time they expect others to offer the highest level of tolerance for their own religion.

Koran 2:193 Fight them until there is no more fitnah and until worship is acknowledged to be for Allah. But if they cease, then there is to be no aggression except against the oppressors.

Koran 2:257 Allah is the ally of those who believe. He brings them out from darknesses into the light. And those who disbelieve – their allies are Taghut. They take them out of the light into darknesses. Those are the companions of the Fire; they will abide eternally therein.

Koran 3:56 And as for those who disbelieved, I will punish them with a severe punishment in this world and the Hereafter, and they will have no helpers.

Koran 3:85 And whoever desires other than Islam as religion – never will it be accepted from him, and he, in the Hereafter, will be among the losers.

Koran 3:151 We will cast terror into the hearts of those who disbelieve for what they have associated with Allah of which He had not sent down [any] authority. And their refuge will be the Fire, and wretched is the residence of the wrongdoers.

Koran 4:56 Indeed, those who disbelieve in Our verses – We will drive them into a fire. Every time their skins are roasted through We will replace them with other skins so they may taste the punishment. Indeed Allah is ever exalted in Might and Wise.

Koran 4:89 They wish you would disbelieve as they disbelieved so you would be alike. So do not take from among them allies until they emigrate for the cause of Allah. But if they turn away, then seize them and kill them wherever you find them and take not from among them any ally or helper.

Koran 5:33 Indeed, the penalty for those who wage war against Allah and His Messenger and strive upon earth to cause corruption is none but that they be killed or crucified or that their hands and feet be cut off from opposite sides or that they be exiled from the land. That is for them a disgrace in this world; and for them in the Hereafter is a great punishment.

This quote above is interesting because the paragraph directly before it in the Koran is often quoted by those who wish to claim that Islam teaches tolerance. Here it is:

> **Koran 5:32** Because of that, We decreed upon the Children of Israel that whoever kills a soul unless for a soul or for corruption done in the land – it is as if he had slain mankind entirely. And whoever saves one – it is as if he had saved mankind entirely. And our messengers had certainly come to them with clear proofs. Then indeed many of them, even after that, throughout the land, were transgressors.

Yet, as has just been seen, in the very next sentence it espouses a directly opposing, violent and intolerant view. So remind anyone who quotes verse 5.32 of the Koran what follows straight after.

This is an excellent example of why the catch-cry "Islam is a religion of peace" is utter nonsense. If it were a religion of peace then its literalists and extremists would be the most peaceable people on earth – more like adherents of Jainism, who do whatever they can to not harm any living creature.

Here are some more examples of Koranic intolerance:

> **Koran 8:12–13** Remember when your Lord inspired to the angels, "I am with you, so strengthen those who have believed. I will cast terror into the hearts of those who disbelieved, so strike them upon the necks and strike from them every fingertip." That is because they opposed Allah and His Messenger. And whoever opposes Allah and His Messenger – indeed, Allah is severe in penalty.

> **Koran 8:59–60** And let not those who disbelieve suppose that they can outstrip Allah's Purpose. Lo! they cannot escape. Make ready for them all thou canst of armed force and of horses tethered, that thereby ye may dismay the enemy of Allah and your enemy.

> **Koran 8:65** O Prophet, urge the believers to battle. If there

are among you twenty who are steadfast, they will overcome two hundred. And if there are among you one hundred who are steadfast, they will overcome a thousand of those who have disbelieved because they are a people who do not understand.

Koran 9:5 And when the sacred months have passed, then kill the polytheists wherever you find them and capture them and besiege them and sit in wait for them at every place of ambush.

Koran 9:29 Fight those who do not believe in Allah or in the Last Day and who do not consider unlawful what Allah and His Messenger have made unlawful and who do not adopt the religion of truth from those who were given the Scripture – fight until they give the jizyah willingly while they are humbled.

Koran 9:41 Go forth, whether light or heavy, and strive with your wealth and your lives in the cause of Allah. That is better for you, if you only knew.

Koran 9:111 Indeed, Allah has purchased from the believers their lives and their properties in exchange for that they will have Paradise. They fight in the cause of Allah, so they kill and are killed.

Koran 9:123 O you who have believed, fight those adjacent to you of the disbelievers and let them find in you harshness. And know that Allah is with the righteous.

Koran 22:19–22 These are two adversaries who have disputed over their Lord. But those who disbelieved will have cut out for them garments of fire. Poured upon their heads will be scalding water. By which is melted that within their bellies and their skins. And for striking them are maces of iron. Every time they want to get out of Hellfire from anguish, they will be returned to it, and it will be said, "Taste the punishment of the Burning Fire!"

Koran 25:52 So do not obey the disbelievers, and strive against them with the Koran a great striving.

Koran 30:60-61 If the hypocrites and those in whose hearts is disease and those who spread rumours in al-Madinah do not cease, We will surely incite you against them; then they will not remain your neighbours therein except for a little. Accursed wherever they are found, being seized and massacred completely.

Koran 47:4 So when you meet those who disbelieve in battle, strike their necks until, when you have inflicted slaughter upon them, then secure their bonds, and either confer favour afterwards or ransom them until the war lays down its burdens. That is the command. And if Allah had willed, He could have taken vengeance upon them Himself, but He ordered armed struggle to test some of you by means of others. And those who are killed in the cause of Allah – never will He waste their deeds.

And from the Hadith and other commentaries:

Sahih al-Bukhari 11:626 Muhammed said: "I decided to order a man to lead the prayer and then take a flame to burn all those who had not left their houses for the prayer, burning them alive inside their homes."

Tabari 9:69 "Killing Unbelievers is a small matter to us." The words of Muhammed, prophet of Islam.

As can be seen, violence is so ingrained in the teachings of Islam, and not merely within a historical context, that Islam has always been at war, either with non-believers or within its own sects. Moreover, given that they are inundated with such frequent calls to violence against non-believers, it is extremely difficult for even "moderate" Muslims to speak out against these teachings, as this would mean they are ignoring and even acting contrary to Koranic doctrine.

On not being true friends with non-Muslims

The following quotes show how the Koran directs believers to avoid entering into any kind of relations with non-Muslims. Combined with the directives above, these suggest that a strict Muslim can never show any genuine respect for other faiths.

Koran 3:28 Let not believers take disbelievers as allies rather than believers. And whoever of you does that has nothing with Allah, except when taking precaution against them in prudence. And Allah warns you of Himself, and to Allah is the final destination.

Koran 3:118 O you who have believed, do not take as intimates those other than yourselves, for they will not spare you any ruin. They wish you would have hardship. Hatred has already appeared from their mouths, and what their breasts conceal is greater. We have certainly made clear to you the signs, if you will use reason.

Koran 5:51 O you who have believed, do not take the Jews and the Christians as allies. They are in fact allies of one another. And whoever is an ally to them among you – then indeed, he is one of them. Indeed, Allah guides not the wrongdoing people.

Koran 5:80 You see many of them becoming allies of those who disbelieved. How wretched is that which they have put forth for themselves in that Allah has become angry with them, and in the punishment they will abide eternally.

Koran 9:23 O you who have believed, do not take your fathers or your brothers as allies if they have preferred disbelief over belief. And whoever does so among you – then it is those who are the wrongdoers.

Koran 53:29 So turn away from whoever turns his back on Our message and desires not except the worldly life.

And from the Hadith:

> **Abu Dawud 41:4815** The Prophet (peace be upon him) said: "A man follows the religion of his friend; so each one should consider whom he makes his friend."

> **Abu Dawud 41:4832** The Messenger of Allah said, "Do not keep company with anyone but a believer and do not let anyone eat your food but one who is pious."

> **Sahih al Bukhari 59:572** Then Allah revealed the Sura: "O you who believe! Take not my enemies And your enemies as friends offering them Your love even though they have disbelieved in that Truth (i.e. Allah, Prophet Muhammed and this Koran) which has come to you … (to the end of Verse) … And whosoever of you (Muslims) does that, then indeed he has gone far astray away from the Straight Path."

On preaching anti-Semitism

No ideology, be it religious or otherwise, should be acceptable if, as part of its official teachings, it espouses hatred towards another group of people, as is the case with Muslim prejudice against Jews. There can never be genuine world peace until these views are placed in context and disavowed by all leaders of Islam, much in the same way as the Vatican eventually publically renounced anti-Semitism in the Second Vatican Council of 1965. That, however is a formidable challenge since, by definition, Islam (remember the word's meaning: submission) cannot disavow any of the comments in the Koran because they are supposedly the actual words of its god, Allah.

Although Muslims often try to portray the Arab-Israeli conflict as a modern political battle, Muslims are actually taught from a very young age to see the Jews as a people who are less than human and who must be fought against. There is only a minor uproar in the Islamic world when Muslims are killed by other Muslims, but when Israeli actions lead to the death of Muslims then the uproar is enormous. Why the imbalance? It all begins with the words of the Koran.

Koran 2:64 But you Jews went back on your word and were lost losers. So become apes, despised and hated. We made an example out of you.

Koran 3:110 You are the best nation produced as an example for mankind. You enjoin what is right and forbid what is wrong and believe in Allah. If only the People of the Scripture had believed, it would have been better for them. Among them are believers, but most of them are defiantly disobedient.

Koran 4:55 Sufficient for the Jew is the Flaming Fire!

Koran 4:160-161 For wrongdoing on the part of the Jews, we made unlawful for them (certain) foods which had been lawful to them, and for their averting from the way of Allah many (people). And for their taking of usury while they had been forbidden from it, and their consuming of the people's wealth unjustly. And we have prepared for the disbelievers among them a painful punishment.

Koran 5:41 O Messenger, let them not grieve you who hasten into disbelief of those who say, "We believe" with their mouths, but their hearts believe not, and from among the Jews. They are avid listeners to falsehood, listening to another people who have not come to you. They distort words beyond their proper usages, saying "If you are given this, take it; but if you are not given it, then beware." But he for whom Allah intends fitnah – never will you possess power to do for him a thing against Allah. Those are the ones for whom Allah does not intend to purify their hearts. For them in this world is disgrace, and for them in the Hereafter is a great punishment.

Koran 5:63 Why do the rabbis and religious scholars not forbid them from saying what is sinful and devouring what is unlawful? How wretched is what they have been practising.

Koran 5:78 Curses were pronounced on the unbelievers, the

Children of Israel who rejected Islam, by the tongues of David and of Jesus because they disobeyed and rebelled.

Koran 33:26 Allah made the Jews leave their homes by terrorizing them so that you killed some and made many captive. And He made you inherit their lands, their homes and their wealth. He gave you a country you had not traversed before.

Koran 59:2 It is He who expelled the ones who disbelieved among the People of the Scripture from their homes at the first gathering. You did not think they would leave, and they thought that their fortresses would protect them from Allah; but the decree of Allah came upon them from where they had not expected, and He cast terror into their hearts so they destroyed their houses by their own hands and the hands of the believers. So take warning, O people of vision.

Koran 59:14 They will not fight you all except within fortified cities or from behind walls. Their violence among themselves is severe. You think they are together, but their hearts are diverse. That is because they are a people who do not reason.

Koran 88:1 Has the narration reached you of the overwhelming calamity? Some faces (all disbelievers, Jews and Christians) that Day, will be humiliated, downcast, scorched by the burning fire, while they are made to drink from a boiling hot spring.

Koran 98:1 Those among the People of the Book (Bible), who disbelieve in Allah and are idolaters, would never have been freed from their false religion if the Clear Proofs had not come to them. An Apostle of Allah came reading out of hallowed pages ... They were commanded to serve Allah exclusively, fulfilling their devotional obligations, and paying the zakat. Surely the unbelievers and idolaters from the People of the Book (Bible) will abide in the Fire of Hell. They are the worst of creatures.

Sahih al-Bukhari 52:177 Allah's Apostle said, "The Hour will not be established until you fight with the Jews, and the stone behind which a Jew will be hiding will say, 'O Muslim! There is a Jew hiding behind me, so kill him.'"

If someone were to say these things at a public event or on TV, they would rightly be condemned. But because they are quoting from a religious text, Muslim clerics can continue to both teach and preach such wretched attitudes.

On slavery

Slavery has been an acceptable part of Islam since its beginnings, and it is only in very recent times that Islam has accepted that it is immoral to "own" another person. There are a number of references in the Koran validating and supporting the idea of slavery, yet there are no anti-slavery comments. Allah is obviously not averse to the concept of owning other human beings. Notably, the last countries on Earth to abolish slavery were all Muslim countries: Saudi Arabia and Yemen (1962), UAE (1964), Oman (1970), Mauritania (1981) and Niger (2003).

Koran 4:36 Show kindness unto parents, and unto near kindred, and orphans, and the needy, and unto the neighbour who is of kin unto you and the neighbour who is not of kin, and the fellow traveller and the wayfarer and the slaves whom your right hands possess.

Koran 4:92 It is not for a believer to kill a believer unless it be by mistake. He who hath killed a believer by mistake must set free a believing slave, and pay the blood-money to the family of the slain, unless they remit it as a charity. If he the victim be of a people hostile unto you, and he is a believer, then the penance is to set free a believing slave.

Koran 23:5–6 And who guard their modesty – Save from their wives or the slaves that their right hands possess.

Koran 24:31 And tell the believing women to lower their gaze and be modest, and to display of their adornment only that which is apparent, and to draw their veils over their bosoms, and not to reveal their adornment save to their own husbands or fathers or husbands' fathers, or their sons or their husbands' sons, or their brothers or their brothers' sons or sisters' sons, or their women, or their slaves.

Koran 24:58 O ye who believe! Let your slaves, and those of you who have not come to puberty, ask leave of you at three times before they come into your presence.

Koran 33:25–26 Allah repulsed the disbelievers in their wrath; they gained no good. Allah averted their attack from the believers. Allah is ever Strong, Mighty. And He brought those of the People of the Scripture who supported them down from their strongholds, and cast panic into their hearts. Some ye slew, and ye made captive some.

Koran 33:50 O Prophet! Lo! We have made lawful unto thee thy wives unto whom thou hast paid their dowries, and those whom thy right hand possesseth of those whom Allah hath given thee as spoils of war.

Koran 33:55 It is no sin for them thy wives to converse freely with their fathers, or their sons, or their brothers, or their brothers' sons, or the sons of their sisters or of their own women, or their slaves.

On apostasy

Apostasy is the renunciation or abandonment of a religious belief system. It may take the form of a complete disaffiliation or, in some circumstances, a declaration that an individual no longer believes in certain aspects of their religion.

Both the Koran and Hadith mention on numerous occasions that an apostate must be punished. As of 2016 over 20 nations (all majority Muslim) have included in their laws criminal statutes forbidding apostasy or allowing it to be prosecuted under other laws. They include: Afghanistan, Algeria, Brunei, Comoros, Egypt, Iran, Iraq, Jordan, Kuwait, Malaysia, Maldives, Mauritania, Morocco, Nigeria, Oman, Pakistan, Qatar, Saudi Arabia, Somalia, Sudan, Syria, United Arab Emirates and Yemen. There are also a few other Islamic majority nations that do not have apostasy laws but prosecute apostasy under their blasphemy laws, for example Indonesia. The penalties for apostasy include fines, jail time, flogging, child custody loss, marriage annulment, and, in many nations, capital punishment.

The United Nations Commission on Human Rights considers the recanting of a person's religion a human right legally protected by the International Covenant on Civil and Political Rights. The UN and progressive non-member states should impose penalties on any nation that ignores such essential human rights, yet they do not. It is even more disgraceful that there are representatives of Islamic theocracies on the UN Human Rights Council.

Often the public face of a majority Muslim country may be forward-thinking and welcoming, but at the same time citizens who no longer believe in Islam are being forced to live in terror and hide their true beliefs for fear of punishment. Moreover, families will often distance themselves or completely renounce their ties to anyone who even begins to question the tenets of Islam. One does not even have to disagree entirely with the Islamic teachings to be considered an apostate. Simply verbalizing or writing, for example, that "humans came to be via evolution" is considered apostasy, as is anything negative said about Mohammed.

This sort of control of followers should not be acceptable. And we should not forget that children brought up in Islamic countries or in Islamic communities within Western countries are forced to live a life without freedom of choice. Living under Islam stifles learning about so many facts and facets of life and other people that it becomes exceedingly difficult for these "Muslims" to have the full rights associated with freedom of thought. How moral is it to threaten people born in an Islamic culture with capital punishment for questioning their religion or wanting to leave it?

So, what do the Koran and Hadith say about apostasy?

Koran 3:90 But those who reject Faith after they accepted it, and then go on adding to their defiance of Faith – never will their repentance be accepted; for they are those who have of set purpose gone astray.

Koran 4:89 They wish you would disbelieve as they disbelieved so you would be alike. So do not take from among them allies until they emigrate for the cause of Allah. But if they turn away, then seize them and kill them wherever you find them and take not from among them any ally or helper.

Koran 16:106 He who disbelieves in Allah after his having believed, not he who is compelled while his heart is at rest on account of faith, but he who opens his breast to disbelief – on these is the wrath of Allah, and they shall have a grievous chastisement.

Then from Hadith the description of the punishment:

Sahih al-Bukari 9:83:17 Allah's Apostle said, "The blood of a Muslim who confesses that none has the right to be worshipped but Allah and that I am His Apostle, cannot be shed except in three cases: In Qisas for murder, a married person who commits illegal sexual intercourse and the one who reverts from Islam (apostate) and leaves the Muslims."

Sahih al-Bukari 4:52:260 Ali burned some people and this news reached Ibn 'Abbas, who said, "Had I been in his place I would not have burned them, as the Prophet said, 'Don't punish anybody with Allah's Punishment.' No doubt, I would have killed them, for the Prophet said, 'If somebody (a Muslim) discards his religion, kill him.'"

Sahih al-Bukhari, 9:89:271 A man embraced Islam and then reverted back to Judaism. Mu'adh bin Jabal came and saw the man with Abu Musa. Mu'adh asked, "What is wrong with this man?" Abu Musa replied, "He embraced Islam and then reverted back to Judaism." Mu'adh said, "I will not sit down unless you kill him as it is the verdict of Allah and His Apostle."

"Most people are bothered by those passages of scripture they do not understand, but the passages that bother me are those that I do understand." – Mark Twain

Morality in general with regard to religions

So, what is more offensive: people choosing to reject or criticize these ideas and words, or the ideas and words themselves? If "hate speech and intolerance" is the argument put forward whenever there is questioning or satirizing of a religion, then surely religious texts should be the first victims of this logic. And while it's generally true that religions should not be defined by the actions of a minority of their adherents, religions must surely be judged on their holy books, as anything within them can be used by their followers to justify their actions. To develop true morality, all religions need to identify and disown the outdated rules, commendations and directives in their texts.

Imagine if the country that you are living in incorporated some of the more extreme rules from the Bible or the Koran into their constitution. Do you think this would create a better and safer and more moral world? Western societies would not be able to function if that happened. Anyone with even a modicum of sanity can see that many religious directives should never be part of a nation's laws. Yet so many people are happy to ignore what such rules are actually saying and allow them to exist within the teachings of a religion.

> "Morality is doing right, no matter what you are told. Religion is doing what you are told, no matter what is right."
>
> H.L. Mencken

Theistic morality refers to the idea that we can't work out that murder or theft is wrong unless some deity tells us so. However, what the laws of religion create are not true morals but simply orders that must be obeyed. True morality is doing what is right, without the promise of heavenly reward or the threat of divine retribution.

Is it axiomatic that whatever a god commands is instantly good? When Yahweh ordered ethnic cleansing in the land of Canaan (Israel), was that morally right, simply because he demanded it? Does a god say that something is good because it is good, or is something good because a god says that it's good? For instance, does a god command us not to rape because it is bad, or is rape bad because a god commands us not to rape?

Religious leaders will often say that atheists must pick and choose what to believe, while divine laws mean that humans don't have to rely on their highly fallible ability to distinguish right from wrong. Yet, as has been seen, religious leaders are required to select which of the rules from their sacred texts should be followed without question and which should be modified or ignored.

When a theist asks the question, "Why do you need to be good if there is no god?", what he or she is implying is that the only thing holding him or her back from committing murder is a belief in a deity that may or may not exist. But if you need the threat of eternal damnation to be a good person, then maybe you need to re-assess whether you really are a good person and are capable of independent moral behaviour.

If only more people could escape the theistic view, then more of us could experience that "light bulb" moment when we realize that the most important person watching and judging our actions is ourself.

> # IF THE ONLY REASON YOU BEHAVE MORALLY IS OUT OF FEAR OF AN INVISIBLE MAN IN THE SKY.........
>
> # PLEASE STAY AWAY IN CASE YOU EVER DOUBT YOUR GOD'S EXISTENCE

Morality is innate in of all of us; if it were not, we would never have progressed this far as a species. From an evolutionary perspective, moral actions allow humans living in large societal groups to cooperate and develop successfully. It is only the mentally disturbed who cannot feel or understand this clearly.

Christopher Hitchens rapidly dispels the issue of morals without religion by asking to "name an ethical statement that was made, or a moral action that was performed, by a religious person in the name of faith that could not have been made as an action or uttered as a statement by a person not of faith. It can't be done. That being the case, we are entitled to say that religious faith is surplus to requirements." Conversely, when asked to think of a wicked thing said or an evil thing done by a person of faith in the name of faith, most people have little hesitation in coming up with an example.

Adhering to the main moral rules of the Old and New Testaments and the Koran is like following the orders of a tyrant. "Obey and worship the laws of God or else you will suffer" is a message repeated throughout all three texts. And these divine orders include the practice of intolerance and the killing of non-believers.

Studies show that normal, healthy individuals will perform terrible acts out of loyalty to an official with a title. The worst atrocities and genocides in history have occurred not as a result of disobedience but of blind obedience. It is sometimes stated by theists that Hitler, Stalin and Pol Pot were all atheists. This is not actually true, but in any case what happened in these situations was that allegiance to the dictator, with its centralization of powers, unquestioning acceptance of a doctrine and hero worship of that individual, became similar to a religion. These leaders used an ideology to control a populace, just as religious leaders might do.

"Too many people are too quick to kill and die for their beliefs and too slow to examine them. I think once we reverse this insanity, the world will be a much more peaceful place." – Michael Sherman

"Religion is an insult to human dignity. With or without it you would have good people doing good things and evil people doing evil things. But for good people to do evil things, that takes religion."

Steven Weinberg
Nobel Laureate, Physics

No society in history became worse off because it became more tolerant and accepting of the view that all of humanity should be seen and treated as equals. It's also true that through time, and most obviously in current-day society, non-religious people are the ones who are most likely to be more tolerant and support equal rights for women, homosexuals and other minority groups. Indeed, when you look at the most secular, atheistic countries or by census those with higher levels of non-believers, such as the Scandinavian nations and Australia and New Zealand, you find that they have the most egalitarian societies and the fewest murders, whereas it is in the world's most religious countries that you find the greatest levels of oppression and the most barbaric actions occurring. The USA, for instance, has the highest per-capita murder rate of Western countries, yet it is among the most religious, and it is notably in those states where religion dominates the local culture – particularly in the so-called Bible Belt – that you find the highest levels of racism, oppression, murders and capital punishment.

Also, if you look at studies of prison populations, the proportion of atheists or non-believers is well below the overall proportion in society. It simply does not hold water that religious people are in any way more moral in their behaviour; in fact, statistics show the opposite. That doesn't prevent religious leaders repeating this falsehood in an attempt to prevent their adherents from seeing that the grass can be greener on the other side.

The lesser position of women in our society does not result from secular views; it is due to the dominance of religious thought and teachings over the last 3,000 years. It is only as a society becomes less reliant on religious views that it can break the shackles of the patriarchy and allow women equal rights and status. Poverty in many developing countries is directly linked to the fact that women are still segregated, not offered the same level of education and work opportunities as males, and not allowed full control of their own bodies or even a say in how many children they wish to bear. Religion has so often chosen to oppress women, separate them, cover them up or hide them away, instead of dealing with the issue of men's urges and discussing how to deal with them from the male side.

Obliging women to cover themselves from head to toe (as in Islam) or having them wear "modest clothes" or wigs to cover their natural hair (as in some forms of Judaism) sends a clear message that the men in charge see themselves and their brothers as little more than lustful creatures who are incapable of self-control and simple human decency. It suggests that all men are potential rapists, if the merest sight of a bit of female flesh could cause them to lose control. Is this the best solution that religion can come up with for dealing with men's sexual urges?

In Judaism, there is a morning prayer that is said by males "thanking God that I am not a woman". How do parents explain this to their young daughters?

With regard to the treatment of women, Christianity is the least offensive of the three major religions; however, equal rights and values for women still do not exist within most Christian systems. Many churches do not allow the ordination of women and most do not for the highest positions. To justify this, church leaders often cite 1 Timothy 2:12: "But I suffer not a woman to teach, nor to usurp authority over the man, but to be in silence."

In many Islamic countries, women are not allowed out of their homes or to drive cars unless they have a male with them. Somehow, even having a twelve-year-old boy in a car suddenly makes it okay for a woman to drive, but having a twelve-year-old girl in the car doesn't. Also, women are not allowed to participate in prayer services as much as men – is their god not really interested in listening to women? What is this teaching females in these countries about their worth or value and what concepts are being reinforced for men here?

There is also a terrible cultural relativism that permeates Western thought with regards to women's rights in Islamic countries. Oppression of women within most of these nations continues, yet many Western people excuse and ignore these actions because they take place under the aegis of a religion. It is simply abominable that we let this institutionalized oppression of 50 per cent of the population go by with nary a thought or concern for these people. No one should have lesser rights simply for having been born where they were born.

In all of the three main religions, the god is usually portrayed as a male-like figure, and in Christianity he is known as the "Father". Surely a deity does not have identifying genitalia or an XY chromosomal makeup? If religions wanted to demonstrate an unbiased approach, surely they would create non-gender-specific words when describing their deities?

What is obvious is that bringing up children within religions teaches boys that they are somehow "holier" and more important than women, and tells young girls that they are, for some intangible reason, of lesser value than boys. It reinforces a sense of entitlement in men because it tells them they have simply been born more special – not that they have done anything significant to earn this status. Absurdly, many people in Western societies who support these religious structures would not accept inequality in the secular world and would demand the same jobs and pay rates for men and women.

This begs the question, why do we continue to give religions a "free pass" when in fact the developing minds of children are far more exposed to these sexist, religious views than they are to, say, issues of inequality in business? While as adults we tend and are able to ignore these outmoded rules, our children take them at face value and absorb them, and this in turn, sadly, enhances their credibility.

Religions tend to throw a few tiny morsels to women, but in general the perceptions are both created and reinforced that women are less important than men. Apart from gay people and people from adherents of different religions, is there any other group that has been more persecuted by religions than women? Were I a woman I would find it extremely difficult to support any religion and, as the father of a daughter, I have done what I can to shield my daughter from and counter where possible the teachings of religions, so that she is never made to feel less important simply because of her gender.

We are all born with both "good" and "bad" tendencies and exactly how these tendencies develop depends on a combination of both genetic and environmental factors. Numerous tests on infants have shown that they will inherently choose what we would call moralistic behaviour over behaviour that favours the immoral. Despite what may have been previously thought, babies are not born with a blank slate on morality. A growing number of studies show that we are born with an innate sense of right and wrong, and that family and society slowly mould our systems.

One of a number of such studies, carried out at the Yale University Infant Cognition Centre, involves a puppet show performed in front of infants aged five to eight months old, during which a character tries unsuccessfully to open a big box. Then a pro-social puppet comes to help open the box. The situation is then repeated, but this time an anti-social puppet slams the box shut. When babies who have watched the performance are afterwards presented with the pro-social and anti-social puppets, the overwhelming majority of them show a preference for the pro-social puppet.[2]

These and similar recent research projects have started to show that aspects of morality are innate. It is thought that even babies can identify good role models. Most humans are indeed more moral than the scriptures they hold to be sacred.

Research in this field has also given rise to the idea of situational ethics, which holds that there are no universal moral rules but that each situation is unique and therefore requires a unique solution. This modern thinking is in stark contrast with religious morals, which are held to be universally applicable and beyond questioning because they originate from a deity. (After all, who are we compared to God?) Those who practice situational ethics approach problems using general moral principles rather than a rigorous set of laws, and are far more likely to modify their principles if doing so may lead to a greater good.

Modern situations require this kind of original thinking. For example, the answers to the ethical questions raised by the imminent presence of autonomous vehicles on our roads cannot come from religious texts; they will have to be worked out in secular discussions. We will not be asking rabbis, priests or imams about, say, how to program a driverless car to make a split-second decision whether to continue ahead and strike another vehicle or deviate from its planned path and possibly hit a pedestrian.

Many advances in scientific fields, such as tissue cloning, IVF, genetic modification and the integration of artificial intelligence present new moral dilemmas. The discussions and decisions will and should be made by scientists, ethicists, philosophers and lawyers; religions should have no presence in these debates. As this book has argued repeatedly, to gain useful knowledge and clear guidance, we must continue to transition away from the religious age and further into the scientific age.

A simple and effective moral rule existed long before the major religions tried to claim ownership of morality. Sometimes referred to as the "Golden Rule", it says, "Do unto others as you would have done to yourself" or, conversely, "Do not do to others as you would not have done to you." Confucius said this 500 years before the birth of Jesus, when he advised, "Never impose on others what you would not choose for yourself." Confucianism, Buddhism, Hinduism and many other religions can in fact be considered far more moral than the Abrahamic religions precisely because they have not endorsed bigotry towards gay people, genocide, rape, slavery or other clearly immoral practices. The proof has really been in the pudding. All too often, followers of a religion will uphold dubious practices prescribed by their doctrine rather than see them as most people outside that system would see them: as immoral actions.

The perniciousness of the view that rules or institutions are more important than the reasonable treatment of fellow humans has been highlighted in recent times with the successive revelations of child abuse perpetrated by religious leaders, particularly in the Catholic Church. The reputation of the church was always seen as far more important than the damage wreaked on any individuals. And, of course, it has now been left to secular institutions to try to offer victims justice, compensation and restitution.

Religions have concerned themselves way too much with sex. People who promote strict religious views on sex may think they are acting morally, but such ideas can lead to worse outcomes for those adhering to them. Again, preaching that condoms shouldn't be used has led to millions suffering from HIV and a huge range of sexually transmitted diseases; and placing unnatural constraints on young people creates guilt and psychological trauma for many young adults.

Furthermore, religious strictures regarding sex tend to focus on participation in sex as the critical issue, rather than the health and welfare issues. Are people who preach such concepts doing so to help those people involved or to placate and appease their god – who despite being the creator of the entire universe seems to have an obsessive interest in what humans on Earth are doing in the privacy of their own bedrooms?

"Men never do evil so completely and cheerfully as when they do it from religious conviction." – Blaise Pascal

Natural morality

What all of this demonstrates is that, despite religions trying to claim ownership of moral rules, if one were to follow even just one religion's textual rules one would in fact live a less moral life than if one ignored religion altogether. The holy books' strictures may occasionally match one's own morals, but this definitely does not make them good moral guides.

We no longer need religious texts for moral guidance. In fact, if people were told they could be transported to those countries or communities, either present or past, where the Biblical and Koranic laws are strongly adhered to, I don't believe that there would be too many volunteers from countries that are currently governed by secular laws. I certainly would prefer to live in a society where justice is meted out while people are still alive.

As a final couple of examples of the absurdity of religious morality, if you were to ask a group of non-religious people whether it is better to raise and eat a free-range or caged chicken, the answer would be pretty clear to most of them. If, however, you asked a religious Muslim or Jew if it is better to eat a caged but Halal/Kosher chicken than a free-range non-Halal/Kosher chicken, you would find that this puts them in a real quandary and they have to go through ridiculous mental gymnastics trying to come up with an answer.

Similarly, if you ask a religious person to decide whether they would prefer their child to marry a kind person from a different religion or an unkind person of their own religion, is it not both deplorable and ironic that they cannot easily and quickly reach the most obvious conclusion?

I hope that this chapter has clearly demonstrated that not only can we be good without gods and religions, but that we can, both as individuals and, even more importantly, as societies, be even *better* without gods and religions than with them.

"Racism isn't born folks, it's taught. I have a two-year-old son. Know what he hates? Naps. End of list." – Denis Leary, Actor and Comedian

7

ON PRAYER, THE SOUL, HEAVEN AND HELL

Religions make many other claims that influence human behaviour, with the role of prayer being an important tenet. Alongside this come teachings relating to what happens if we act in certain ways or propitiate our deity, and the rewards that may come with this. So how do these teachings sit within our modern world and our greater understanding of how things work?

Prayer

Prayer is defined as an "address as a petition to God or a god in word or thought" (*Merriam-Webster Dictionary*), but often when we think we are praying we are simply wishing or hoping for something. When we have family or friends who are sick, we naturally want them to feel better quickly, but much of the time we are not truly praying to whichever deity we believe in but are rather just creating an outlet for a desire for a positive outcome.

We have already looked at the creation and early evolution of the prayer process in Chapter 4. What we need to do now is critically assess the modern prayer systems and the evidence for their success. In this discussion, either what prayer does intrinsically for the individual praying or the resulting outward physical evidence may measure success.

Why do people pray?

Without doubt, praying can have many benefits for an individual, both psychological and physical. When you are stuck with a problem, you might pray for an answer, and this act of praying can help to calm, relax and reinvigorate you, and possibly give you a fresh perspective on the problem. It can reduce anxiety and allow you to feel that you may be helping others. It has also been suggested that if a person knows he or she is being prayed for it can be uplifting and increase morale, thus aiding recovery.

For the person praying, the act may have a similar effect to meditation or Tai Chi, in that it can help one focus on problems and devise tactics to overcome them. Praying to a deity can also alleviate some guilt or responsibility for an action that may have caused the problem, by including the deity in the recovery process. Whether or not the deity exists seems to make little difference to believers, as long as they feel that the deity *could* exist.

Prayers said, or hymns sung, by a large group of people can of course provide a similarly uplifting effect to that of attending a music concert. That is why so often there are songs and other music at prayer services. It is the harmonies and the crowd singing in unison that resonates, more than the actual words. Religious institutions realize this, and often the most effective services involve a good number of tuneful prayers or, better still, a choir to really increase the volume, connection and positive sensations. Church organs, which create a deep, powerful sound, also add to the atmosphere – believers want their god to seem powerful.

Houses of worship also attempt to influence our senses in ways that shape our religious experience and make prayer more satisfying. The most imposing ones usually have high ceilings and vertical lines, drawing our eyes upwards to the heavens, and use windows and recesses to create contrasts between light and darkness, to impart a sense of contemplative awe. Smaller, plain houses of worship just don't have the same effect.

The togetherness and sense of connectedness with others present excites the congregation and encourages them to return; they may even be aware of people in congregations all around the world saying and doing the same things. It is this feeling of community rather than the prayers or hymns themselves that instill a sense of well-being.

However, the number of attendees at religious services in educated, Western countries has been falling rapidly over the last few decades; many church congregations have just a few elderly parishioners, while others have had to close their doors. In an attempt to defy the death throes of religion in Western society and maintain interest in the idea of communal prayer, Christian leaders in the United States are using major marketing and razzle-dazzle to keep religion going, and it has become big business. Some of the TV preachers, or televangelists, are now worth many millions of dollars and their slick performances are helping to keep a modern form of Christianity alive.

Studies of prayer

Studies have looked at the physical effects of prayer from a variety of perspectives. One well-known multicentre randomized study of over 1,800 patients assessed whether being prayed for by others brought any benefits.[1] It compared those who knew that they were being prayed for to those who didn't know they were being prayed for, and to those who were told they were being prayed for but in fact were not. The outcomes for all patients were almost the same, except that, surprisingly, those in the group who knew they were being prayed for had a few more post-surgical complications.

Scientist Francis Galton hypothesized, tongue-in-cheek, that if prayer were effective, members of the British royal family would live much longer than average, given that millions regularly pray for their well-being. He also prayed over randomized plots of land to see if the plants would grow any faster, and found no benefits. Sam Harris, an author and neuroscientist, has noted that most studies that purport to demonstrate the effectiveness of prayer often involve illnesses that normally resolve themselves anyway, with or without the intervention of an all-powerful divine being. He suggested a simple experiment to settle the issue: "Get a billion Christians to pray for a single amputee. Get them to pray that God regrow that missing limb. This happens to salamanders every day, presumably without prayer; this is within the capacity of God. I find it interesting that people of faith only tend to pray for conditions that are self-limiting."[2]

Perhaps most significantly, people who pray appear to suffer the same degree of sickness, disease, syndromes and general life issues as those who do not pray. Moreover, people experience the same incidences of illness and disease whichever deity they pray to. And atheists have the same rates of recovery as those who have prayed or been prayed for. Given all that, why do people continue to believe that their prayers will have an effect? Surely, on some level, people who regularly devote time to prayer must realize that their praying does not affect outcomes; if so, do they ever feel cheated by the systems they have allowed themselves to be enveloped in?

Most people recognize that the sacrificial rituals and dances to rain gods and the like that were practiced by our ancestors now hold no credence. So, is it not time to now admit too that incantations and the recitation of words of prayers have no effect either?

Prayer has been used for millennia to try to cure or affect disease processes, with no proven benefit. Where people feel it has helped them, it is more akin to the placebo effect, whereby a doctor gives a patient an ineffectual substance in place of a real medication and the patient benefits by simply believing the treatment will work. Whether such an approach involves a placebo, meditation, simple positive thinking or prayer, it should not, however, be confused with real, directed medical treatment.

Through testing and steady research, science, on the other hand, has established that many diseases are caused by bacteria and viruses (rather than being the retribution of an inadequately appeased deity) and has created antibiotics, vaccinations and other medications to treat these afflictions. Thanks to advances in modern science, life expectancy has increased rapidly and the quality of life, even for those affected by illness, has increased remarkably in recent times. In contrast, prayer has changed nothing.

> BELIEVERS, THINK FOR A MINUTE ABOUT ALL OF THE THINGS THAT YOU WOULD DO IF YOU WERE GOD.
>
> PREVENT FAMINE, WIDESPREAD DISEASE AND UNNECESSARY SUFFERING, GENOCIDES, MURDERS, RAPE, CREATE WORLD PEACE?
>
> CONTEMPLATE THAT YOU WORSHIP A GOD WHO HAS DONE NONE OF THESE THINGS.

Praying for what?

Prayers to the current deities yield exactly the same results as those to previous deities throughout the ages, yet somehow present-day religious adherents view their prayers and rituals as more valid or reasonable. In part, that may be because they often seek more modest, less clearly defined responses – instead of requesting rain for crops, people pray for smaller immeasurable outcomes. It's almost as if they do not expect quantifiable results but still participate "just in case". Meanwhile religious organizations like to use phrases such as "God moves in mysterious ways" to suggest that people should continue to pray and that their prayers might be heard (even if they are not acted upon!).

This means that prayer in modern times suffers from confirmation bias, the tendency to interpret information in a way that confirms a preconception. It works for theists in this way:

- If a positive outcome follows a prayer, then God did it.
- If there was no positive outcome, then maybe God has an alternative and better plan for you.

In Biblical times, the god of the Old Testament advised that if one prayed to him and followed his rules, he would provide fertile fields and food for livestock and look after his followers (Deuteronomy 11). But the land of Israel remained fairly barren and unproductive until the last few decades, following the introduction of specialized irrigation, desalination plants and advanced horticultural practices. In a short time, science achieved what Yahweh, over centuries, had failed to bring about.

Theists often argue that God is not responsible for a famine, yet their argument falls apart the moment these same people say grace at the dinner table. Why not also pray to end famine? For if prayer truly did work, then famine could be eradicated swiftly. Is it so difficult to accept the position that people in wealthy countries have enough food to put on their plates not as a result of praying to a god, but because they are fortunate enough to have been born and raised in an educated society with a developed agricultural market?

What about when natural disasters occur? To pray after a tragedy indicates that one either follows a god who is happy to cause such incidents or one who is impotent to or disinterested in stopping them. Believers who say, "Thank God I survived" are being thankful that their god just wreaked havoc and killed others instead of them. Why not recognize that natural disasters happen and that fewer deaths have occurred of late because of science and better preparation, and not as a result of prayer or because those spared are better people than those who are affected?

With most religions, the deal is that the deity will give you unconditional love provided that you pray to him and meet all of his conditions. Of course, the bar is set so high as to be unattainable, so you just can't get off the hamster wheel of praising and attempting to follow all the rules (unless of course you leave the god concept behind). Many people cling to religion on the basis of what's known in Western philosophy as Pascal's Wager. This is the idea, formulated by the French philosopher and mathematician Blaise Pascal, that it is a safer position to believe in and pray to a god because there is infinite gain if you are correct but only finite loss if you are wrong. What this obviously fails to take into consideration are all the different gods and the different prayers and prayer regimes that they each call for. It would be narrow-minded to only pray to the god of our parents; to follow through on this concept properly one would have to learn the Old Testament, New Testament, Koran and the Vedas and so on, and pray to Yahweh, Jesus, Allah, Shiva, Vishnu and others, in case the god you follow is not the "true god"! The mindset underlying Pascal's Wager point of view is therefore nonsensical.

From all points of view praying to a deity is absurd. Even if you accept the idea that "he gave you life, so he should be thanked", there is no other moral situation where that alone is a reason to elevate and glorify someone. Someone (or something) should only be seen as worthy of praise on the basis of their actions, and must also be judged on the misery that they cause or let happen. The existence of widespread sickness and suffering and the lack of clear response to prayers shows that no deity is worthy of such unrequited acclamation. One should not automatically worship one's parents simply because they gave birth to you; it must be because they provide a lifetime of continuous affection and support. Parents who do not interact with or look after their children are usually put in jail or have their children taken away from them.

The relationship between religions and free will is also baffling. If a deity gave humans free will, how can everything be part of that god's plan? Given the unpredictability of free will, how can he possibly be all knowing? If, on the other hand, everything is part of a god's plan, then we don't actually have free will. And that means that any time we "sin", our god had planned this for us and it is therefore not our fault! Why do we need religious rules or prayer at all if a god has preplanned everything for each and every one of us? Surely a loving god would prevent innocent people from being harmed, unless he didn't really care about us, in which case why deify him?

* * *

"A man who prays is the one who thinks that God has arranged matters all wrong but who also thinks that he can instruct God how to put them right." – Christopher Hitchens

"I cannot believe in a God who wants to be praised all the time." – Friedrich Nietzsche

"Prayer – the use of undignified begging to persuade the non-existent to do the impossible." – Bill Flavell

"One day when I was praying, it suddenly occurred to me that I was talking to myself." – Peter O'Toole

"Prayer, in my opinion is an act of doubt, not an act of faith. For if you truly trusted your god's plan, surely you wouldn't pray for anything." – Michael Sherlock

"Like chronic gambling, with prayer you never talk about all of your losses." – Anon

"Prayer is like masturbation: it feels good for the person doing it but does nothing for the person they are thinking about." – Anon.

"I asked god for a bike but I know god doesn't work that way, so I stole a bike and asked for forgiveness." – Anon.

"Pray: it's least you can do. Literally. The least." – Anon.

* * *

Side effects

Not only is prayer absurd and ineffectual, but it also promotes negative views of life and dangerous mindsets.

As medicine advances rapidly and religious views do not, the involvement of religious bodies in medical care is resulting in significant conflicts. Many large hospitals in major cities around the world have affiliations with certain religions and, accordingly, doctors who work within these hospitals have certain ideological restrictions placed upon them. In many Catholic hospitals, for example, pregnancies cannot be terminated beyond a certain point, even if it is known that the foetus will not survive and potentially dangerous or life-threatening complications may affect the mother. This can instantly complicate the patient–doctor relationship and in some situations the mother may have to swiftly find another doctor or even an alternative hospital to carry out a procedure.

Stem-cell research is starting to provide breakthroughs in the treatment of various conditions, but many religious leaders speak against it because it conflicts with their teachings. Imagine being a cancer patient who has been under the care of an oncologist for a number of years and you are then told there is a new treatment option that may help you, but that your doctor cannot use the treatment because he or she is employed by a hospital with strict religious views.

Prayer can be taken to the most awful extremes when children are ill. Some religious parents will refuse to take their children to a doctor and instead insist only on prayer to cure them. In recent times, many children and adolescents in the USA and around the world have died from preventable diseases, including untreated diabetes, appendicitis, and other infections. These innocent human beings are being denied the rights to a life because of the absurdity not of *their beliefs but of those of their parents. By all means, adults have the right to be martyrs, but they should not have the right to make martyrs of their children.*

MUSINGS OF A SURGEON ...

If you are going to thank your god for me having operated successfully on you, then you can sue him if anything goes wrong.

Prayer can lead to laziness or a fatalistic view of daily life. If you take the view that through prayer alone things will happen, then you may actually be held back from achieving. For example, if you want a promotion, you need to work harder, not simply pray. If you want to do well on a test, go study. For adherents to claim that you have to do both is to say that the prayer process is in reality irrelevant (though they will still not see it that way!).

A "prayer culture" can also have many deleterious effects on believers. If their prayers are not answered, those who are suffering may feel that they themselves are responsible for the lack of improvement. Worse still, they may start to feel guilty, wondering if they have been praying wrongly, or what else could have done to improve the situation, such as attending their place of worship more often. They may lie in bed asking themself what they have done wrong that their god is not helping them as they have requested. Maybe they are not good enough for their deity to intervene.

"When all is said and done, more is said than done." – Aesop

Time better spent

It really is time for us to become more scientific with regards to prayer. We need to give ourselves the time and space to review and assess the success of prayer instead of continuing to blindly follow what we have been told to do. We need to look at whether it is more beneficial to assist the sick and dying in other ways – for example, instead of spending an hour or two at a church, synagogue, mosque or temple praying for someone, wouldn't it be better to call or visit that person or offer support in other, much more practical, ways?

In most of the poorest countries in the world you will find groups of Western missionaries, many of them Christians. It's true they are there partly to help with practical issues, but usually with the ulterior motive of establishing Christian institutions and communities. Imagine if instead of teaching these people to pray to their god, they taught scientific truths, such as how to halt the spread of diseases like HIV. Imagine if their religious beliefs did not stop them explaining contraception and they could thereby prevent much of the pain and suffering caused by sexually transmitted diseases. Imagine if these volunteers were able to spend more of their time building clean water supplies, or providing higher-quality education to pass on skills that might lead to jobs. Imagine if these volunteers did their work purely for altruistic reasons and not to create and reinforce their own religious views.

> A FRIEND ONCE TOLD ME THAT SHE WAS
> PRAYING FOR STARVING PEOPLE IN AFRICA.
>
> I TOLD HER THAT HER GOD MUST HAVE
> LISTENED BECAUSE THERE ARE MILLIONS
> OF THEM.

After yet another mass shooting in the USA in October 2015, President Obama finally stood up for common sense by announcing, "Our thoughts and prayers are not enough." Unfortunately, the current crop of religious politicians in America have reverted back to only offering the hollow platitudes. These are the only people capable of changing gun laws, yet they feel that they are fulfilling their duty by repeatedly just offering their "thoughts and prayers" after every incident. Until this ridiculousness is called out as next to useless, and while faith is still seen as more important than real-world actions, lives will continue to be lost. If only the populace would demand that this mindset was kept out of government policies.

All of the times that you prayed for strength in a difficult time and you somehow got through it, accept it was you who succeeded, by yourself, and not thanks to a god. Conversely, when you helped out others and did a good deed, you did it because it was you and not because you would receive bonuses from a god. It's time to take some credit for your actions, instead of always passing it on to a deity.

Prayer is unfortunately one of the last great bastions of anti-intellectualism, and an affront to human intelligence. Deep down most people know that it has no effect, yet they continue to be involved in prayer services and spend money supporting and building places of worship.

It still amazes me that so many intelligent people can compartmentalize the ineffectiveness and ridiculousness of prayer. It just goes to show how difficult it is to shed [or break free from] habits and beliefs ingrained during childhood. It is time to move on from this superstitious nonsense.

"Imagine that all the money we spend on crosses and stars and half moons was spent instead on food for the hungry. Imagine all the land we use to build churches, synagogues and mosques was used instead to build hospitals and schools. And imagine all the time we take to learn passages from the Bible and the Torah and the Koran was used instead to learn a little something about the person sitting next to us." – Steve Hofstetter

* * *

A brothel was being constructed next door to a church, so the priest decided to get his congregation to join with him in a prayer vigil. Every morning, noon and night prayer sessions were held from the moment construction began. The day before the official opening, a storm came, lightning struck the brothel and it burned down to the ground.

The church folk were very smug and commented about the "never-ending power of prayer".

Two weeks later the brothel owner sued the church, the preacher and the entire congregation on the grounds that they were "ultimately responsible for the demise of the building and business".

In its response to the court, the church vehemently and vociferously denied any and all responsibility or any connection to the building's demise.

The presiding judge commented: "I don't know how I am going to decide this case but it appears from the paperwork that we now have the owner of a brothel who staunchly believes in the power of prayer and an entire church congregation that thinks that it's all bullshit!"

* * *

On heaven and hell

All three of the religions that have been discussed make grand claims about their god being "all-loving" and "all-forgiving" and that there will be rewards in death for those who praise him sufficiently and follow all of his rules. But all three also claim that if you do not obey the rules or praise God/Allah enough, then you are a sinner and will be punished and tortured eternally.

Never has there been any evidence of either the good place you might end up in (heaven) or the bad place (hell) to validate these concepts. They are unverifiable tenets of each of the religions, designed to control the thoughts of believers. It's as if religions infect believers' minds with an imaginary disease and then claim to have the only cure. They hold this carrot and stick above adherents to keep them as a part of their flock. And often because these ideas have been taught to people since childhood by important figures in their lives, they are accepted as truisms.

By promoting the concept of heaven, religions are actually devaluing the lives that we live – after all, what can our relatively short lifetimes be worth compared to an eternity of bliss? Such thinking can lead people to be more apathetic about combatting real-world issues. Why stress about climate change when you believe that your god/s can fix the problem? Why care about environmental issues if you see life as just a tiny fragment of your existence? Even worse, attributing such importance to the afterlife can lead people to perpetrate appalling acts – it's the kind of thinking, for example, that compels and justifies many acts of terrorism.

Conversely, those who choose not to believe in an afterlife have a greater appreciation of this life and are generally less likely to kill other people; they understand how terrible it would be to end someone else's existence.

As John Lennon put it in his immortal song "Imagine":
Imagine there's no heaven

It's easy if you try

No hell below us

Above us only sky

Imagine all the people

Living for today....

The concept of hell is an awful one to be indoctrinating children with. Would we allow schoolteachers to tell our children that they will burn in a huge fire if they misbehave in class? If not, then why do we let preachers and religious parents traumatize children with such threats? In most Western schools, teachers are no longer even allowed to "send children to the corner" due to concerns about the psychological effects this may have, but threats of eternal damnation appear to be fine as long as they are a part of religious instruction. Indeed, there are almost no limitations on the abhorrent teachings with which we can indoctrinate our children in the name of religion.

COMMENTS CONSIDERED TO BE CHILD ABUSE – If you disobey me, I will take you underground and torture and burn you eternally.

COMMENTS NOT CONSIDERED TO BE CHILD ABUSE – If you disobey me, God will take you underground and torture and burn you eternally.

The fact that religions have to use fear to get children to behave shows the limitations of their ideas. If after so many years this is the best way they can teach young people about right and wrong, then they can only be viewed as deplorable. Other organizations that use fear to control populations are regarded as terrorist organizations and in that context we can quite clearly see that using such tactics is immoral.

There is a terrible irony within Christian theology in that Jesus offers to save you if you follow his teachings; but save you from what? From what he will do to you or allow happen to you if you don't follow his teachings?

> ## USING FEAR OF AN INVISIBLE AND INTANGIBLE BEING AS A TOOL TO FRIGHTEN CHILDREN IS THE WORST POSSIBLE FORM OF BULLYING

Devils and demons

The concepts of Satan, devils and demons in Christianity and the similar figures of Iblis and Shaytan in Islam are also puzzling. If God/Allah is all-powerful, then he knowingly allows these figures to use their powers to make humans commit major sins (otherwise why would these gods have created them?). If that were not the case, he would eliminate these figures and leave humans to commit only minor improprieties. Or as Christopher Hitchens once put it: "God creates you sick and commands you to be well."

Is it not also a bit peculiar that the only people who seem to be "possessed by demons" are religious zealots? Why do we not see hundreds of atheists on TV being possessed by demons? Is it that demons only exist when the concept has been implanted into the minds of adherents?

Religions have had thousands of years to provide evidence for their claims, yet all they have are error-riddled threats. Adherents often fall back on such arguments as "Just you wait until you're dead, and then you'll see." This is patently ridiculous.

The "soul"

One of the ideas that religious adherents cling to is the notion of the soul. As defined in the *Merriam-Webster Dictionary*, the soul is "the spiritual part of a person that is believed to give life to the body and in many religions is believed to live forever." Ask someone to describe what a soul is and one typically receives a response along the lines of "eternal, indefinable, the cause of certain actions, the essence of a person" and so on.

Yet there is no evidence of such a thing existing. It is again merely a gap in our understanding of how we as human beings perceive and respond to stimuli and what makes us all individuals. It is our varied complex biochemistry, there is nothing ethereal about it.

Meanwhile, as in many areas of life, science is beginning to shed light on human identity, particularly research into the brain and biochemistry. Studies of people who have suffered brain traumas and diseases show that related changes in behaviour are physical, often biochemical, reactions. Degenerative diseases such as Alzheimer's can slowly erode our personality, sense of self and understanding of the world around us. If our emotions and perceptions were part of our soul, then the disease would not affect these capacities – yet it does! The soul therefore does not control our character, emotions or behaviour. Our souls do not suffer from depression or various emotional states; we do, as biological beings. And, fortunately, that means that personality disorders and personality changes, which are caused by chemical imbalances, can now be treated with medications.

Imagine a person who many people would describe as "having a beautiful soul", or a "Christ-like character" – someone who gives to others, is a calm and caring person, says their daily prayers and is the most benevolent and considerate person one could possibly imagine. Then imagine getting this person addicted to the drug ice (crystalline methamphetamine), so that they are continuously under its influence over a number of months. They will almost certainly become violent, withdrawn, non-communicative, selfish and unhelpful. What was once a "beautiful soul" will become an irreversibly dangerous and potentially harmful individual with little "goodness" or "godliness" left in them. If this is possible, then we must accept that a single simple chemical can damage the soul, or that what we refer to as the soul in this context is actually a number of biochemical processes we are only beginning to understand.

We don't as yet understand the amazing process of a memory. How we can recall images, events, sounds, smells and even emotions that we felt yet we can accept that biochemical processes somehow create them. Our heart beats thousands of times per day, hormones are produced as required, our brain creates memories and we might have 50,000 thoughts in a single day. All of these things occur without us consciously thinking about them, yet we can show that they occur as a result of physiological processes. We do not require a soul to subconsciously drive us. When we are young we have next to no personality; it is something that develops as we experience life, and neuronal connections are created. The development of our personalities does not require a soul.

How will we view the concept of the soul once brain transplants become successful? Imagine if the brain of Stephen Hawking (who suffered from motor neuron disease) could have been successfully transplanted into the body of another person (possibly some-one who had suffered a severe brain trauma). He could have been out of his wheelchair communicating more freely with the world. If that happened, would religious adherents believe his soul had been transported into his new body along with his brain? If so, then one's personality, thoughts and character traits are, again, merely the result of biochemical processes within the brain. I look forward to the day when brain transplants are successful, so that the concept of a soul can finally be put to rest.

Religions nevertheless like the idea that we have a soul and that for our souls to have the best possible outcomes in the afterlife we have to follow their rules. However, they struggle to answer certain obvious questions. For example, given that human beings are just a branch on the evolutionary tree of life, when along this pathway did we develop souls? Did Neanderthal people have a soul? Do other mammals have a soul? Did dinosaurs have souls? Do insects or bacteria have souls? Do plants have souls? If all living things have a soul, then how does a god manage to judge their "behaviour" and decide whether they are deserving of entry into heaven?

As discussed earlier, many "simpler" creatures appear to have the rudimentary beginnings of awareness of self, and this seems to increase with the size and complexity of the brain and nervous system. Perhaps what people refer to as a soul is merely this awareness. Anyone who has a close relationship with a pet cat or dog might agree that they too can seem to have a soul.

Another pertinent question that religious adherents need to answer is: when along the developmental pathway of a living thing does the soul appear? Is it at the point of conception when the sperm penetrates the egg? Is it only once the brain and neural pathways are sufficiently developed within the foetus? Or does a soul form only at birth? If so, then doesn't that suggest it is a by-product of physical neuronal connections? That being so, could the soul just be another name for biochemically induced self-awareness?

All religions teach about souls and what happens to people when they die. To make extraordinary claims you really need extraordinary evidence. Yet not one such claim regarding the soul can be substantiated. The reality is that these ideas are nothing more than hope, desire and wishful thinking. Like the notion of an all-powerful deity, they were concocted thousands of years ago and passed down through the generations – concepts that can neither be proved nor disproved.

A small percentage of religious people nearing death appear to derive pleasure and relief from the thought of their soul entering an afterlife, but the majority of believers still seem to fear death. This suggests that most of them do not fully believe in the stories they have previously subscribed to. If heaven and the afterlife exist, why are religious adherents not all excited to be heading there? After all they will supposedly be reunited with their families, other loved ones and even pets, and meet angels and enter the warm embrace of their deity. Why are they not thrilled and joyful?

We would all love to watch what happens to our children and grandchildren or would love to come back some time in the future and meet our descendants, but wishing for this does not make it real. Only the institutions that peddle such ideas benefit from them – the Catholic Church taking money for indulgences (payments to be absolved of sins), for example, or the Islamic terrorist groups that lure suicide bombers, shooters and stabbers with contrived promises of eternal bliss in the afterlife.

* * *

"I don't believe in an afterlife, so I don't have to spend my whole life fearing hell, or fearing heaven even more. For whatever the tortures of hell, I think the boredom of heaven would be even worse."
– Isaac Asimov

"Do I think that I am going to paradise? Of course not. I wouldn't go if I was asked. I don't want to live in some fucking celestial North Korea for one thing, where all I get to do is praise the leader from dawn till dusk."
– Christopher Hitchens

"Go to heaven for the climate, hell for the company." – Mark Twain

"Demand money with the threat of violence and you'll get arrested. Do it with the threat of eternal damnation and it's tax deductible."
– Steve Hofstetter

"Most people can't bear to sit in church for an hour on Sundays. How are they supposed to live somewhere similar to it for eternity?"
– Mark Twain

"Considering how many scientists are non-believers I'm sure that they will have hell air-conditioned by now." – Anon.

"We have two lives and the second one begins when we realise that we only have one." - Confucius

8

CAN WE MOVE ON FROM RELIGIONS?

Despite the contradictions inherent in religions and the lack of evidence that faith and prayer do any good whatsoever, many people still find it difficult to give up their religious beliefs. Why is that? And how can we convince more people to move on, and how do they do that?

Why do people cling to religion?

There are many completely understandable reasons why people are reluctant to abandon religions. They relate in part to certain highly effective methods religious organizations use to engage and ensnare adherents, but also in part to our doubts, fears and psychological makeup.

Early indoctrination

One of the smartest strategies of religious groups is to get in early and indoctrinate children. If we were told nothing about religion until the age of 16, much in the same way that we are not taught about political ideologies, economic ideologies or views on sexual activities until then, we would be able to make better decisions as to the validity of each faith. Very few well-educated adults, having had no prior exposure to the texts and associated rituals of each religion, would start to believe them to be truths. Missionaries, notably, despite their "bribing", still struggle to convert adults who have already been exposed to worldly knowledge. That's also why there is so little changing of religions among educated adults.

As Richard Dawkins has noted: "Isn't it a remarkable coincidence that almost everyone has the same religion as their parents? And it always just happens to be the right religion. Religions run in families. If we'd been brought up in ancient Greece we would all be worshipping Zeus and Apollo. If we had been born Vikings we would be worshipping Wotan and Thor. How does this come about? Through childhood indoctrination."

The fact that the only way we find out about the god of our family's religion is via other human beings or books should be evidence enough that gods are a human invention. If gods were real, then why would we not have any direct communication with them in a real sense? Surely if such gods wanted interaction they would communicate clearly with us to avoid any possible doubt or confusion?

Small stuff

Religious structures can also achieve control of thought processes by restricting discussions to narrow topics but allowing limitless discussion and refinement of rules within these areas. They are then able to build upon each previous set of rules to the point that no one dares to question the validity of the original concept. A good example of this relates to the laws in the Jewish religion of acceptable foods and ways to kill and eat animals (known as Kosher laws). There are only a few sentences on these views in the Old Testament, yet through the centuries layer upon layer of rules and interpretations have been added by rabbis and other scholars, to the point where those trying to obey the rules must have multiple sets of cutlery for different foods, different sinks to wash in, and, in modern times, even specially manufactured kosher products (such as toothpastes and sunscreens).

All these complex conditions conceal the fact that the strictures have little biblical authority. If they were really the wishes of an omnipotent, omniscient being, then surely they would have been spelled out precisely in the Old Testament. Why is there so little information on this topic there? Was there a need for brevity in a book that (supposedly) covers generations and goes into so much detail about other laws?

I also wonder what Jews and Muslims think when they ponder the fact that 75 per cent of the world does not follow their dietary rules, yet nothing bad happens to those non-believers. How can pork be against a god's rules yet so many people eat it without any ill effects? To everyone else the rules are obviously nonsensical, but those trapped inside the religion cannot see that their dietary choices have absolutely no effect when it comes to placating a god or improving their lives. And for those who argue that they feel reassured to be following the dictator's rules, they are obviously so far under the spell of their belief systems that they have forgotten to ask the most obvious questions.

Cognitive dissonance

Through this early indoctrination and focus on narrow areas of behaviour, religions often manage to indoctrinate people for life. Another contributing factor is a psychological phenomenon called cognitive dissonance. This term was coined by psychologist Leon Festinger in the 1950s and it refers to the fact that, in the words of the *Merriam-Webster Dictionary*, "when confronted with challenging new information, most people seek to preserve their current understanding of the world by rejecting, explaining away, or avoiding the new information or by convincing themselves that no conflict really exists."

Cognitive dissonance happens regularly with people of religious persuasion when they are questioned about the stories in their "holy books". In discussions, most people accept that every living creature wasn't created in a few days and that Adam and Eve weren't created instantly from dust (and Adam's rib) and that we are all descended from these two individuals (or from Noah's family, given that humankind was supposedly wiped out and had to start all over again). Yet because we have heard these stories since childhood, and usually hear about evolution only later in life, many people find it difficult to fully accept evolution and completely disregard the Adam and Eve story.

The two concepts are often compartmentalized and separated because it is just too uncomfortable for us to accept that we were lied to by the people we trusted most: our parents and teachers. (This is in contrast to Santa Claus and the Tooth Fairy because our carers usually tell us at a certain point that these characters are in fact fictional and non-existent.)

Ideas taught to us as children and repeated on a regular basis by those who are considered important and reliable sources of information are major influences on who we become and what we believe. There are sound biological reasons for this: to survive we must usually trust our parents and leaders, as they have survived by following what they were taught. How do we know as children, when we want to go play outdoors that we need to avoid slow-moving worm-like creatures, otherwise known as snakes, because they could kill us? Because our elders have told us this repeatedly. We must believe what we are told, even if we have never seen any evidence for those claims.

Herd mentality

We often cling tightly to our existing beliefs much more than we need to. It is exceedingly difficult to change the way we act and view the world when the views that we currently hold have allowed us to survive successfully to this point in our lives. Moreover, as a variety of behavioural experiments have shown, it is hard to change your belief system when you are surrounded by others who adhere to it, even if the evidence is to the contrary. A well-known experiment, conducted by psychologist Solomon Asch in the early 1950s, resulted in what became known as Asch's Paradigm. In the experiment, one male college student, unbeknownst to him, was placed in a room with seven other male college students who were "actors". All were shown a card with a line on it, followed by a card with three lines on it (labelled A, B, and C, respectively). Participants were then asked to say aloud which of those three lines matched the line on the first card in length. Each line question was called a "trial". Prior to the experiment, all of the actors were given specific instructions on how they should respond to each trial. Specifically, they were told to unanimously give the correct response or unanimously give the incorrect response. The group sat in a manner so that the real participant was always the last to respond.

Overall, there were 18 trials, in 12 of which the "actors" gave the incorrect (but unanimous) response. In this situation, 75 per cent of the real participants gave an incorrect answer to at least one question.

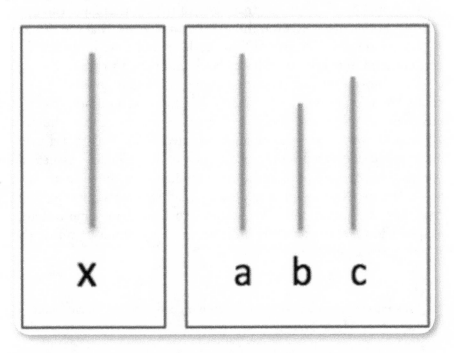

An example of the line problems shown to participants

What this shows is that despite our thinking that we freely decide all that we believe, it is often very difficult to break away from the pack. Many other behavioural experiments also show that we look for confirmations of our beliefs rather than falsification of them and, when shown examples of the same situation but with opposing results, we will support that which is more consistent with our own beliefs rather than challenge ourselves. If the models upon which people have built their entire lives and belief systems are threatened, then of course that can be challenging and uncomfortable for them, and they often feel it is safest to avoid thinking critically about the issues.

Desperate times

Another reason why people cling to religion is adversity. When things aren't going well and our normal remedies and support systems are failing us, we are often more open to out-there beliefs and "snake oil salesmen". For example, many people who have not had success with conventional medicine in the treatment of their cancers will explore a variety of other avenues, even though they may know that the chances of success are low. "Desperate times call for desperate measures" is a concept used in many situations to hook into people's psyches.

The unfortunate reality is for as long as humans continue to fear death, there is always the possibility of religions continuing to exist. After all, religions and gods were invented partly to help humans rationalize death and imagine an alternative to the idea that a living creature once deceased is only a collection of decomposing tissues and organs. The afterlife promised by many religions is the ultimate sales pitch. It appeals to people's egos as well as their fears, by suggesting that they are special and may continue to live on in some different shape or form. It is extremely difficult for many people to refuse this (albeit baseless) offer from religions.

* * *

"It's easier to fool people than convince them they have been fooled." – Mark Twain

"One of the saddest lessons of history is this: if we've been bamboozled long enough, we tend to reject any evidence of the bamboozle. We're no longer interested in finding out the truth. The bamboozle has captured us. It's simply too painful to acknowledge, even to ourselves, that we've been taken. Once you give a charlatan power over you, you almost never get it back." – Carl Sagan

"In the long run, nothing can withstand reason and experience, and the contradiction religion offers to both is palpable." – Sigmund Freud

"Religion is something left over from the infancy of our intelligence, it will fade away as we adopt reason and science as our guidelines." – Bertrand Russell

"Mythology is someone else's religion, past or present, different enough from your own for its absurdity to be obvious." – Anon.

Reviewing the evidence

We must, however, keep reminding ourselves that the failings and limitations of religions are very clear in this era of scientific discovery. Even at a most basic level, religions do not stand up to any kind of scrutiny.

A human construct

One of the many problems with current religions is that they impose certain rules for which there is no evidential support or sound reasoning, other than "it's written in the book that I choose to believe in". This has allowed adherents to justify bigotry by quoting rulings or pronouncements from their texts. Yet many of these rules will be contradicted in another place within that same book.

When asked to validate the religious system that one follows, many theists fall into a circular reasoning that goes a bit like this:

"The Bible/Koran/Torah is the word of God…"

"But how can you be sure that it's the word of God?"

"Because the text tells us so."

Using a book to prove the existence of the god of that book would in any other circumstance be seen as a poor way to confirm a truth. The books assessed in isolation cannot be seen as self-authenticating; they require corroborative evidence, of which there is none for any of the supernatural claims. Theists will, however, still use this argument as a way to validate their book and god; yet they do not accept the same kind of "proof" when disregarding the gods of other religions.

When people ask me if I have proof that their god doesn't exist I say, "Sure, I have many books that say that your god doesn't exist, and that everything you attribute to your god can be explained (or will eventually be explained) by scientific evidence set out in many other books. The difference is that my evidence is repeatable and testable by you or anyone else." Is it possible for a religious person to prove that their holy book is the "word of god" without using the book itself as their proof? The answer is a clear-cut no.

When we all appreciate that religions are human constructs, we will be able to better understand both why there are so many contradictions within each religion and why there are so many different religions. And why the same problems that have always plagued humanity continue, despite the teachings and rules of religions.

Over thousands of years nothing of significance has been resolved by religion, whereas science and secularism are slowly providing answers to many problems, mainly because they commence from unbiased starting points and are not shackled to any mistruths.

Until we stop giving credit to deities for their accomplishments, we will never take responsibility for our atrocities. Organized religions will, however, credit their god for a person's accomplishments while laying blame on the individual for his failures. Through the millennia, many immoral actions and beliefs have occurred because of misunderstandings of causal relationships. Witches were burned because it was thought that they caused crop failure, and still in many Christian communities natural disasters, or "acts of god", are, despicably, said to have been caused by promiscuity, homosexuality or other "sins".

"Properly read, the Bible is the most potent force for atheism ever conceived." – Isaac Asimov

> THERE'S NOT A SINGLE RELIGION THAT
> CAN SURVIVE THE TWO WORDS
> "PROVE IT"

The limitations of faith

Religion doesn't just distract from clear thinking, it also asks us to deliberately replace reason with the opposite, faith. And the problem arises that when people operate according to faith they can no longer be reasoned with, which can lead in turn to potentially dangerous situations. People who rely on faith and old texts as guiding principles are much more likely to use their own interpretations of those texts to justify behaviour that would in most other situations be seen as inappropriate.

Faith is not a reason to believe in a deity. Uttering "because I have faith" only changes the question from "Why do people believe?" to "Why do people have faith?". The important difference is that evidence has been removed from the list of possible answers. It therefore becomes just something that you want to be true. Religious, or blind faith, should not be the basis of important real-world decisions.

Likewise, theists make vague statements along the lines of, "There must be a god, look at rainbows, or a baby smiling, or all that has been 'created'." But such examples provide no evidence in any way.

Secular moral philosophy ended slavery, implemented suffrage, set up societies to protect animals and continues to fight for equality. If the religious structures and laws had everything correct, why would we have needed "The Universal Declaration of Human Rights", which came into being in 1948? Why do we need secular laws and courts and why have they now replaced religious legal systems in most countries? Is it because the laws laid down in the old texts can be updated, improved upon and made more relevant to our times? We only require improvements to systems that are inadequate. And if gods supposedly gave them, are these gods therefore inadequate?

* * *

"Faith: not wanting to know what is true." – Friedrich Nietzsche

"To learn who rules over you, simply find out who you are not allowed to criticize." – Author uncertain, but often attributed to Voltaire

"Yes I do have proof God does not exist. It is perfect and irrefutable. I'm not going to show it to you, however. You cannot detect it in any way. You cannot deduct it from the laws of logic either. You might claim that I do in fact have no such proof, but you have no proof that I don't. Sound familiar?" – Rune Friberg

"Where there is evidence, no one speaks of faith. We do not speak of faith that two and two are four or that the earth is round. We only speak of faith when we wish to substitute emotion for evidence." – Bertrand Russell

"The difference between faith and insanity is that faith is the ability to hold firmly to a conclusion that is incompatible with the evidence whereas insanity is the ability to hold firmly to a conclusion that is incompatible with the evidence." – William Harwood

"The way to see by faith is to shut the eye of reason." – Benjamin Franklin

"To understand via the heart is not to understand." – Michel de Montaigne

"Isn't it enough to see that a garden is beautiful without having to believe that there are fairies at the bottom of it too?" Douglas Adams

* * *

BEST MIRACLES GOD CAN ACHIEVE

4000 BC – create the entire universe

3500 BC – flood the planet

3000 BC – cause 10 plagues, part the Red Sea

30 AD – walk on water

600 AD – make a horse fly

Present day – appear in clouds or on toast

The burden of proof

The most effective opponent of theist beliefs is education. That is why for centuries the leaders of the church (and more recently Islamic leaders) have had scientists confined or killed, or forced them to disavow their scientific understandings. In the 17th century Galileo was tried by the Catholic Church and found "vehemently suspect of heresy". He was forced to recant, and spent the last nine years of his life under house arrest. In 1616, an Inquisitorial commission unanimously declared heliocentrism (the belief that Earth revolves around the Sun) to be "foolish and absurd in philosophy, and formally heretical since it explicitly contradicts in many places the sense of Holy Scripture".

Most religions have at various times condemned those who have spoken against any of their so-called facts. They are fearful of scientists getting to the real truth and keen to stifle the voices of reason and keep people in ignorance. They can see that continuous advances in science threaten their authority. As the astrophysicist Neil Degrasse-Tyson has said:

Does it mean if you don't understand something, and the community of physicists don't understand it, that means God did it? Is that how you want to play this game? Because if it is, there's a list if things in the past that the physicists at the time didn't understand and now we do understand. If that's how you want to invoke your evidence for God then God is an ever-receding pocket of scientific ignorance that's getting smaller and smaller and smaller as time moves on.

Indeed, ignorance is receding in all fields of science – biology, chemistry, physics, medicine – and, as a result, religious theories are losing ground. So many phenomena that were once explained as the actions of a wrathful god, such as diseases and extreme weather, have in recent times been understood and shown to be predictable and testable. Cures and remedies have been discovered.

We can now determine the age of Earth and of stars, we can date fossils and provide evidence that man was not created instantly, a few thousand years ago. Yet when one asks religious adherents for evidence of their gods' actions or for any archaeological proof of events recounted in their scriptures, they cannot provide any. There is no scientific refutation for radiometric dating or an anti-evolutionary stance, only old books.

Religions and their leaders have claimed for millennia to have the answers to the big questions regarding the origins of life, languages, morals and societal rules, and they have long been the source of information on how to live life. But now that we have secular governments and laws and science to teach us real truths, religious leaders play an ever-diminishing role in society.

In response to criticism, theists often shift the burden of proof, asking non-believers to disprove religious beliefs. But this is to ignore that it is impossible to disprove something for which no credible evidence has been presented. The onus should be on believers to prove that their god and associated stories are real – and that every other god and its associated stories are not real – if they want to argue from this position. Otherwise, if we accept something just because it is not disproven, then we have to accept all made-up things as possible facts. This is not a cogent argument; it is merely a list of things which have not been disproven. One could include leprechauns and fairies and Russell's teapot.[1]

Saying "I don't know how X happened" is not evidence a god exists. Not understanding is a feature of magic shows, which are replete with "how did that happen, that's amazing" moments; but this does not make the illusions real. Somehow in these circumstances, we accept that we may not understand the magic, but we do not attribute it to "special powers".

Likewise, when someone claims that they have seen a miracle, we can appreciate that that is what they believe, but that does not mean that it is true. Many people believe that they have been abducted and probed by aliens or seen Elvis, but do we believe them? No. However, we understand that they strongly believe the illusion or fantasy. Like watching great magic, it may in fact not be what it appears to be, even though it feels so real.

Dreams work similarly. Nearly all of us will have woken up during the night from a dream because the story that our mind created felt incredibly real. We often need to wake properly and consciously double-check with the rational side of our thinking processes to realize that what we have just seen was not real. What this shows is that we are even capable of fooling ourselves!

PROOF THAT YOUR GOD DOESN'T EXIST

1. Think of a god of another religion that you don't believe exists.

2. Determine your standards of proof as to why you don't believe that it exists (despite the supporting stories that its adherents accept as truths).

3. Now apply those same questions and standards to your own god.

4. Is your god still true?

* * *

"Extraordinary claims require extraordinary evidence." – Carl Sagan

"If there is a god, he will have to beg my forgiveness." – phrase carved into the wall of a concentration camp cell by a Jewish prisoner

"Gods are fragile things; they may be killed by a whiff of science or a dose of common sense." – Chapman Cohen

"The lack of understanding of something is not evidence for God. It's evidence of a lack of understanding." – Lawrence Krauss

"The invisible and the non-existent look very much alike." – Delos McKown

"The proof that God does not exist is the complete lack of evidence that he does." – Anon.

"I believe in evidence. I believe in observation, measurement and reasoning confirmed by independent observers. I'll believe anything no matter how wild and ridiculous, if there is evidence for it. The wilder and more ridiculous something is, however, the firmer and more solid the evidence will have to be." – Isaac Asimov

"I listen to all of these complaints about rudeness and intemperateness and the opinion that I come to is that there is no polite way of asking somebody: 'Have you considered the possibility that your entire life has been devoted to a delusion?' But that's a good question to ask. Of course we should ask that question and of course it's going to offend people. Tough." – Daniel Dennett

What are the alternatives?

Even after accepting the sound and rational arguments against belief in deities, some people still seek comfort in non-theistic forms of religion. Others renounce their religious beliefs entirely and accept their new status as a non-believer, of whatever hue.

Deism

An interesting alternative to the traditional theistic form of religion is deism, defined by the *Merriam-Webster Dictionary* as "a movement or system of thought advocating natural religion, emphasizing morality... denying the interference of the Creator with the laws of the universe". Deists believe that there may have been a being or force that created all that we see and that that force set all of the laws of physics, chemistry and biology in place, but they do not believe that this being or force interacts with human beings on the tiny speck of dust we call Earth.

This is a crucial and hugely significant distinction. An interventionist god is the one that exists in the sacred texts and stories of a particular religion, a deity who supposedly interacted with humans sometime in the past, who gave advice on how to live and who performed miracles. A list of all the interventionist gods would include all of the Egyptian, Assyrian, Mesopotamian, Greek, Roman, Viking, Minoan and other gods that have come and gone in the last 5,000 years, as well as those people still believe in, such as Yahweh, Christ, Allah, Vishnu, Shiva and Brahma. Clinging to these gods can lead to stifled thinking and potentially dangerous actions. Deists, on the other hand, do not teach intolerance of others and do not adhere to any set doctrines. They have freedom of existence, and complete freedom to make choices.

The decision that people who believe in a god must make is what sort of a god are they willing to believe in. Do they want to believe in a god who needs to be praised all the time? One who needs to be prayed to but doesn't respond? A god who cares what you wear, what you eat, how you have sexual relations, who watches and judges you every second of your life but doesn't interact with you at all?

A full discussion and review of this idea of a god is required by society if we are to live a more peaceable and tolerant existence.

> PHILOSOPHY is like being in a dark room and looking for a black cat
>
> THEOLOGY is like being in a dark room, looking for a black cat that isn't there and shouting "I found it!"
>
> SCIENCE is like being in a dark room and looking for a black cat with a flashlight

Non-belief

There is no doubt that with improved education, more and more people in Western countries are abandoning religious beliefs altogether. For example, according to recent research in the traditionally religious USA, the number of "Nones" – those who are religiously unaffiliated – has risen sharply in recent times. General Social Survey has been conducting surveys since 1972. At that time, the proportion of the religiously unaffiliated in the USA was just 5 per cent; by 1990 it was 8 per cent and in the 2016 study that number had jumped to 22 per cent.[2]

In Pew Research polls from 2007–14 the percentage of adults who describe themselves as Christians dropped from 78.4 per cent to 70.6 per cent. This means that the number of unaffiliated has now overtaken the number of Catholics in America (20.8 per cent) as well as mainstream Protestants (14.7 per cent).[3] Along with this, the same study showed a concomitant rise in religious intermarriage, with 39 per cent reporting that they are in religiously mixed marriages, up from 19 per cent of those who got married prior to 1960.

In Britain the proportion of non-believers is even greater. A 2016 YouGov poll showed a four-point decline in the percentage of people who believe in a higher power, from 32 per cent in February 2015 to 28 per cent in 2016. Britons' belief in God has long been in decline, but normally at a slower rate of about 1 per cent per year. Meanwhile the proportion of atheists – people who say they do not actively believe in any kind of god – has risen from 33 per cent to over 40 per cent in the last few years.

On top of this, the age breakdown of religious belief in Britain shows that the youth are becoming irreligious at a much greater rate:

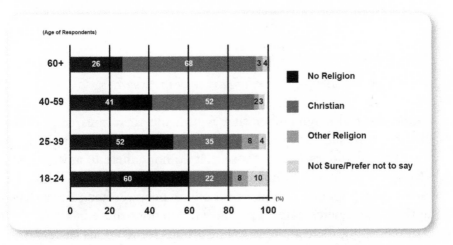

British YouGov poll, 8–9 February 2015, showing marked drop-off in religious beliefs among British youth

Similar results are even being seen in the USA. The chart below shows that among the Millennials, the future of humankind, there is a very large drop-off in belief in a god and the relevance of religions. Once the so-called Silent Generation and Baby Boomers are no longer around, the percentage of the population believing in a personal god will drop even further.

It is evident that worldwide the youth of today with easy access to an unprecedented quantity of information are, for the first time in history, no longer reliant on parents or elders for knowledge. With this comes a major disbelief in the stories of religions and gods with the next generation no longer accepting the mythologies of religious teachings. It is the start of the death of religions.

RELIGIOUS VIEWS AND BEHAVIOURS IN AMERICA

	Silent Generation (born 1928–1945)	Baby Boomers (born 1946–1964)	Generation X (born 1965–1980)	Older Millennials (born 1981–1989)	Younger Millennials (born 1990–1996)
Pray daily	67%	61%	56%	46%	39%
Believe in god with certainty	71%	69%	64%	54%	50%
Religion is very important in their lives	67%	59%	53%	44%	38%

Source: 2014 Religious Landscape Study, conducted June 4–Sept 30, 2014
Pew Research Centre

Drop-off in religious views in America

One must also remember that worldwide there are many other belief systems, such as Hinduism, that do not follow the single deity view of the world, as well as those that do not adhere to any god-belief systems, such as Buddhism, Confucianism and Taoism. China, the world's most populous nation, at 1.3 billion people, often rates as having the highest percentage of people who do not believe in a god.

Interestingly, there are now online groups for religious leaders who no longer believe in their god/s or their mythologies and need assistance in dealing with this. A relatively new one, the Clergy Project (clergyproject.org), is an American-based not-for-profit organization that helps current and former clergy transition into secular employment. The organization was established in 2011 and has already assisted over 700 clergy. This is a remarkably high number in a short timespan, considering that (1) only a small percentage of clergy would know of the organization and (2) in the early stages it would require an immense amount of courage for them to act on their changed beliefs. Clearly, it is not only those brought up in a secular lifestyle who can see that alternative views of the world exist and offer better explanations.

There is also an international group that assists lay people to transition away from religion, called Recovering from Religion. It provides a support network for people who have left or are in the process of leaving their faith, to help them deal with the impact of this transformation on their lives. It even offers a telephone hotline for "people in their most urgent time of need", as well as a range of online tools and practical resources.

It is deplorable that religions can have such a strong grasp on humanity that support systems like these are required. It's ironic that religious groups, who are supposed to be the most supportive of us all, are the very people who impose severe psychological punishments, even on family and friends, for simply seeing the shortcomings of their own religion. The distress experienced by some people as a result of these punishments is now a recognized psychological condition, Religious Trauma Syndrome, which has been compared to Post-Traumatic Stress Disorder.

Statistics suggest that there will be a continuous upswing in non-believers over the next few decades. Worldwide, however, the overall trend may start moving in the opposite direction by about 2050 because religious adherents in developing countries have much higher birth rates than those in developed countries. Despite the pressures of burgeoning populations on the environment, religious bodies will continue to promote having large families and to object to contraception, in order to keep bolstering their numbers. And the environmental damage will continue to escalate due to the religious "arms race" between Christian and Muslim populations in the developing world.

Atheism

An important distinction in terms must be made so as to help people understand the full spectrum of choices. Not believing in a god or gods is different to saying that someone believes that there is no god. Unfortunately, the most common word that has been used to describe a lack of belief in a personal god is "atheist". Contrary to what most people think, the term "atheism" is widely used not to refer to a particular belief, but to a rejection of belief generally. Atheists have no defined worldview and no book of myths or doctrines to believe in or follow. Taking this position is merely saying, "I do not see any or enough evidence for the existence of any god that you present to me".

Most atheists that I interact with see themselves as agnostic atheists. This is not a contradiction in terms, as the following chart explains:

Theism	I believe in a god but I can't say for sure a god exists.	I believe in a god and I know for sure a god exists.
Atheism	I don't believe that a god exists but I can't say for certain.	I don't believe that a god exists and I know this for sure.
	Agnostic	Gnostic

"Atheist" is in fact a word that need not exist; after all, if we don't believe in aliens we do not call ourselves "non-alienists" or "a-alienists". And nothing else links atheists, no specific views on science or morals. It is usually not an active form of belief, just a non-belief in all of the currently promoted deities. If religions eventually disappear, the word "atheist" will vanish with them. Atheism is not an entity of itself; it merely exists because theistic views exist.

"I reject the label atheist because defining me in terms of the things that I don't believe would require an infinite list of nouns." – Brian Cox

ATHEISM

BELIEVING IN ONE LESS GOD THAN MOST THEISTS.

REALLY, THAT'S ALL THERE IS TO IT.

Once this is understood, it may also become apparent that the word "atheist" is not really how most non-believers wish to describe themselves. It is not a positive description of what one believes; it is just a word to describe something one doesn't believe in. A more positive term for those who are not believers is "secular" (as opposed to religious), as it more aptly describes how non-believers make their decisions as they live their lives. There seems to be a growing support for the use of this term, which is defined in the *Merriam-Webster Dictionary* as meaning "of or relating to the physical world and not the spiritual world; not overtly or specifically religious".

Scale of disbelief

Richard Dawkins, when asked whether he had a disproof of "God", stated that he could not be 100 per cent sure that there is no god, as that is impossible to prove. He continued, "It's very important to make a distinction between 'I don't know whether X is true or not, therefore it's 50/50 likely or unlikely' and that's the kind of agnostic that I'm definitely not. I think one can place estimates of probability on these things and I think the probability of any supernatural creator existing is very, very low."

Dawkins also simplified the issue by creating a useful scale called the "Spectrum of Theistic Probability", in his book *The God Delusion*.[4] It suggests people generally belong to one of the following categories:

1. Strong theist. 100 per cent probability of God. In the words of C.G. Jung: "I do not believe, I know."
2. De facto theist. Very high probability but short of 100 per cent. "I don't know for certain, but I strongly believe in God and live my life on the assumption that he is there."
3. Leaning towards theism. Higher than 50 per cent but not very high. "I am very uncertain, but I am inclined to believe in God."
4. Completely impartial. Exactly 50 per cent. "God's existence and non-existence are exactly equiprobable."
5. Leaning towards atheism. Lower than 50 per cent but not very low. "I do not know whether God exists but I'm inclined to be sceptical."

6. De facto atheist. Very low probability, but short of zero. "I don't know for certain but I think God is very improbable, and I live my life on the assumption that he is not there."
7. Strong atheist. "I know there is no God, with the same conviction as Jung knows there is one."

When asked where he lay on the scale, Dawkins rated his position as about a 6.9, as he felt that it was impossible to provide 100 per cent support for the full 7 on the scale.

Believers in a god reject the gods of all other religions, so they are atheistic with regard to every other of the 3,000-plus gods that have been a part of human history. In fact, we are all born atheists; we are not born Christian or Jewish or Muslim or Hindu or Buddhist. Up until the age of at least three, a child's brain cannot absorb any of the stories or beliefs that define a religion.

* * *

"Religion is a phase a species goes through when it evolves enough intelligence to ask profound questions but not enough to answer them." – Bill Flavell

"The fact that opinion is widely held is no evidence whatever that it is not utterly absurd." – Bertrand Russell

"One can't prove that God doesn't exist, but science makes God unnecessary." – Stephen Hawking

"The word god is for me nothing more than the human expression and product of human weakness, the Bible a collection of honourable but still purely primitive legends which are nevertheless pretty childish." – Albert Einstein

"When a religious person says that the reason you don't understand their faith or believe the fictitious stories in their scriptures is because you are not looking at the issues with your 'heart', what they are really asking is to suspend your reason and use your imagination. Now I would suggest that if you have to use your imagination to see their god, then their god is more than likely imaginary." – Michael Sherlock

"Religion: It's given people hope in a world torn apart by religion." – Jon Stewart

"I don't know if God exists, but it would be better for his reputation if he didn't." – Jules Renard

"The problem with religion, because it's been sheltered from criticism, is that it allows people to believe en masse what only idiots or lunatics could believe in isolation." – Sam Harris

"Religion is an illusion and it derives its strength from the fact that it falls in with our instinctual desires." – Sigmund Freud

"People when they say that this is evidence of Almighty always quote beautiful things. They always quote orchids and hummingbirds and butterflies and roses ... But I always have to think too of a little boy sitting on the banks of a river in west Africa who has a worm boring through his eyeball turning him blind before he's five years old. And I reply and say, 'Well presumably the god that you speak about created the worm as well', and I find that baffling to credit a merciful god." – Sir David Attenborough, BBC interview, 2008

"Ignorance is the soil in which belief in miracles grows." – Robert Ingersoll

"If there is a god, atheism must seem to him less of an insult than religion." – Edmond de Goncourt

"Religion is an advertising campaign for a product that doesn't exist." – Clive James

"Why don't I believe in God? No, no, no, why do YOU believe in god? Surely the burden of proof is on the believer. You started all of this." – Ricky Gervais

"Is god willing to prevent evil but not able?
Then he is not omnipotent.
Is he able but not willing?
Then he is malevolent.
Is he both able and willing?
Then whence cometh evil?
Is he neither able nor willing?
Then why call him god?" – Epicurus, Greek philosopher

Or the modern version:

Innocent people suffer or die every day and God does nothing. Is this because:

1. He doesn't care.
2. He is unable to do anything.
3. He is indifferent to suffering.
4. He is absent.

Choose wisely

And some quotes from social media that I have come across over the years:

"If you viewed your religion with as much scepticism as you view the religion of others, you too would be an atheist."

"God is an interesting concept. To some people it is so obvious that there is a god, while to others it's obvious that there is not, and the truth is not somewhere in between."

"I have no evidence of any 'god' but tons of evidence of humans inventing the most imaginative of things."

"It is strange that if God exists, he would create a universe where it appears that he does not."

"I've seen nothing to convince me that 'God's will' means anything other than 'I don't want to have to think about this.'"

"If theists all shut up, the gods would be speechless."

"The fact that a human being has to tell you about the existence of their god shows that their god does not exist."

"If all religions advocate peace, then why aren't their extremists extremely peaceful?"

And finally, from Freddie Mercury/Queen:

"I don't believe in Peter Pan, Frankenstein or Superman; all I want to do is bicycle."

9

GOOD AND BAD

Religions have created and refined many features that cater to our basic human needs. They serve a useful purpose. However, can philosophies without theistic beliefs and rules serve humanity better? I think that this is beyond doubt, and this is the point from where the discourse needs to commence.

It's difficult to imagine a world without religions, but it is not only possible, it is also highly probable, that there will come a time when all of the current religions no longer exist. Having said that, there are many aspects of religions that people enjoy. We need to assess which of these are beneficial and worth maintaining, and which features need to be eliminated.

Preserving the good

Religions have served many useful purposes to humanity and still continue to do so. There are many aspects of and practices associated with the cultures of religions that are positive and could be retained, albeit with some adjustments.

Community

Religions currently provide a sense of community, creating places where like-minded people can spend time together. One only has to attend a religious service to feel the sense of connection between disparate people. When a person is familiar with and can follow along with a service, the use of repeated rituals provides a sense of belonging.

Religious organizations often facilitate involvement in many other communal activities. They can serve as hubs for social gatherings, and they can often encourage members to help other people in the community, be it the sick, the less fortunate or those who need support with life issues. For people who have moved to a new community, a religious centre can often be an excellent starting point for creating new connections, as adherents are usually warmly welcomed into a congregation and there are instant familiarities. This helps new arrivals put down roots, which, in turn, further strengthens the community.

Religion can also provide structure in life, offering guidelines for day-to-day living and for specific situations. From when we are young, it is evident that in order to feel comfortable and confident in our daily lives we need structure and routine so that we gain a sense of security and feelings of achievement.

Religious debates and sermons, even ones about religious texts, can be thought-provoking and stimulating and lead to fascinating philosophical discussions. Most congregants look forward to these discourses for the general insights they provide into human behaviour or as parables about life and morals. That's not to say, however, that these discussions validate the existence of a god or the truths of the texts. Many early Greek philosophers also created fascinating fables and parables that intrigued the people of their time and continue to fascinate us today.

Probably the greatest benefit created by religions is in binding people together. Sharing religious beliefs, or religious culture, can create a continuum of mindset through many generations of a family, and can reinforce the sense of togetherness. Even those who are not related will share a bond and understanding if they have grown up with the same religious traditions.

Tribalism is an innate part of all of us and religion certainly helps us to feel that we are part of a particular and often large tribe. But the question that we must ask is this: is the religious form of tribalism the one that we want to keep for humanity? Are there other less divisive tribalisms that can create and maintain similar positive bonds between family members and groups of human beings?

I certainly feel no need to be a part of a religious community when I belong to so many other social groups. Taking one away still leaves plenty of others. As an example, I belong to the greater community of my family and friends, and we share many, many experiences, ideals and practices, as well as the strongest possible bonds: these are connections with *real people*, with whom I can interact whenever I want. This network also involves me in other clubs, sports and activities, including those that my children participate in. Sports clubs in particular, whether that means participating in a sport or just supporting a favourite team, provide many hours of enjoyment and camaraderie.

I am also a part of the greater community of my profession. There are conferences, study groups, research journals and general rules and procedures that are adhered to worldwide. I was also a supporting member of our city's zoo for a number of years. You can of course join walking clubs, photography clubs, music appreciation groups, artistic groups, volunteering organizations and so on. And if you are looking for spirituality it can be achieved in many more ways than those a single religion offers. In fact, being obliged to attend religious services on a regular basis can really narrow your options! To become a more balanced person in life requires an individual to have the chance to explore and take on a far greater variety of lifestyle views and choices.

Charity

Religious groups have been instrumental in providing for those less fortunate, both within their societies and in other countries. Many, many people have donated their time and energy through religious organizations to help others, often by providing food, shelter, education or the basic necessities of life. Every developing country in the world is supported by religious groups of various shapes and forms. They have helped set up or improve schools and hospitals, and provide financial assistance as best they can.

In reality, however, this picture is not as pretty and simple as it has just been painted. Each religious sect or organization sets conditions for its assistance and has ulterior motives, most often to convert those they are helping to its belief system. Assistance almost never comes without strings attached. Religious organizations in developing countries often behave similarly to former Western colonial powers, in that they try to establish a base of converts who will then bring about changes to the educational systems and social and healthcare policies of the nation that will support their belief systems.

The imposition of conditions and restrictions on charitable assistance has throughout time led to much pain and suffering in the developing world, particularly where local cultural identity has been eroded and where sex education has prohibited the use of contraception. The only way that the developing world will be able to lift itself out of the mire is through the empowerment of women – by giving them equal rights and access to education and employment opportunities as well as control over their reproductive systems. In places where this has been tried, it has worked. Yet many religious organizations unfortunately preach against this strategy. How much better it would be if these groups would teach that one can create a better world by having fewer children, to help relieve pressure on the environment from a burgeoning human population. The lack of focus on this issue perpetuates the continued suffering of millions of people in the developing world. It should always be at the forefront of any discussions on the "good" that missionaries do.

If religious organizations were truly acting out of pure altruism they would happily donate money to non-biased secular organizations to achieve the best outcomes for those in need. After all, religions are among the wealthiest institutions on the planet, with the Catholic Church being the richest in the world. and, unlike almost every other organization, they do not even have to submit financial reports, they do not pay federal taxes or taxes on their investments, and they receive various tax exemptions. (This means that, like it or not, we are all financially supporting religious institutions.) The fact that they don't, and would never, support secular organizations is an indication of the problems we face.

"When the missionaries arrived the Africans had the land and the missionaries had the Bible. They taught us how to pray with our eyes closed. When we opened them, they had the land and we had the Bible."

Jomo Kenyatta, first president of Kenya

We want to continue the charitable work that religious institutions have done, and in recent times many secular groups have been created to provide similar assistance. While their presence is still much smaller than that of religious organizations, their numbers and support systems are growing. There is nothing good that a religious organization can do that a secular organization cannot do as well if not better, and the opposite is certainly not the case – this is an extremely important point.

The many important secular organizations include:

- UNICEF
- Doctors Without Borders
- Amnesty International
- Greenpeace
- Rotary International
- Oxfam
- Fairtrade Foundation
- WaterAid
- World Wildlife Fund

– and many, many, many more.

Moreover, within most countries there are thousands of non-religious volunteer organizations that do a power of work in communities. Certainly, where I live the endless phone calls for donations, sales of raffle tickets, and collectors at traffic intersections are evidence of this.

We can all help continue charitable work in developing nations and help reduce the impact of religious strictures by supporting these new secular organizations and by making sure our donations go to them rather than religious groups.

Culture

Without a doubt, religions have given rise to fascinating cultures that have in turn produced extraordinary institutions, structures and works of art, as well as cuisines, festivals and other traditions that enrich our lives.

Religious practice and worship have inspired countless magnificent paintings and sculptures and many outstanding pieces of music. Music of course plays a central part in religious services of all kinds, and there is no doubt that it helps bring people together – just hearing a religious song that has been a part of previous services can bring one into the fold of the community. Think of all the great religiously inspired works in music – masses, choral compositions, symphonies and so on – that even non-believers love. Religious music can reach deep within us all. Imagine how disconnected one would feel in religious services if there were not a single tune, hymn, melodic incantation or song. Without a doubt, congregants would find the services boring and would not be able to connect in the same way.

All of this, along with the sense of community religion can create, makes many people reluctant to abandon their religious culture altogether. It's not surprising then that in current times there are many people who still wish to maintain some of the cultural aspects of their upbringing while distancing themselves from the texts and the beliefs they uphold. "Cultural Jew/Christian/Muslim/Hindu" may not seem like an ideal description, especially as there may be certain perceptions created by using such terms, but it may be the best that can be achieved for many in the current climate. It is not necessarily a sign that these individuals are confused; it is merely that they wish to keep certain aspects of their lives and family history alive.

For example, there are many Jews who no longer believe the stories or rules of the Old Testament but wish to preserve many of the cultural aspects of their religion and upbringing. They maintain their regular Friday night/Shabbat/Sabbath dinner with family or friends as a way to end the working week, and they continue to enjoy foods associated with Jewish culture. Many of these foods have penetrated the broader world menu, such as potato pancakes and donuts at Hanukah, honey and apples for the Jewish New Year, and of course chicken soup for a Friday night – or to cure any ills.

Jewish people, even non-believers, are also justifiably proud of their culture's contributions to intellectual achievement – a disproportionate percentage of Jews have won Nobel prizes through the years, Jews have also played a large role in the development of the film, television, music and comedy industries, and there is a large body of distinctively Jewish literature. Most secular Jews still like to feel connected to their culture and appreciate their connection with the long history of Israel. As Rabbi Steven Carr Reuben has noted, "What gives Jews our identity is not so much belief as it is belonging – the sense of belonging to the Jewish community, belonging to the Jewish people, being part of a family literally that goes back to Biblical times." Interestingly, 32 per cent of Jewish American millennials told a Pew survey in 2013 that their Jewish identity is based on ancestral, ethnic and cultural connections rather than religious ones.[1]

People of a Christian background make up a very large proportion of the world's secular population. Many still refer to themselves as Christians but, day to day, live essentially secular lives. They enjoy their Christian heritage, including the religion's extraordinary art and music and its health, welfare and educational systems, and they participate in festivals and enjoy associated culinary traditions. But they do not believe in the religious claims of Christianity and often do not agree with the church's position on sexuality and science, or its failure to acknowledge "the problems of the real world".

Because the Koran is supposedly the exact words of Allah and apostasy is seen as a crime in many Muslim countries and in some Muslim communities elsewhere, it is generally much more difficult for Muslims to live a secular existence. A shift in this direction is occurring in a few Islamic nations, however. According to a recent Gallup poll, the Muslim countries with the highest proportion of irreligious Muslims are Turkey (73 per cent), Azerbaijan (51 per cent) and Lebanon (33 per cent). Although Turkey is leading the way, there have recently been some teething problems there, as is to be expected when secularism clashes with a religion as strong as Islam.

There are also, however, many millions of Muslims who have left such countries to move to more secular nations in order to enjoy the extra freedoms that they provide. This has allowed these migrants to actively participate in secular societies while maintaining some of their favourite traditions and rituals. They can choose to associate themselves with their culture without necessarily practising the religion or adhering to its more extreme views. For instance, they may not attend regular prayer services, abstain from alcohol or enforce or endorse the seclusion or subservience of women. To these people, there is no contradiction in being a non-theistic Muslim, just as secular Jews and secular Christians feel they can retain their culture without keeping the faith.

Religious holidays, festivals and ceremonies

One of the clearest signs of this growing tendency towards secular forms of traditional cultures is the way in which religious festivals and holidays are observed and celebrated. Often these are the main times when people in developed countries acknowledge their religious backgrounds, even if for the rest of the year they are fairly removed from them.

Many religious holidays have been altered so much in the last few centuries that much of their original purpose and meaning has been lost. Perhaps most obviously, for the majority of Christians in Western societies Christmas has become an almost entirely secular celebration of consumerism, during which families get together mainly to eat, sing songs and share presents. Themes and icons have developed around Christmas that have nothing to do with the original story of a Middle Eastern Judean desert person: Santa Claus and his reindeer, the North Pole, Christmas trees with fairy lights and so on. There are also many foods associated with Christmas that are unique to many countries – such as fish in parts of Italy; puddings, mince pies and fruit cakes in other European countries; and turkey in the USA – yet have little or nothing to do with the religious origins of the event.

Similarly, for most people, Easter is now more about having a four-day weekend to spend with family and friends than about celebrating the resurrection of Jesus. Chocolate eggs have become synonymous with Easter, yet people who lived in the Middle East 2,000 years ago would never have heard of such a thing. It just goes to show how symbolism can be created and changed over time to whatever society chooses. On top of all this, fewer and fewer people are now attending church services over these peak Christian occasions. In fact, these festivals have become so separated from their religious beginnings that many non-Christians also participate in them.

While Islamic festivals are generally more strictly observed, many secular Muslims still participate in the feast of Eid al-Fitr, which marks the end of Ramadan, as a way to enjoy traditional foods and celebrate being with family.

Clearly, religious celebrations change over time and people can now use them to maintain a historical and cultural connection with their religious past. Taking this further, many of these festivals could gradually become more inclusive, drawing participants from other cultural backgrounds (as Christmas and Easter already do) in a way that is highly appropriate in a modern multicultural society.

Halloween is a good example of a blended, modernized celebration that has not only become a part of Christian society but also, in recent times, a worldwide secular festival celebrated by people of many religious backgrounds. It is thought to originally have been a pagan or Celtic harvest festival dedicated to remembrance of the dead but has gradually evolved into a non-denominational, all-inclusive festivity. Anyone and everyone is now comfortable partaking in Halloween, yet it was previously a holiday celebrated by a completely different religious group.

Could other currently popular religious occasions be modernized and secularized in the same way, so that some of their enjoyable cultural aspects can be maintained? Yom Kippur, the Day of Atonement, is the holiest day on the Jewish calendar, a 25-hour fasting period. People attend synagogue all day and then have family get-togethers at sunset to break the fast. It is a time of reflection and thanks. A secular form of this festival could be developed, whereby instead of spending the day repeating prayers in Hebrew (which most Jewish congregants don't even understand), people could spend the day discussing real-world issues and engaging with their community to create real-world solutions. The event would promote togetherness and the day-long fast could be maintained as a way of reminding people how fortunate they are and to be thankful for that, as with the World Vision

40-hour Famine. Religious faith and prayers would not be required, however. The period of Ramadan could possibly be adapted similarly as could the Christian sin/confession/atonement practice to create a trans-religious concept.

Religious ceremonies could also be adapted to create secular versions; for example:

- a secular christening/baby-naming ceremony
- a coming-of-age ceremony at age 15–16, whereby the person is transitioned out of adolescence by presenting a speech about their passions and what they intend to do to make their life and the lives of others better
- non-religious wedding ceremonies. When one looks at the many different ways that weddings are currently celebrated, it is clearly possible to extract many interesting features from religious and cultural ceremonies that add great meaning to the occasion. I personally would love to include aspects of Indian/Hindu weddings, Greek weddings and even Japanese tea ceremonies
- secular funeral rituals and grieving processes; these could be altered to be far more honest and positive and yet still be reflective
- other milestone events, such as father-son, mother-daughter and parent-child rituals and occasions. Some could be designed to ensure that grandparents still have a strong educative and interactive presence within the family.

We already have many "World Days", most of which pass almost unnoticed. If we focused on them more and promoted them better they could replace many of the religious festivities:

January 23	International Freedom Day
January 26	International Environmental Education Day
January 27	International Outer Space Day
January 30	International Nonviolence and Peace Day
February 4	World Cancer Day

February 20	World Day of Social Justice
March 3	World Wildlife Day
March 8	International Women's Day
March 20	International Day of Happiness
March 21	World Poetry Day
April 7	World Health Day
April 29	International Dance Day (just for some fun!)
May 15	International Day of Families
June 5	World Environment Day
July 30	International Day of Friendship
August 12	International Youth Day
September 5	International Day of Charity
October 1	International Day of Older Persons
November 13	World Kindness Day

This is not to forget that most countries already have a number of secular holidays, such as New Year's Day, Thanksgiving, Memorial Day and usually a founding day of some sort.

Currently the USA has a National Day of Prayer. Imagine how beneficial it would be if, instead of spending a day sitting in a room praying and achieving, well, as much as prayer does, we all gathered in groups to discuss pressing social and global issues and how we can all work together to help others and the environment. Or we held a National Day of Thanks. Imagine the positive effect it could have on our children to promote ideas of togetherness and mutual assistance instead of teaching differences and indoctrinating them with fear of a malevolent deity.

So much could be achieved by further secularizing religious festivities and ceremonies, and it's not difficult to imagine that one day there will be greater emphasis on some of these far more beneficial and inclusive options. We just need to begin to embrace them.

Acceptance of others

Why is it that we can both accept and embrace multiculturalism – people of different backgrounds living in one country – and enjoy their foods and history and culture, yet we can't do the same for people from other religions? Is it because religions preach and point out not only the differences between their adherents and others but also that their way is the only true way?

Most Europeans of today can travel to Germany and happily deal with the German people only a few decades after the country's nationalism and policies created a continental war leading to the deaths and suffering of tens of millions. Why can Americans and Japanese get along, holiday in each other's countries and be interested in each other's culture and history, yet only two generations ago they fought against each other in a war that killed so many innocent people? How can we as societies move on in these circumstances, yet harbour grudges from hundreds or thousands of years ago once religion is involved? Why do the teachings of religions create such an instilled point of difference, dislike or even hatred?

> SOMETIMES THE NICEST PEOPLE YOU MEET ARE COVERED IN TATTOOS AND SOMETIMES THE MOST JUDGMENTAL PEOPLE YOU MEET GO TO CHURCH ON SUNDAYS

Eradicating the bad

While there are a number of positive aspects of religion that are worth preserving there are many more negative aspects that we cannot and should not continue to tolerate. They need to be identified and discussed in order for us to move forwards and create new and improved societal systems.

You are never good enough

One of the most contemptible aspects of religions is the guilt that they impose in order to maintain control of their followers. They preach to children and adults that we are all born flawed and are never good enough. It is terrible how adherents are made to feel guilt for acting within the normal and otherwise acceptable realms of human behaviour. Believers are made to feel culpable just for being human.

There are too many artificial rules and teachings in religions that are either nonsensical or impossible to follow, which as a result make people feel inadequate and unable to reach those "standards". Any belief system that preaches that you are worthless unless you follow its doctrines is poisonous to the human psyche and must be recognized as such. We don't accept this in any other communal situation.

Living with a deity belief, especially in those religions that require prayer, means that you must accept that you were created flawed but have to be perfect. So even though your god made you imperfect (in his image!), you have to spend the rest of your life praying constantly to request forgiveness for the errors made by the manufacturer.

We don't teach our children about a single political party, yet we have no issue with teaching them about only one religion. This is why most religions have procedures, celebrations and rites of passage for babies, so that they instantly (and not of their choosing) become one of flock. Religions get their talons into children as early as possible.

> "A child is not a Christian child, not a Muslim child, but a child of Christian parents or a child of Muslim parents. This latter nomenclature, by the way, would be an excellent piece of consciousness-raising for the children themselves. A child who is told she is a 'child of Muslim parents' will immediately realize that religion is something for her to choose – or reject – when she becomes old enough to do so." – Richard Dawkins, The God Delusion

Many branches of Christianity have labelled the mistake made by Adam and Eve in the Garden of Eden as the "Original Sin" and consider this as an important tenet of their belief systems and practices. Because of this story everyone is said to be born a sinner and must spend the rest of their life repenting. There are many occasions when being in religion is like existing under a dictatorship. There are plenty of rules that must be followed, adherents are made to feel guilty by the ruling body, and all the while one must praise the dictator. These teachings undoubtedly lead to unnecessary life stresses and many family break-ups and suicides.

The requirement in many religions for constant praise of the god-head suggests that the supposedly all-powerful deity is somewhat insecure. And the fact that followers cannot question anything and must just accept that "that is my god's rules" reinforces this view. Even the existence of blasphemy laws is tantamount to saying that your religion or deity is not strong enough to accept criticism – which, iron-ically, should be considered blasphemous in itself!

Blasphemy laws are another way in which theists attempt to force people to adhere to or respect their religious beliefs. By silencing those who don't agree with them, religious leaders enjoy special protections that other educators do not. Apparently, the god/s of these religions are not able to protect themselves.

In contrast, secularism/atheism is like living in a democracy where you cannot be convicted of thought crimes and where you are free to criticize and change your opinions and the way you choose to live your life. You must still follow rules, but these rules are created by demo-cratic processes, in other words by the people who agree to follow these rules. You cannot be found guilty of invented "crimes", nor must you spend so much time lauding your leader.

Religions often resort to psychological warfare and name-calling for anyone who even thinks about leaving their "warm embrace". They have an extensive list of derogatory words to describe those who choose to transition away from religion: heathen, infidel, apostate, godless (said with the appropriate tone), pagan, heretic, gentile, impi-ous, unbeliever, unholy, sinful and so on.

It is accepted that many people do like the rules of religions; they like to be told what to do and how to do it, and by following these rules they feel like they have at least accomplished things. Religion provides a comfort, and whether it is true or false seems irrelevant, as long as there is even the slightest possibility of it being true. Being offered that support, as against the alternative of the world not owing us anything, is very tempting and too hard for many people to pass up on. It is seen by many as a very reasonable proposition to trade some freedom for the possibility of greater things.

Psychologically, the relationship is similar to the feelings of comfort we had in childhood, when we had fewer freedoms but knew there was someone watching over us and looking after us. More disturbingly, it also resembles the well-known "Stockholm Syndrome", described in the *Merriam-Webster Dictionary* as "the psychological tendency of a hostage to bond with, identify with or sympathize with his or her captor." As noted in Wikipedia, "These feelings are generally considered irrational in light of the danger or risk endured by the victims, who essentially mistake a lack of abuse from their captors for an act of kindness."

Religion and death

People often draw comfort from their religion when it comes to dealing with death and mourning. Religions provide rules and advice on how to honour the dead, plan and conduct funerals and how long and in what way we should mourn our lost loved ones. They reassure their followers that the deceased has gone to a better place. This can all be a great comfort at a difficult time.

But each religion of course has its own slant on things (and after all, they can't all be right), and some rules are not only nonsensical but potentially damaging to individuals in a fragile state. So, we must ask if these rules should be accepted and adhered to, or whether we would all benefit from an entirely different, secular approach to dealing with death.

For instance, do religious beliefs really provide comfort? From my observations and experiences, religious funeral services seem to have the most crying and wailing, whereas secular people appear to have accepted the cold, hard facts earlier on. Should we be encouraged from a young age to take a more matter-of-fact view of death?

And what about the judgments pronounced by religions? Do they exacerbate the stresses on dying individuals and their families? And are the very particular and often restrictive rules of religions regarding death and mourning capable of dealing with each situation as a unique problem, or are they mostly a one-size fits all approach?

Within Judaism, for example, adherents are not allowed to have tattoos on their bodies and in some branches of the religion they cannot have elective cosmetic procedures. These rules are based on the concept that your body belongs to God and you are merely a transient user of it. Some sects do not allow burial of such people within Jewish cemeteries and, even if they do, there may be last-minute stresses for families in conversations with religious leaders about whether they will or won't be accepted. Cremation is also forbidden, so there goes the option of having your ashes scattered over your own special place.

One of the greatest stresses regarding both Jewish and Muslim death and mourning is the urgency with which the religions say the deceased must be buried. Unless there are extenuating circumstances, burial should happen on the day of death or the next. Often family and friends do not make it to the funeral of someone close to them because of this rule, and it seems despicable to put this extra stress on people who are already in a trying situation. It must be awful for a person not to be able to attend the funeral service of a loved one and then have to carry unnecessary guilt for the rest of their lives.

Aspects of organ donation are forbidden within certain religions. Now that we have the means to successfully donate our organs after we no longer need them, surely the most considerate and moral act is to allow or even encourage people to donate body parts to people in need? What better work could be done with one's body than to help improve and prolong the life of another individual? Surely an omnipotent god is not so malevolent as to require human body parts after death? The only impediments to more of us doing this are outdated interpretations of a few sentences in old religious texts.

Religious views on "the sanctity of human life" have also influenced governmental views on euthanasia, forcing medical treatment and suffering to continue beyond when they rightly should. We have no problem euthanizing our favourite pets when we see that they are suffering, but cannot do the same for our loved ones; instead, we have to watch them suffer and slowly die. We must limit the influence of such religious beliefs on secular laws. It's fine for religious adherents to hold their views, but these should never form the basis of a society-wide ban on easing suffering.

In Islam, there is an expectation for women to be "circumspect" for over four months after a husband's death, but there are no restrictions on men having new relationships as soon as they wish. So, not only do religions make restrictive, controlling rules in life, these rules may continue even after one's death.

Within Catholicism, a family member cannot be buried with Catholic burial rites if they were "guilty" of apostasy, heresy or schism, or if they were manifest sinners, or if the granting of church funeral rites to them would cause scandal. The Catholic Church has only recently allowed for cremations.

I think it's vital that we adopt and make available new secular strategies for dealing with death and mourning, in order to counter the damaging influence of religion in this sphere. Could trained psychologists or grievance counsellors do things better, without some of the restrictions created by each religion? This would allow people who have much broader views to provide support and advice during the most confronting time of life. It would also allow someone who is dying to decide for themselves what sort of services and follow-on they would like for their family. There is no singular "right way" to grieve, so why be restricted by the rituals of one narrow belief system when experienced counsellors can help provide many options?

Sexuality

Most religions preach that the natural desires and pleasures of sex are evil or sinful. Yet if there is any action that is utterly natural, it is sexual desire. Without strong sexual urges, life would not be perpetuated. Religion should be preaching that sexual desire is a positive affirmation in a relationship and to be encouraged, rather than telling us it is only for procreation and must otherwise be suppressed. As humans, we have moved past the point where sex is only for having children, and it is time that religions caught up with and embraced this idea.

Some religions have created all-powerful identities associated with virginity. They have created a pedestal for the concept of one's first sexual encounter (mostly for females), placed a value on it and used the term as a tool to control adherents. This labelling causes insecurities, repression and anxiety. It is absurd and disgusting that religions place such a high value on virginity. When someone decides to have their first sexual encounter, it is only the business of that individual, and it should have nothing to do with religious leaders or rules.

Instead of teaching children to repress sexual feelings, with all of the associated psychological traumas that may entail, we should merely educate them about sex, birth control and disease prevention. Sexuality is something which should be explored positively and people should be encouraged to understand and enjoy it.

Thankfully some nations are starting to ignore religious teachings when it comes to sexual issues. In a momentous vote in 2015, Ireland held a referendum on same-sex marriage. Yes, the Ireland that was once almost an extension of the Vatican and remains a stronghold of Catholicism. Thankfully, a very high number of voters, and especially those from the younger generations decided to put religious teachings aside and say that all human beings should have equal rights. On that one day, Ireland proved to the world that the claws of religion are beginning to recede, even in former religious hotspots.

Circumcision

Another common religious practice that must be re-examined and rejected is circumcision. To start with, let's not call it circumcision; it should be called what it truly is: genital mutilation. Somehow this 3,000-year-old, unnecessary procedure has been passed from generation to generation to the present day, and as a result has gained a high level of societal acceptance.

Yet only in the context of religious thinking could circumcision be seen as an appropriate action. Imagine if the god of the Old Testament had called for the removal of a finger or toe instead? This may seem abhorrent, unlikely or bizarre to you, but that is only because of the society you were brought up in. Had this god requested it be the little finger or toe, we would see that as being completely acceptable because "that's what God said". Actually, it almost seems more acceptable than the idea of cutting off part of a penis, where a mistake could be far more costly.

Surely if you want to show devotion to a deity and belief system, it should be through regular good behaviour and not disfigurement of the body. And if you need a physical reminder of your faith, then maybe that suggests its teachings are not so memorable.

I also wonder if, with new gene-control treatments such as CRISPR, a genome editing technique, at some stage in the future we will be able to modify our genes for non-growth of a foreskin. If this were to occur, what position would religious adherents take? They like to support their position by saying that circumcision has health benefits (mostly preventable with other techniques), but would they argue against the use of the technology because it would prevent them from making a physical covenant? If gene technology were to eliminate foreskins, would they want an alternative part of the body to be cut or would they just refuse to use the technology?

If we were to change the laws and ban the procedure on minors until the individual is old enough to make his own decision, how many men would opt to have the procedure done? Likely there would be a sharp drop-off because it would now be adults deciding if they truly believed in the religious doctrines of their parents.

Worldwide there are reported deaths from ritual circumcision: there are bacterial and herpetic infections, disfigurements and revisional surgeries. To ignore this is to ignore our obligation to act morally towards the most innocent humans and those who need the most protection – newborn children. To fall back on the generational view of "but it's written in the Bible" is a complete abrogation of responsibility, and is the adult version of "but he told me to do it" (often referred to in modern world as the "Nuremberg Defence"). We teach children that such behaviour is unacceptable, so why do we allow adults to get away with it simply because they have certain personal beliefs?

In many secular societies, one can get into legal trouble for spanking a child, whether you are a parent, a teacher or someone unrelated, but if you want to butcher your child's genitals, well, apparently that's fine. Only under the guise of religion can one seem to get away with almost anything. How has humankind reached this insane position?

Female genital mutilation occurs commonly in Islamic countries in line with the Koran's views that men should control women's sexuality, even though the Koran does not specifically make mention of the procedure. It has absolutely no health benefits but has many life-long detrimental effects. According to the World Health Organization website it is:

> recognized internationally as a violation of the human rights of
> girls and women. It reflects deep-rooted inequality between the

sexes, and constitutes an extreme form of discrimination against women. It is nearly always carried out on minors and is a violation of the rights of children. The practice also violates a person's rights to health, security and physical integrity, the right to be free from torture and cruel, inhuman or degrading treatment, and the right to life when the procedure results in death.

A UNICEF report in 2013 found that over 125 million women and girls in 29 countries had been genitally mutilated.[2]

> IN ANY NORMAL SITUATION, IF SOMEONE HELD DOWN A TERRIFIED LITTLE GIRL AND SEWED UP HER GENITALS AND CUT OFF HER CLITORIS, THEY WOULD BE SEEN AS A MONSTER AND BE LOCKED AWAY. HOWEVER, WHEN MILLIONS OF PEOPLE DO IT AND IT IS ENDORSED BY A RELIGION, IT IS INSTANTLY ACCEPTED AS "PART OF THE CULTURE".

Refusing to face facts

Perhaps one of the most dispiriting and objectionable aspects of religion is the way its adherents refuse to accept evidence demonstrated by science. It is still discouraging that so many people can employ the results of scientific research when they listen to the radio, watch television, use a cell-phone operating via satellites, use nuclear energy to power these devices, utilize CT-scans and medicines on a daily basis and read that we have unravelled the human genome, but they still won't endorse the far simpler processes of dating fossils, understanding evolution or measuring the size and timescale of our universe. Only a religious indoctrination can allow this to be so, and most people who actively reject evolution do so because of religious reasons and not because they have put time into reading widely and understanding it.

There are no scientists in any of the varied fields of evolution who can find any evidence against it, despite the potential rewards for doing so being so great! Ask an evolution-denier what evidence they would need to allow them to accept evolution as true and they will be unable to provide a valid response. Therefore nothing can change their minds, as a result of their rigid indoctrination.

Religion is a dogma that struggles to change, whereas science is a continuous process of learning and understanding. Left to religion we would still think that epilepsy was caused by demons and that a sufferer or their family must have done something to offend a god.

Religion does not just ask for faith, a word that it has tried to own, but in fact it asks for "blind faith", a completely different way of viewing things. And ironically for the only species on the planet capable of reason, religion is the one sphere of human endeavour that requires devolution of our abilities. It asks us to suspend our reasoning and just believe that what we have been told by our family and community are truths. And this is why it is dangerous and why people from the outside of a religion can see that it is wrong (even though they may not be able to see that their own religion is false too).

* * *

"If you are a priest and you write a brilliant article that explains why the Pope is wrong, you will get ex-communicated. If you're a brilliant theoretical physicist and write a brilliant article that explains why Einstein is wrong you will win the Nobel Prize." – Sean M. Carroll

"No amount of experimentation can ever prove me right; a single experiment can prove me wrong." – Albert Einstein

"That which can be destroyed by the truth should be." – P.C. Hodgell

"People don't want to hear the truth because they don't want their illusions destroyed." – Friedrich Nietzsche

"The deepest sin against the human mind is to believe things without evidence." – Aldous Huxley

"Name one scientific theory that was later replaced by a religious interpretation? You can't? Strange how it only works the other way around. Religion: 4,000 years of constant back-pedalling." – Anon.

* * *

When I look at friends who have struggled to fall pregnant and the many stresses that this creates, I feel their pain and disappointment. Religious people will simply say it must be accepted as their god's will and that they must just move on and accept this situation. I am then heartened to hear that a good percentage of these people have utilized science and gone through IVF and are subsequently able to conceive and achieve one of life's ultimate experiences. We must take the terrible teaching of "gods will" out of such situations.

One of the other predominant views of life created by religions is that we are the pinnacles of creation and that life exists only on this single, small planet, and that a god is highly interested and involved in the minutiae of everyday human life. Opposing this is the view that we are connected to every other living thing on this planet, and that there is potentially so much more out there. How would religious views of this change if we found out that a far more "advanced" alien species existed? We could be the simple and "irrelevant" life form.

Carl Sagan stated in his book *Pale Blue Dot: A Vision of the Human Future in Space*:

> How is it that hardly any major religion has looked at science and concluded, "This is better than we thought! The Universe is much bigger than our prophets said, grander, more subtle, more elegant?" Instead they say, "No, no, no! My god is a little god, and I want him to stay that way."

The most amazing thing about science is that it allows absolutely anyone to be the first person to discover or explain something new. The potential satisfactions and rewards of working in scientific fields are totally different from those of any other endeavour.

Religions almost always provide comfort, and many religious people may find what they perceive as coldness in the facts of science. Not everyone wants to know the sometimes brutal and harsh realities of life, and religions allow people to stay removed from this. They also tend to separate humans from all other living things and make out that we are special. Again, this appeals to the human ego and can be tantalizingly more attractive to many than the honesty that science provides. It is, however, a fabrication based on no evidence.

There is nothing inherently wrong with living this way; however, as described earlier, these belief systems lead to actions by believers. Meanwhile, those who do not live with deity belief (likely at least 1 billion people) find much more comfort in knowing that they are living this one life with a different kind of wonderment, and a stronger connection with *all of nature* instead of a single deity.

For too long, religions have been given a free pass to make up concepts that in any other sphere of thought would be seen as absurdities. A major truism of religions is that they show that people will believe utter nonsense based on zero evidence. Religion tries to explain the explicable by invoking something inexplicable. As Sam Harris once put it, "The point is that religion remains the only mode of discourse that encourages grown men and women to pretend to know things they manifestly do not (and cannot) know. If ever there were an attitude at odds with science, this is it."

Despite adherents wishing otherwise, science and religion barely overlap when viewed from the scientific perspective. Religions have no tools for determining whether or not their claims are true. As much as religions say that one can't test for their god/s, this is not in fact true, because religious people make factual claims. These include the effectiveness of prayer, their creation mythologies, interaction with people, miracles and so on. None of these, however, have any evidential backing despite opportunities to do so, and this is a really important concept to understand. Religions make real-world claims that they cannot back up. They make claims that are testable, yet they come up with zero.

Repeated studies of the beliefs of the world's top scientists, including the Fellows of the UK-based Royal Society and the US National Academy of Science show that over 90 per cent do not believe in an interactive personal god.[3] That there are a few who do does not show that science and religion can co-exist as ways of thinking; it simply results from the fact that there are a few outliers who display a common psychological process known as compartmentalization – they are somehow able to keep the two thought processes separate when they switch from professional time to personal time. They just lock their personal views in a separate box and leave it outside the laboratory when they walk through the doors. The figures do, however, show that the scientific method is incompatible with the religious method. In science, faith is never the way to form views, but in religion it is the main way.

A religion, old or new, that stressed the magnificence of the universe as revealed by modern science might be able to draw forth reserves of reverence and awe hardly tapped by the conventional faiths.

Discrimination

It's bad enough that religious organizations are able to get away with internal discrimination regarding positions that females and others can hold in their organizations, but it's even worse that they can do the same in more secular bodies. In many community groups with religious backing, bigoted views affect the treatment of those who wish to partake in or become more useful in such organizations. For example, in many sections of the Boy Scouts, the Salvation Army and other social groups, the leadership does not allow gays or atheists to join or hold senior positions. How can this be possible when these organizations are not specifically religious institutions?

In fact, there are still seven states within the USA that have laws on their books that ban non-believers from holding senior government positions. The typical wording in each is along the lines of "no person who denies the existence of a Supreme Being shall hold any office under this constitution". Imagine if these words were said about Muslims, Jews, Hindus or Buddhists.

How about if a school employee comes out as gay or transgender, against the belief system of that school; does the school have the right to instantly dismiss this employee? Are they entitled to refuse to hire such a person in the first place?

There is a myriad of situations where religious beliefs can affect the lives of non-believers in significant and often detrimental ways. Should we really allow this? We need to make sure that any religious organization that seeks or receives government funding to provide any community services must abide by secular laws, even when they contradict their own internal belief systems.

False leaders

Another pernicious religious influence we must try to counter is the widespread automatic respect and deference shown to religious leaders, even by secular institutions. Even if we want to continue some of the good that religion does, we must ask ourselves: do we want religious leaders to continue to have authority and play leading roles in society, or could we train (or do we already have) secular leaders who could do a more effective job?

Religious leaders are first and foremost supposed to be educators. But, in reality, these persons of faith have been teaching us and our children falsehoods as facts, have been preaching moral concepts which have too often been abhorrent, and have incited hatred towards others or stated that those who do not accept and follow their teachings are wrong and lesser human beings. These are the people whose predecessors, throughout the ages, supported the Crusades, the Spanish Inquisition, pogroms, Nazism, slavery, bigotry against gays, and the treatment of women as possessions and/or inferior beings. Some still impel people to become martyrs by perpetrating suicide killings of innocent people. In every religion, leaders preach intolerance of others (and not just their beliefs). They were preaching from the pulpits during the massacres in Rwanda, during recent Sunni-Shia violence and in Protestant-Catholic conflicts.

For too long we have accepted that describing a religious leader as a "person of faith" somehow automatically confers on them an elevated standing in society. Religious leaders are really just shamans, interpreters of old myths and rules, their antiquated costumes somehow imparting an air of "specialness" in our modern world.

Throughout the ages and even in modern times, trusting these people blindly has been shown to be a dangerous policy, often allowing religious leaders to get away with preaching that is false and hateful, while perpetrating atrocious crimes. For example, as is now widely known, church officials and leaders have participated in widespread pedophilia, and, just as despicably, tried to cover it up and pressurized affected parties not to discuss the matters further. Even today, church leaders continue to hide the guilty parties, fight charges in courts all around the world and conceal or modify evidence. Such situations occur because religion will often put doctrines and the religion itself before people, ritual before individuals, and "sacred" principles before human dignity. Religion has always been and continues to be based on preserving the faith at the expense of the individual, without truly questioning whether its beliefs were ever correct in the first place.

Religious leaders are the people who preach and force followers to genitally mutilate their children, just so that they can prove that these innocent victims are good enough to belong to their ideology. These are the people who have claimed, and in many parts of the world continue to claim, that natural disasters such as disease epidemics and storms are punishment for poor behaviour. It is interesting that these words come from human preachers while their gods remain silent. (I also wonder how those same preachers explain storms that occur on other planets. The Great Red Spot on Jupiter is a storm that has been raging for at least hundreds of years. Is the god of Jupiter angry at the actions of life forms living somewhere on that planet?)

These are people who re-enforce divisions in society by instilling an "us versus them" mentality in their followers, specifically the idea that only adherents of their religion know the truths.

These are the people who continue to preach and teach that Earth and everything on it are only thousands of years old, and continue to teach creationism as factual even though it has been proven otherwise.

This does not mean that every person of faith is a bad person. They are mostly only trying to do good by following their doctrine, but it must certainly be acknowledged that being a religious leader should not automatically confer an elevated status. Too many of these people have been a negative influence on societies, and their teachings must continue to be questioned or totally discarded.

Think of the greatest ideas, understandings and inventions of the last 200 years. They all came about through the scientific process and are backed up with solid evidence. Whereas thousands of years ago religions claimed to have come up with the great understandings and teachings, now nothing new comes from religions. They are only reactive bodies trying to determine religious rules for new situations while being bogged down in ancient views and concepts. We see the Pope struggling to decide how to deal with his flock's use of modern contraceptive techniques; rabbis discussing whether to allow the implementation of pre-set power settings on a Sabbath; and imams debating whether women should be allowed to drive cars on their own.

> "Imagine the people who believe such things and who are not ashamed to ignore totally, all the patient findings of thinking minds through all of the centuries since the Bible was written. And it is these ignorant people, the most uneducated, the most unimaginative, the most unthinking among us, who would make themselves the guides and leaders of us all; who would force their feeble and childish beliefs on us; who would invade our schools and libraries and homes. I personally resent it bitterly."
> - Isaac Asimov

Believers will continue to spout, "But religion does some good", and yes this is true, but it is like saying, "He may abuse his wife but he often buys her flowers." Yes, there is some good there, but one must not accept it without also acknowledging the bad and trying to rebuild a different and far better system.

Traditionally, religious leaders have provided advice on a wide range of life issues, including marriage, relationships, feelings of guilt or inadequacy. But we now have counsellors and other professionals who specialize in each of these areas. These are the people we should now be turning to for advice. We no longer go to shamans for chests pains; we see cardiologists and physicians. The same should be happening when it comes to dealing with psychological well-being.

"The most dangerous aspect of religion is it's tendency to glorify the absurd and justify the abhorrent." – Stifyn Emrys

New views

Many people, however, still prefer to stick with religious structures because they feel there are no other options that echo their morals and views on life. We are presently in an interim period where we are just starting to create effective and highly regarded alternatives to religious bodies. Among the most interesting of these to emerge recently is Sunday Assembly. This is a group of non-religious people who want some of the benefits of community created by religions but without a god and its rules. It was founded in England in 2013 and there are already over 70 chapters in eight different countries. Local branches organize speakers, there is singing, and action groups have been created as well as general support systems.

I am not advocating for an instant and sudden shutdown of religions because that is not going to occur any time soon. But one would hope that with education, the theistic views and their associated texts will gradually come to be seen as no more than fascinating narratives of their times. As these texts diminish in importance, their associated cultures will be able to adapt and adopt more effective and appropriate tools for dealing with modern life. And some of the more positive aspects of religions may continue, albeit after being adapted to a more holistic view of the world instead of a restrictive, conflict-creating ideology.

What is evident is that religion is a lot like smoking. We were once told that it is fine and even good for you, but through education and patient research we have learned that, even though some people still enjoy it, it causes unacceptable and dangerous side-effects. Just as increased scientific knowledge and more effective education have convinced us of the dangers of smoking, so the same processes are showing up the flaws in religious stories and practices. Education has led to a massive decline in smoking in developed countries and, like cigarette companies, religions now find themselves increasingly relying on the poor and uneducated in developing countries as their major customers.

While people will continue to search for something that provides answers and meaning in their lives, we must accept and make plain to others that the existing major religions are most definitely not the answer. It may sometimes look like they have an answer, but it will be the wrong answer. If you were to scrounge through the junkyards of most societies you would undoubtedly discover a broken clock somewhere. That clock that is no longer working or of any benefit to the previous owner will still be correct twice each day. Religions are much the same, and should be consigned to humanity's scrapheap.

* * *

To finish this chapter, here's a classic joke from comedian Emo Phillips, which explains quite succinctly one of the many divisive aspects of religions:

Once I saw this guy on a bridge about to jump. I said, "Don't do it!"

He said, "Nobody loves me."

I said, "God loves you. Do you believe in God?"

He said, "Yes."

I said, "Are you a Christian or a Jew?"

He said, "A Christian."

I said, "Me, too! Protestant or Catholic?"

He said, "Protestant."

I said, "Me, too! What franchise?"

He said, "Baptist."

I said, "Me, too! Northern Baptist or Southern Baptist?"

He said, "Northern Baptist."

I said, "Me, too! Northern Conservative Baptist or Northern Liberal Baptist?"

He said, "Northern Conservative Baptist."

I said, "Me, too! Northern Conservative Baptist Great Lakes Region, or Northern Conservative Baptist Eastern Region?"

He said, "Northern Conservative Baptist Great Lakes Region."

I said, "Me, too! Northern Conservative Baptist Great Lakes Region Council of 1879, or Northern Conservative Baptist Great Lakes Region Council of 1912?"

He said, "Northern Conservative Baptist Great Lakes Region Council of 1912."

I said, "Die, heretic!" And I pushed him over.

10 THE MEANING OF LIFE AND SPIRITUALITY WITHOUT RELIGION

I'd better start by apologizing if you skipped forward to this section looking for a stroke of genius, a definitive answer to the question, "What is the meaning of life?". The reality is that after thousands of years of humankind trying to come up with a convincing response to this question, we still don't have one.

But asking that question is like asking what is the meaning of the universe. Does it have to have meaning? Does it owe us a meaning? The universe has no meaning, no sentience; it is just a physical existence. Is there meaning to life for an amoeba, a slug or a bird? Or an embryo of a few thousand cells that dies in utero, or a baby that lives only a few hours? Are we humans so special and removed from every other creature on the planet that only we must have an explanation for our existence?

The question is a collection of words that works grammatically but has no validity. One can pose the questions "What does sound taste like?" or "What is the meaning of the planet Neptune?" because they are grammatically correct, but they make little sense otherwise and therefore there are no answers to them. Of course, that hasn't stopped philosophers asking the meaning-of-life question for thousands of years. Douglas Adams in his book *The Hitchhikers Guide to the Galaxy* came up with the answer "42", which is as reasonable a response as any other.

We humans are unique creatures in that we are able to look around and ask questions about the world around us, but this does not mean that any and every question is valid. In fact, maybe we would enjoy life more if we stopped asking that big question and simply learned to appreciate what we actually have and what we actually need as human beings to lead happy and fulfilling lives!

Religious belief leads to a common catch-cry that "there is no meaning to life without God". This statement needs to be clarified because its subtext is actually "I need to have a higher controlling power and a promise of possible rewards (or an afterlife) to make my whole life's journey worthwhile." Does this also mean that if a believer found out that their god was nothing but a fabrication, would they then consider that their life had no meaning? This is one of the more detestable mindsets that religions can create.

What much research shows is that human beings simply need to have a sense of purpose for life to have meaning, and that the source of that purpose is not so important. In other words, as long as we feel like we are contributing to the world, life has meaning for us.

You can be extremely happy and satisfied living a life guided only by logic and reason. Some theists claim that life would be cold or hollow without belief in a god. In fact, science opens your eyes, mind and heart to the pure natural beauty of things, leading you to a beautiful place called reality. There can be enormous wonderment in looking up at the night sky and all of the stars once one has even a basic comprehension of cosmology. You can experience an almost primal feeling standing in front of a large waterfall or watching animals migrating en masse across the African plains. And that's not to mention the deep feelings brought to life by love and friendships, music, the arts and other forms of experience. One does not need a god to have spirituality.

* * *

"It's a strange myth that atheists have nothing to live for. It's the opposite: we have nothing to die for, we have everything to live for." – Ricky Gervais

"Amazingly, there really are people who think, 'It would be unpleasant if X were true (e.g. no life after death), therefore X can't be true.'" – Richard Dawkins

"I do not fear death. I had been dead for billions and billions of years before I was born, and had not suffered the slightest inconvenience from it." – Mark Twain

"Since our inner experiences consist of reproductions and combinations of sensory impressions, the concept of a soul without a body seems to me to be empty and devoid of meaning." – Albert Einstein

*　*　*

We humans are also unique in that we understand that our lives have a finite lifespan, which can be estimated reasonably accurately by looking at our genetics, where we live, our lifestyle and so on. What we don't comprehend quite so well are the vast aeons of time that have occurred before our own existences and the vast aeons of time that will occur after our existences. Millions of years are incomprehensible to us, let alone billions.

Nevertheless, as an overarching concept, we understand that we are here for quite a short time. This understanding falls down, however, when we start to think that we may still exist forever after our deaths. Nurtured by religious belief systems, this is simply wishful thinking that we are superior to all of the other creatures that exist and have existed. The fact that many people wish that an afterlife were true does not make it so. When we understand evolution, we can begin to accept that we die exactly as every other living creature has done before us. We are not "special" in this respect.

Compared to the idea of an eternal afterlife, our lives look transient and insignificant. As a result, believing in an afterlife tends to belittle the efforts and achievements of our earthly lives and devalue our relationships with our families and friends. Conversely, not believing in an afterlife enhances our current existences. I personally find it far more awe-inspiring to know that the atoms and molecules I am made of were once part of the Big Bang and so many other prehistoric living things and that in the future they will be a part of other living things long after I am gone.

While most religions claim that they alone are the holders of spiritual beliefs and experiences, in fact spirituality can be found all around us – and we don't even need to look hard to find it, as we do with deity beliefs. As noted above, many people find spirituality in beautiful music, in arts and in appreciating the magnificence of the natural world. Others derive spiritual comfort from mental exercises such as mindfulness and meditation.

We are all different (thankfully) and we all find different things that move us or connect us to others. If we believe that spirituality is found only in belief in the god that we were taught about as children, then we are missing so much. Could someone brought up in one religion feel spiritual about aspects of a different religion? If not, then religions really do narrow the possibilities for us all.

In this context, Buddhism is a fascinating belief system, for it focuses on core spirituality and connections with both one's inner being and the outside world. It is probably one of the clearest proofs that a god is not essential for people to have spiritual experiences or feel enlightened, for practising Buddhists constitute one of the most spiritual groups of people on the planet.

Most of us have some sort of yearning for transcendence, but it should not have to be confined to the strictures of Islam or Christianity or Judaism. One can feel it in a myriad of ways and it is a shame that followers of individual religions are required to adhere to the teachings of their religion alone. How much greater would their lives be if they had no spiritual restrictions placed upon them and could be awe-inspired by anything and everything?

On that note, I will end this chapter by quoting the Dalai Lama's views on why religions are now irrelevant and where we need to be heading, with regard to both religions and spirituality: "All the world's major religions, with their emphasis on love, compassion, patience, tolerance and forgiveness can and do promote inner values. But the reality of the world today is that grounding ethics in religion is no longer adequate. This is why I am increasingly convinced that the time has come to find a way of thinking about spirituality and ethics beyond religion altogether."

11 WHERE TO FROM HERE?

Living without religion may not appeal to everyone. A secular life is based primarily on truths, while emotional comforts may appear to come second. With religions, these two priorities are often the opposite way around, and comfort from beliefs (or discomfort from obedience to rules) is the utmost priority.

Interestingly, in the many discussions that I have been a part of or observed, non-religious people seem to be more at ease with life and death and what they wish to get out of their lives in comparison to adherents, who tend to be constantly looking for something extra or a connection to something they are unlikely to find. The believers appear to be living lives of "never good enough" or "striving to follow the God-given rules". And, yes, most of us would like to be on a constant path of self-improvement; however, who is one trying to be a better person *for*? Among believers, it is mostly for their god/s, while among non-believers it is mostly for humanity and all other living things.

It is completely understandable that people will continue to find comfort in religion. I have even heard people argue that religious people are happier (not that this is borne out in studies, or of great relevance; after all, what is the relevance of an alcoholic being happier while they are "under the influence"?). Yet I see so much evidence that points to the contrary.

It has also been said that most people require religions because they create a social order and framework for life. But I contend that we now need something beyond religion. Something that provides structures and philosophies but is a way of life that is also amenable to change. A philosophical approach that accepts that everyone can interpret life in their own individual way, not one that is inherently divisive in its rules and teachings. We really require something more than what religions currently deliver, and need to remove many of their negative features from our lives.

Education alone is not enough

Many studies have shown that countries that are more secularized rate highly in relation to happiness and success (by many different measures) while conversely, many of the most religious societies tend to have the least freedom, societal support and happiness. Whether this means that countries are more successful because they are more removed from religious views or that people become less religious because they live in more successful societies is up for discussion. Most likely it is due to both factors.

In the more developed nations, statistics support the theory that those with lower levels of religiosity enjoy superior community and individual benefits. One only has to look at the most religious countries in the world to see this – often they have higher levels of poverty, greater income inequality, little universal healthcare and decreased life expectancies. The least religious advanced nations, on the other hand, such as the Scandinavian and Western European countries and Australia and New Zealand have the most successful societies.

What this tells us is that if people feel like they are being taken care of by their governments, communities or fellow human beings, then they have less need for a supernatural deity to look after them. This is a critical issue to take on board if we wish to make a better world and rid ourselves of the problems created by religions: not only must people be better educated and presented with a broader information base, but societies must also raise their standards of living to help break the shackles. The bar must be raised in all communities around the world. People will not give up their religious security blanket unless there is an alternative support system.

As Karl Marx once wrote, "Religious suffering is, at one and the same time, the expression of real suffering and a protest against real suffering. Religion is the sigh of the oppressed creature, the heart of a heartless world, and the soul of soulless conditions. It is the opium of the people." What he was alluding to is that if society does not support individuals then religions may fill the void.

The Pew Research Centre has found in studies that women tend to affiliate with religion more than men, and consider religion more important in their lives. That, however, changes when women have more opportunities. Women who are in the labour force have religious views more in line with men, while women out of the labour force tend to be more religious.[1]

In his 1954 book *Motivation and Personality*, psychologist Abraham Maslow discussed a hierarchy of human needs. This is often depicted as a pyramid, as seen below, with the most fundamental needs at the bottom. It has been shown that the more these needs are met, the more easily people can be weaned off religion and learn to see the benefits of a secular or science-based society. When any of the categories in the hierarchy are lacking, religion tends to fill the gaps. Therefore, a general raising of the bar with regards to food, shelter, security and safety can have a profound effect on how people within a society are able to view and understand the world.

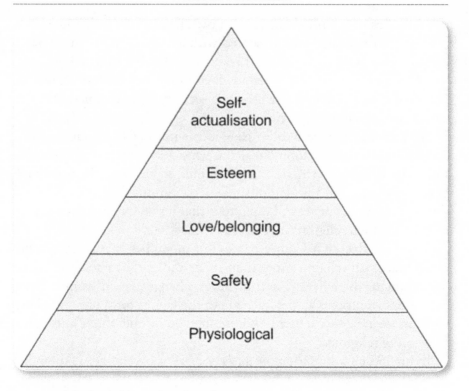

Maslow's hierarchy of needs, represented in pyramidal form

Speaking out

It is not the intent of this book to disparage individuals directly but rather to question belief systems. And no belief is beyond questioning. One must be able to back up one's beliefs with reason in order for them to be upheld by society as valid, especially as so many beliefs lead to actions that affect other people.

We have little issue with individuals ridiculing and arguing against people's political opinions, economic views, ideas on horoscopes and fortune tellers, even views on such things as parenting, diets and so forth, so we should certainly not have to hold back when question- ing scientific or religious ideas. Science has been built up on that very foundation: questioning and assessing validity. It is only through meticulous repetition of experiments, be they physical or theoretical, and by continually re-assessing information that we have got to where we are today.

An unfortunate political correctness has taken hold in the Western world, whereby people feel they have a right to be offended by anyone or anything said. On this slippery slope, open and frank discussion can become suppressed. People being greatly offended by someone simply questioning their beliefs is unreasonable. There are of course ways to question without being offensive, and there are many situations when people are rightfully offended, but to allow someone to pull out the "offended card" any time they are questioned is not acceptable because it may stifle important discussions that need to be had. And if you do not speak out against religious beliefs, then it is reasonable for others to assume that you accept or endorse them.

Every ideology must be able to be subjected to open and free examination and discussion as to its value to society. Islamophobia is not racism any more than communistophobia or astrologyophobia would be, because Islam, like communism or belief in astrology, is merely a set of ideas; it is not a race. Races are immutable, unchangeable parts of our genetic makeup that we are born into and have no control over, whereas religions are ideas that we can opt into or out of or change our level of allegiance to at any point in our lives. Challenging someone's belief should be called "beliefist", not racist. Anti-discrimination laws are designed to protect people, not ideas.

***

"It's now very common to hear people say, 'I'm rather offended by that' as if it gives them certain rights. It's no more than a whine. It has no meaning, it has no purpose, it has no reason to be respected as a phrase. 'I'm offended by that.' Well so fucking what? – Stephen Fry

"If someone tells me that I've hurt their feelings, I say, 'I'm still waiting to hear what your point is.' In this country I've been told 'That's offensive', as if those two words constitute an argument or a comment. Not to me they don't." – Christopher Hitchens

"Taking offence has become America's national pastime. Being theatrically offended supposedly signifies the exquisite moral delicacy of people who feel entitled to pass through life without encountering ideas or practices that annoy them." – George Will

"Ridiculing ideas is what makes progress. So if I offend some of you I don't mean to offend you personally. I may offend some of your ideas but that doesn't bother me at all. In fact, if you confront my ideas it will lead to a discussion. What does offend me of course is offending personal freedom and equal rights." – Lawrence Krauss

"I see offence as the collateral damage of free speech. I hate the thought of a person's ideas being modified or even hushed because someone somewhere might not like to hear them. Outside actually breaking the law or causing someone physical harm, 'hurting someone's feelings' is almost impossible to objectively quantify." – Ricky Gervais

"Nobody has the right to not be offended. That right doesn't exist in any declaration I have ever read. If you are offended it is your problem, and frankly lots of things offend lots of people." – Salman Rushdie

"If you are offended by reading views that disagree with yours,

then yes, you will be offended. However, it is not gratuitously offensive, it simply puts an argument, and if your views are not strong enough, as I believe they are, you will be able to defend your views. You will not say 'Oh it's offensive, it's offensive.' You will say 'No, you are wrong here and you are wrong here and you are wrong here' and that's what you should do."
– Richard Dawkins

"Everyone is in favour of free speech. Hardly a day passes without its being extolled, but some people's idea of it is that they are free to say what they like, but if anyone else says anything back, that is an outrage." – Winston Churchill

Moving on

It is now time to dispense with myth and superstition altogether as ways for living our lives. If we do not do so, how are we to choose which superstitions and religious rules to accept? Do we accept virgin sacrifices or throwing people into volcanoes to appease the weather gods? Do we allow female genital mutilation because it is a continuum of the teachings of a text written by ignorant, misogynistic men? Should we continue to permit community leaders in many African countries, be they political or religious, to preach fables about how diseases such as HIV are transmitted? Or preach adherence to a specific interpretation of a sentence in the Bible to prevent the use of condoms, thereby allowing millions of people to suffer and die? Surely in order for us to continue to improve our societies and claim to have a morally correct existence we should insist that this way of making decisions is no longer acceptable.

An essential distinction must be made here: people have rights, ideas do not. In order for us to maintain free democratic societies, we must protect the ability of all people to question and even offend others' views. We have no right not to be offended in a free society, or else the society will slowly regress to an un-free state. Most people are only offended when their belief systems are questioned and they themselves have doubts as to their veracity.

The current situation in many societies is the opposite of what is required. How can we accept that people are so offended by criticism or ridiculing of their beliefs that they think it reasonable to hurt or kill those critics? For a free and democratic society to be successful, surely those entrenched beliefs should be devalued, not the questioning or satirization of them.

You may believe whatever you choose, that is your right. You may not, however, demand that others respect those beliefs without question. Claiming you have a right to your opinions and beliefs is one thing; expecting that they be listened to, respected and accepted without criticism is a type of fascism. If we accept the often-repeated statement that "we should respect everyone's beliefs", then we are agreeing to tolerate the ideologies of white supremacist organizations, apartheid systems, or any other bigoted ideology or belief system that people can conjure up.

If you follow this chain of thought, you should be able to see that it is a poor position to uphold. Again, we should accept that everyone has a right to believe what they want, but such beliefs do not have a right to be automatically respected and in very many cases should be stridently rejected. For instance, should we allow a community to have an ideology that includes acts that physically and emotionally traumatize the children brought up in it or oppress its women? (Unfortunately, we already do.)

As much as we like to think that we are islands, able to have whatever beliefs we like, the reality is that our beliefs lead to actions that affect others, be it our children, our family or the broader society. Many theists want their rules to be applied across entire communities or countries. They want to tell two consenting adults that they can't have a registered union; they want to control sex education in schools or try to force abstinence on teenagers. They want to ban or limit a variety of contraceptives and to disallow abortions in any situation. They want reduced rights for women and to force them to dress the way men demand them to.

The truth is that those who belong to and support an organized religion are upholding systems that promote bigotry and the oppression of women and minorities, as well as a divisive "us versus them" mentality. As much as we like to think that our religious beliefs do not teach this, the evidence is to the contrary, as has been shown. Those who support religions in any way must accept that they are creating or maintaining a foundation that allows for religious fundamentalists. They permit false, dangerous and extreme teachings to persist. Without the support of "everyday" moderate religious people, the more fundamentalist adherents would be isolated members of society, standing on the street corners with their eccentric teachings and beliefs painted on homemade posters.

Many, many people are suffering and dying and will continue to suffer and die because of religious views. If you support even moderate religious organizations and say nothing against religions, then you are allowing this to continue. If you truly believe that other people should not suffer just because they are different, then you must speak out against religious texts, teachings and practices. If you want to fight for equality for women but aren't willing to criticize religions, then you are not really fighting against the greatest oppressor, the one that instills this inequality in children.

Looking at all the turmoil around the world, and the problems created by people who are so aggressive in either their religious beliefs or pride in their local history and nationality, if these mindsets continue in the next few decades then with the improvements in weapons technologies there will almost certainly be a gross destruction of humankind.

We must eliminate both nationalistic and religious dogma and the hatred that they inspire very soon, otherwise our lives or the lives of our children and grandchildren are under threat. The situation is comparable in many ways to climate change, in that we must collect and share the evidence, educate everyone and then bring about the required changes at individual, community, national and global levels; if not, there is potential for catastrophe in the not-too-distant future.

Many world leaders, including the presidents and prime ministers of the most powerful countries, regularly state that we must oppose and fight terrorism. The problem is, however, being fought mostly as a short-term problem. The "war on terror" has been largely unsuccessful, with terrorist acts continuing and new terrorist groups being created. Ground warfare is useful in preventing or trying to prevent imminent attacks, but to end the cycle, the opposite must occur. What is required is evidence-based education of the youth and those who teach them intolerant and mythical views of the world. We need to raise future generations with a secular mindset, not a religious one. As Einstein famously said, "Peace cannot be kept by force, it can only be achieved by understanding."

We must teach that old grudges from hundreds or thousands of years ago need not be perpetuated. We must undermine divisive ideologies; we must name and shame them. We must bring everyone to the realization that we are all part of humanity, that we are all 99.9 per cent similar, and that it is just our xenophobic education that is and has been the problem. Neither weapons nor tolerance for all belief systems are the means of eliminating the problems caused by adherents; only education and societal support can work. We must openly speak out against religious belief systems, and, yes, it will take generations for this to become effective.

Peaceful pluralism

Most parents who send their children to a religious denominational school do so with the thought that teaching children religion is a good thing because religions preach peace and tolerance. In fact, it is often the opposite. Segregating children from an early age and teaching them that a particular view is the only correct one, and other views are wrong, reinforces divisions in society; it also implies that segregation is not just acceptable but divinely ordained. We should be teaching our children to respect pluralism and, most importantly, the right of every person to question anything. If religions really are about peace and tolerance, then why are the most devout people not the most peace-loving and tolerant people on the planet?

Respecting pluralism does not, however, mean that you must automatically respect everyone's beliefs, just their right to have their beliefs. The only way people can view all others as equals is if they drop all constructed barriers that force them to view other people negatively. We must become more tolerant of all people (but not necessarily beliefs) and realize that the views that have been ingrained in us may in fact not be as true as we were taught.

People ask, "Why try to change things? It's impossible to bring about such huge changes; it'll never happen." To me, religions as a collective are like an alcohol or drug addiction that needs to be studied and then treated or cured. The process certainly won't be completed in our lifetimes, but we can all play our part. And what an accomplishment it would be, if we did get rid of religions, to say that it all started in the early 21st century.

There will of course be resistance, firstly from ourselves, feeling that it is just too difficult, then resistance from the communities that we belong to, and finally resistance from those political leaders, business leaders and religious leaders who are in control. But, as Lao Tzu philosophized, "The journey of a thousand miles begins with a single step." If, at the end of our lifetimes, we have contributed to making the world of the future a better place, contributed but one step on this journey of humanity, then we have done something good and will be able to feel satisfied with our life's achievements.

> # CHANGE
> If we think that it's too difficult,
> then it will never happen.
> If we try, we may lose, but if we don't
> try then we've already lost.

If there are any belief systems that you feel may affect your life negatively or the lives of your children or grandchildren, then surely it is beholden upon you to stand up against them? One only has to look back to the 1930s and 40s when an ideology grew over a number of years while most people just watched without acting. Nazism brought about a war that lasted for six years and engulfed not only continental Europe but also many other countries around the world. It led directly to the deaths of an estimated 60 million people (3 per cent of the world's population at that time) plus another 20 million deaths from war-related famine and disease. On top of that, a huge number of other people were affected by losing loved ones and friends. It was a situation that we would never want repeated, but that is what could happen if we do nothing. If the next big war is a religious war, then there will be a major decimation of populations and the planet's resources, because nothing inspires people more than acting on religious beliefs.

Without a doubt, tribalism will always be a part of humanity but when it is based on falsehood and bigotry and preaches hatred to the point of causing violence then not only should these beliefs be questioned, surely it is essential that we stand up against them and try to eliminate them.

What can we do?

The point of this book is not to present a definitive explanation of the issues; it is rather to provide a useful starting point for continuing to ask questions of ourselves, of our communities and of the world as a whole. You can choose to take on as little or as much as you feel comfortable doing, but I hope that, armed with some new thoughts, questions and information, you may choose to try to bring about some effective change.

That may involve simple steps like admitting that the stories that form the bases of religions are fabrications, myths and story-telling. As soon as people accept this premise, they start to see religious issues in a new light. Maybe when we talk to our children about the Bible or the Koran we will now more comfortably tell them that they are not accurate representations of what really occurred, that these books are simply a fascinating snapshot of and insight into our ancestors' understandings and knowledge 2,000–3,000 years ago, and that this was how people tried to explain the many great mysteries of the time.

Another important thing that we can do is to have the courage to not be "politically correct" and not allow dangerous ideas to persist by saying, "It's their belief and everyone is entitled to believe what they want." The world can only get past humankind's biggest hurdle if none of us supply oxygen to the fire. Humanity will be at risk if we do not take steps and speak out against religions.

An overwhelming majority of people have been affected or suffered in some way as a result of tolerance of all religions and their teachings. Even if we find it difficult to dispense with the rituals and cultural traditions of our religions, we should at least reject and oppose religious teachings because of their institutionalized sexism and bigotry and what they are instilling in our children and grandchildren.

Does this mean that one has to suddenly change one's life and completely walk away from one's past? Of course not. As discussed earlier, there are a number of important things that can be retained from the cultures of religions; they just need to be slowly modified to the point where people no longer act on the teachings of ancient texts or feel that their view is divinely endorsed.

On the other hand, some people may read this and feel that they now want to more whole-heartedly distance themselves from some of the hateful, divisive or bigoted aspects of religions and take a firmer stand against them. That might involve not attending places of worship, except for special occasions for family and friends, and choosing not to pray to the deity while there. It may mean no longer providing financial support to a religious institution or abandoning some of its rituals.

I hope readers of this book continue to read more, watch more and learn more, for this discussion is just the start. And with more knowledge comes greater confidence to talk more openly about one's views. To partake further in the discussion, you could join one of the many groups and societies worldwide that promote the evidence against religions, campaign for separation of religion from government, and highlight misleading or destructive ideologies. Often they provide free information, newsletters and weekly or monthly emails. A simple search through social media will also allow you to see what others are discussing.

One of the most important actions you can take is to "come out of the closet" and simply admit that you are secular rather than religious, that you enjoy aspects of the culture of your religious upbringing but do not believe in the gods and stories of religions. A campaign that has started recently, called Openly Secular, encourages people to feel comfortable and confident enough to say that they consider the secular view and understanding of the world and our way of life to be more reasonable than religious explanations. The only way to reduce the negative effects of religions will be through more and more people publicly distancing themselves from them.

Some groups are seeking to change certain entrenched religious symbols, such as the motto "In God We Trust" on US currency (which only appeared on paper currency in 1957) or the words of the national anthem of the United Kingdom, "God save the Queen/King". Achieving these alterations would have mainly symbolic value; however, it would in turn help reduce support for deity belief systems.

Other people are already standing up to governments and trying to ensure that government monies are not spent supporting religious views in any way. Court cases seeking changes in this regard are underway around the globe. It is essential that governments, the secular bodies that run most aspects of a society (except in theocracies), should always be kept completely separate from religious teachings and religious institutions. That means not only that governments should not interfere with religious bodies (unless they are breaking secular laws), but also that religious bodies should not interfere with government. And, yes, this, very importantly, includes schools and legal views and processes.

I am not suggesting that religious education should be forbidden, but I am saying that there should be no public funding of religious education, except as a way to understand the history of religions and their associated cultures. Secular governments should at the very least be entirely neutral on religious "education"; otherwise they are subsidizing childhood indoctrination. If we could achieve this, within a number of generations religions would begin to fade away.

I am very disappointed that some of the taxes I pay are used to fund the brainwashing of minds that are too young to understand whether or not what they are being taught is truth or mythology. A child who is taught a religion in isolation will undoubtedly develop a view that followers of other religions are wrong (which ironically is true). They should be taught that *all* religions are as wrong as each other! Education should be about freedom, not indoctrination. Our taxes should not be used to fund religious schools whose main purpose is to promote divisive beliefs, preserve falsehoods and deny evidence. Imagine if your government funded schools that taught as their core teachings paganism or witchcraft or voodoo. If that would not be acceptable, then why is the pushing of any religion on children acceptable?

> # BIRDS RAISED IN A CAGE THINK FLYING IS AN ILLNESS.
>
> # PLEASE DON'T TREAT OUR CHILDREN THE SAME WAY.

It is also wrong that religious institutions are almost automatically granted tax-free status. It is fair enough that their charitable work be treated as such, but we should not be rewarding religious establishments for the majority of their enterprises, which are simply furthering their own goals and maintaining their own existences.

Fortunately, many associations are now campaigning on these issues. Examples of these groups and their philosophies include:

- The American Humanist Society – "Humanism is a progressive life-stance that, without supernaturalism, affirms our ability and responsibility to lead meaningful ethical lives capable of adding to the greater good of humanity."
- The British Humanists – "We work on behalf of non-religious people who seek to live ethical lives on the basis of reason and humanity. We promote Humanism, a secular state, and equal treatment of everyone regardless of religion or belief."
- The Richard Dawkins Foundation for Reason and Science – "Our mission is to support scientific education, critical thinking and evidence-based understanding of the natural world in the quest to overcome religious fundamentalism, superstition, intolerance and human suffering."

There are secular and atheist societies in most countries and many have get-togethers featuring guest speakers and even some singing (if you can't beat them join them!). As these groups grow, religious institutions will wane and their influence will decrease. And if we continue on this trajectory, the term "atheist" will eventually no longer be required, as everyone will use science instead of religion to understand the world.

CONCLUSION

One of humankind's greatest achievements will be when the last churches, temples, mosques and synagogues have closed their doors and slowly become relics like Angkor Wat or the famous Greek, Roman or Egyptian temples. It will mark the point in time when humans no longer have to rely on myth and superstition to guide their behaviour, when differences in people can be celebrated by all rather than used by some as a justification for preaching intolerance. There will never be peace for humanity or equality for women as long as religions exist. It's time for humanity to put the religious phase of "knowledge" and existence behind us and move on to an evidence-based existence.

What we need to do is sort the wheat from the chaff and create philosophies rather than religions for those people who require or enjoy some of the features that existing religions provide. This book does not provide all of the solutions or ways forward – maybe that will come in a successive book! The hope is that readers will take on board the evidence raised and just begin to contribute to improving this world by abandoning ancient superstitions. I encourage you to think while you are sitting in your place of worship reading from your holy scripture to question what you are reading. Question the validity of the stories that your religious leader is re-telling and question if these fully comply with your understanding of the world.

It must be acknowledged that it is a challenge to try to change people's beliefs simply by presenting contrary evidence. After all, people often can't be reasoned out of a belief that they didn't first arrive at through reasoned assessment, and most religious beliefs were created through childhood indoctrination.

Thank you for reaching this point. I hope that it has allowed you to open your mind and think afresh about some of the points raised. I realize that most readers will be adults who are well into their lives and some will think there is little to gain by changing their beliefs and practices now. Doing that requires a very high degree of altruism because most of the effects will not directly benefit you, but rather future generations. It requires you to say, "I will do my little bit for the world of the future that I will likely not experience." Having said that, the greatest freedom in life comes from living by reason and truths. That alone should be motivation enough for us all to discard religious texts and their gods.

The hope is that some day religious beliefs will be gone and that even during the phase of transition they will be no more significant than personal interests and hobbies, little more than a collection of traditional cuisines, family customs and modernized historical festivities.

We should all fight against religions while the following are still happening as a result of religious teachings (and I'm sure that you can think of other items that could be added to this list):

- children are being taught myths as facts
- school boards still have to waste time and money battling to teach evolution in schools
- schools refuse to teach evolution properly to our youth because it contradicts their religious beliefs
- religions use their gods and their rules as tools of fear
- children are told about hell in scary and graphic detail and it is used as a psychological tool against them

- children are having their genitals cut because of *their parents'* beliefs
- newborns die or require surgical revisions due to complications from genital surgery
- the world accepts young girls undergoing genital mutilation because it is part of a religion's culture, and defend the religion but not the young girls
- children need to have armed guards at their schools and practise "lockdown procedures" to protect them against religiously inspired violence
- children and adults are told that they are born sinners (and that only through religions can they be made well)
- religious people pray to heal their children instead of seeking medical help, and these children needlessly suffer and sometimes die because of their parents' negligent and grossly irresponsible beliefs
- children are being killed by parents who say that they were commanded to do so by their god (this is still occurring!)
- religions see the reputation of their institution as more important than their congregants, as borne out in child sexual assault and rape cases
- children are forced into arranged marriages
- religious people teach that people with autism may be possessed
- people (and especially children) are taught that people from opposing belief systems are heathens and infidels and many other derogatory names
- religions inspire scapegoating and honour killings
- religions impel people to have what any rational person would otherwise see as bigoted views
- the books that form the bases of religions are considered sacred, even though they inspire so much poor behaviour (yet people can see the issues created by other people's religious texts!)
- religious believers hound, torture or kill people they believe participate in witchcraft
- religious teachings create a view that two human beings of

different religious beliefs shouldn't marry

- religious people deny equal rights in marriage equality
- it is taught that women are of lesser value
- while girls are prevented from attending school
- women face restrictions with regard to the leadership roles they can hold within religions
- women have lesser rights in their familial roles due to religious practices
- religious preachers tell the women in their congregations to submit to their husband's sexual wishes
- women must get permission from their husbands to obtain a divorce
- females (including young girls) are told while they are menstruating that they are impure and in some systems excluded or banished
- religions squeeze money from their followers, often those who can least afford it, while these organizations are the wealthiest the world has ever seen
- adults of the opposite sex are not even allowed to shake hands or make simple physical contact
- it is taught that males and females cannot have any sexual contact until they are married
- non-heterosexuals are treated as outcasts simply for their sexuality
- non-heterosexual youth are taught to hate, fear or dispel their sexuality and feelings, or that they will burn in hell for eternity
- non-heterosexuals are being tortured and killed
- businesses are allowed to discriminate against certain customers on the basis of their own religious beliefs
- rape victims are being charged with adultery
- people who disavow religions or speak against them are called apostates and are considered criminals, jailed, tortured, hounded or murdered
- people who choose to question or disavow their religion are treated poorly or ex-communicated by their family and/or community
- even where there is supposed to be separation of church and

state, governments continue to fund religious organizations, provide them with tax breaks, pay for prayer rooms, employ swearing on the Bible for secular processes, and include the word "god" on currencies and in national anthems and so on

- politicians, the only people who can alter gun laws, continue to offer "thoughts and prayers" after each mass shooting, and see this as being the best use of their positions
- governments do not allow non-believers to hold office
- political leaders talk openly about *their* god and religion (obviously at the expense of other beliefs or non-beliefs)
- governments and the populace confuse freedom of religion with governmental support of religions
- non-believers are not allowed to hold high positions in what are essentially non-religious organizations
- in divorce settlements judges and courts deny or place conditions on the granting of custody of children to atheist parents
- government employees can refuse to marry people because of their own religious beliefs
- religious schools and institutions have exemptions on whom they can hire, even though the positions may have nothing to do with religious instruction
- doctors and hospitals are allowed to refuse to offer accepted medical treatments because of *their* religious beliefs
- parents place their god ahead of their family when discussing or listing their priorities in life
- people and their families have to suffer in pain and have torturous ends to their lives rather than dying with dignity in a controlled environment and time of their choosing
- people are suffering and/or dying from sexually transmitted diseases when condoms can prevent this
- religions continue to be based on ideas that believers say are not verifiable with real-world tools yet cause real-world problems
- religious leaders teach that natural disasters are punishments for sins
- religions teach that eating certain foods or eating a food that has not been prepared to a god's liking makes you a sinner

- religions teach that we must suffer not only because of our own mistakes but also because of the sins of our forebears thousands of years back
- we continue to call the current violence "terror attacks" when we should have the guts to call them what they are: religious-inspired attacks (then we can fight the true cause – religious texts and teachings – and not just the people who act on them)
- religions peddle made-up stories about what happens to us after we die
- religions use these stories and implications of guilt to influence people's behaviour
- religions stand in the way of four of the most important freedoms; freedom for women, free speech, free will and free thought
- and, most importantly, supporters of religions say that non-believers are immoral or have no need to act morally, while those religious adherents are the ones responsible for all of the above immoral actions!

It's time to dispense with religions and their mythologies. Let's make the world a more inclusive and better place.

CREDITS

Front cover design courtesy of "bravoboy" at 99designs.com

The following cartoons were provided by my lifelong friend Andrew Weldon:
Chapter 5: God on a cloud
Chapter 7: Prayer
Chapter 9: "God!"
Chapter 11: Intolerance

Andrew's cartoons have been widely published in Australia and internationally. He has been a contributor to *The Age* newspaper for many years and he has been a regular cartoonist for *The Big Issue Australia* since its inception in 1996. His cartoons have also appeared in *The New Yorker*, *The Spectator* (UK) and *Private Eye* (UK), and in The Chaser publications and website. He has published two book collections of his work as well as several acclaimed children's books.

Chapter 5, image "EVERY SINGLE ACTION OF GOD IN THE BIBLE, THE QURAN AND THE TORAH TOOK PLACE INSIDE THAT LITTLE CIRCLE" kindly reproduced with permission from @AtheistWorld

Chapter 9, image of Jomo Kenyatta courtesy of Wikipedia

ACKNOWLEDGMENTS

I would firstly like to thank my parents for raising me with a sense of wonder about the real world and for promoting the mindset of "If you have a question, look it up in the encyclopedia." This was in the pre-Google days! They complemented this with a diet of David Attenborough documentaries and similar nature-based programs.

I am also grateful to my family for supporting this whole process that has taken over three years. I tried my best not to let it interfere with time with them by working on it early in the morning, late at night or on my days off. They were also at times a great help with creating some of the images for their less-than-computer-savvy father/ husband. They have always been supportive of the concept of me trying to make even a tiny positive change to the world. I love them all very much and hope that this book in some way improves their future.

To my very close group of friends, colloquially known as "The Camping Group", who provided early assessment of the manuscript and put up with my arguments and discussions as I began to slowly understand and clarify my position and knowledge, thanks guys.

Thanks to cartoonist extraordinaire and lifelong friend Andrew Weldon for his four great contributions. I hope that readers will feel that they added a little something extra to the reading experience.

I'm also grateful to Maureen Beigel for looking over my manuscript a few times in the early days and providing her editing skills and feedback in the early developmental stages, and to Manfred Spanger for his final textual analysis and advice and the many and varied conversations that we have had about this topic over the last few years. And to the nicest and most friendly Astronomer that I know, Perry Vlahos, for his assistance with checking the details in Chapter 1.

I would also like to mention in general all of the people and organizations who are active on the internet and social media publishing articles and information promoting a positive view of the secular and rational way of thinking. This starts with people such as Richard Dawkins and the Richard Dawkins Foundation for Reason and Science, who actively interact with people all over the world, regularly disseminating research articles and discussion points. It also includes the many different scientists and orators whose presentations and debates can be viewed on YouTube. If you only watch one video or person, please begin with anything by the late Christopher Hitchens. He provided so much intellect and wit in all of his discussions that I would be surprised if anyone who saw him speak live was not taken by his "slap you in the face, drag you to think" charm.

I must also thank the many anonymous people all around the world who have created great memes about religions and gods, which provided the foundation for my simplified book-friendly versions. I hope that this counts as an acknowledgement to those creative people. At times while writing this book, I felt as much a collator as a writer, as many of these ideas have been voiced by others. I just hope that the format in which I have presented them makes for easy and stimulating reading.

I would like to name a few social media people and sites that drew my attention to the damage caused by religions and the mindsets that they create. They include from Twitter: @AtheistRepublic, @ center4inquiry, @CEMB_forum (Council of Ex-Muslims), @ AtheistAus, @RitaPanahi, @aliamjadrizvi, @MaajidNawaz, @Ayaan,

@MrAtheistPants, @Antitheistnz, @SecularBloke, @MrOzAtheist, @godless_mom and @GSpellchecker

And thanks, finally, to my editor, Scott Forbes, for all of his help and feedback in putting the finishing touches to the manuscript. I really enjoyed working with you and am very thankful to you for the way you provided feedback so constructively yet positively.

If there are any inaccuracies, omissions or errors in quotes, please feel free to contact me so that they may be amended for updated versions of this book, via the website for the book at www.beyondgodthebook.com

ENDNOTES

Preface

1 See, for example, "Religion and Views on Climate and Energy Issues", Pew Research Centre, 22 October 2015.
2 Just as this book was being completed, the newly formed US Government, which includes an abundance of anti-science evangelicals, announced that it is withdrawing from the internationally recognized Paris Climate Agreement.
3 World Wildlife Fund website, accessed 2017.

Chapter 1

1 If this is of interest to you, further research and reading can be found in the works of people such as Lawrence Krauss (notably his A Universe from Nothing) and other cosmologists/physicists.

Chapter 2

1   Marc Bekoff, "Do Animals Know Who They Are?", Psychology Today, 6 July 2009.

Chapter 6

1   See https://en.wikipedia.org/wiki/Trolley_problem
2   See https://www.ncbi.nlm.nih.gov/pmc/articles/PMC3076932/

Chapter 7

1   H. Benson et al, "Study of the Therapeutic Effects of Intercessory Prayer (STEP) in Cardiac Bypass Patients: A multicentre randomized trial of uncertainty and certainty of receiving intercessory prayer", American Heart Journal, April 2006.
2   Debate between Sam Harris and Rick Warren, 2007.

Chapter 8

1   An analogy posited by philosopher Bertrand Russell, which suggested that there may be a teapot orbiting around the Sun that was too small to be seen even with the strongest telescopes. He explained it thus: "But if I were to go on to say that since my assertion cannot be disproved, it is intolerable presumption on the part of human reason to doubt it, I should rightly be thought to be talking nonsense. See "Is there a god?", unpublished article commissioned by Illustrated magazine, 1952.
2   See https://gssdataexplorer.norc.org/variables/287/vshow
3   Pew Research Centre, "America's Changing Religious Landscape", 12 May 2015.
4   Richard Dawkins, The God Delusion, Bantam Books, 2006.

Chapter 9

1   "A Portrait of Jewish Americans, Pew Research Centre, 1 October, 2013; http://www.pewforum.org/2013/10/01/jewish-american-beliefs-attitudes-culture-survey/
2   Female Genital Mutilation/Cutting: A statistical overview and exploration of the dynamics of change, 22 July 2013, http://data.

unicef.org/resources/female-genital-mutilationcutting-statistical-overview-exploration-dynamics-change/

3   E.J. Larson and L. Witham, "Leading scientists still reject God", Nature 394 (6691), 1998, pp. 313–14.

Chapter 11

1   "The Gender Gap in Religion Around the World", March 2016; http://www.pewforum.org/2016/03/22/the-gender-gap-in-religion-around-the-world/

CPSIA information can be obtained
at www.ICGtesting.com
Printed in the USA
LVHW030906110323
741404LV00004B/389